HARRAP'S

VERBES ANGLAIS

HARRAP

Édition publiée en France 2004
par Chambers Harrap Publishers Ltd
7 Hopetoun Crescent, Edinburgh EH7 4AY
Grande-Bretagne

Édition précédente publiée en 1998

ISBN 0245 50539 3

Dépôt légal : décembre 2003

Maquette et photocomposition : Chambers Harrap Publishers Ltd, Edinburgh

Impression et reliure : G. Canale & C., Italy

Rédactrice
Nadia Cornuau

Coordination éditoriale
Anna Stevenson

Direction éditoriale
Patrick White

Prépresse
Vienna Leigh
Sharon McTeir

Marques déposées

Préface

Cet ouvrage se concentre sur un aspect essentiel de la grammaire anglaise, à savoir la formation et l'utilisation des verbes. Les chapitres de la première partie de l'ouvrage ont pour but de faciliter et d'appronfondir l'étude de la structure du verbe. Ils permettent d'éclaircir les spécificités de la langue anglaise en examinant notamment la forme des temps, l'emploi des auxiliaires, du gérondif, des modaux, etc. Tous ces termes grammaticaux sont expliqués de façon claire et précise tout au long de l'ouvrage.

Dans la deuxième partie, on s'intéresse davantage à une structure verbale réputée difficile : les "phrasal verbs" (verbes composés ou verbes à particules), éléments dynamiques et essentiels de la langue anglaise. Après un chapitre entier consacré à l'emploi des particules, illustré par des exemples et leur traduction, vous trouverez un dictionnaire de verbes à particules dans lequel plus de 1 000 verbes ont été analysés et mis en contexte.

Les éditions Harrap tiennent à remercier Lexus qui a rédigé l'édition précédente de cet ouvrage.

TABLE DES MATIÈRES

1	Les formes verbales : concepts de base	9
2	Les auxiliaires	11
3	Les modes et les temps	13
4	Les verbes modèles	16
5	Le passif	19
6	Liste des verbes irréguliers	22
7	Les contractions	30
8	Les questions	32
9	La forme négative	35
10	Le présent	36
11	Le passé	39
12	Le futur	43
13	L'infinitif et le gérondif	49
14	L'impératif	55
15	Le conditionnel	57
16	Le subjonctif	61
17	Les auxiliaires modaux	63
	can-could	63
	may-might	66
	must-had to	68
	ought to	70
	shall-should	71
	will-would	72
	used to	74
	dare, need	74
	have, get	75
18	Les particules des verbes composés	76
Dictionnaire des verbes composés		107
Index		239

1 LES FORMES VERBALES : CONCEPTS DE BASE

Les concepts de base décrits dans cette section sont l'infinitif, le participe présent et le participe passé.

a) L'**infinitif** est la forme de base du verbe qui ne porte pas d'indication de personne et qui, en anglais, peut être précédée ou non de **to**. C'est celle donnée, par exemple, dans le dictionnaire des verbes composés de ce livre ou dans l'index. Le verbe à l'infinitif employé sans **to** s'appelle le **radical**. **Watch** est à l'infinitif dans les exemples suivants :

   do you want **to watch** TV?
   est-ce que tu veux regarder la télé ?

   I can't **watch**
   je ne peux pas regarder

   Pour les différents emplois de l'infinitif, voir chapitre 13.

b) Le **participe présent** est la forme du verbe qui se termine en **-ing** :

   is anyone **watching** TV?
   est-ce que quelqu'un regarde la télé ?

   they were **watching** us
   ils nous regardaient

   Le participe présent s'utilise pour mettre un verbe à la forme progressive. Comme le montre le deuxième exemple (**were watching**), il peut s'employer pour former d'autres temps que le présent.

   Le gérondif se forme comme le participe présent (**supposing you're right...** *en admettant que vous ayez raison...*).

   Pour les détails concernant la formation du participe présent, voir chapitre 4. Pour le gérondif, voir chapitre 13.

c) Le **participe passé** anglais est la forme verbale employée notamment après l'auxiliaire **have** pour former le "present perfect" (**it**

has rained *il a plu*, **you have tried** *tu as essayé*, etc.). Pour les verbes réguliers, le participe passé a la même forme que le prétérit simple, c'est-à-dire : radical + **-(e)d** :

watch - watched
dance - danced

Pour les détails concernant les modifications orthographiques du participe passé, voir chapitre 4.

Les participes passés des verbes irréguliers sont donnés dans la liste page 22. En voici quelques exemples :

go - gone
teach - taught
stand - stood

2 LES AUXILIAIRES

Un auxiliaire modifie le verbe d'une phrase. Les verbes **be**, **do** et **have** sont appelés des auxiliaires ordinaires.

Ils fonctionnent aussi comme verbes à part entière et dans ce cas ils signifient : être (be), faire (do), avoir (have).

Les auxiliaires sont employés pour former les temps composés des verbes :

what **are** you doing?
qu'est-ce que tu fais ? (maintenant)

what **do** you do?
qu'est-ce que tu fais ? (en général, d'habitude)

what **have** you done?
qu'est-ce que tu as fait ?

Les formes de ces auxiliaires au présent et au passé sont :

BE

	SINGULIER	PLURIEL
PRÉSENT		
1ère	I am	we are
2ème	you are	you are
3ème	he/she/it is	they are
PRÉTÉRIT		
1ère	I was	we were
2ème	you were	you were
3ème	he/she/it was	they were

DO

	Singulier	Pluriel
Présent		
1ère	I do	we do
2ème	you do	you do
3ème	he/she/it does	they do
Prétérit		
1ère	I did	we did
2ème	you did	you did
3ème	he/she/it did	they did

HAVE

	Singulier	Pluriel
Présent		
1ère	I have	we have
2ème	you have	you have
3ème	he/she/it has	they have
Prétérit		
1ère	I had	we had
2ème	you had	you had
3ème	he/she/it had	they had

3 Les modes et les temps

Les modes

Les modes font référence à l'attitude d'une personne par rapport aux propos qu'elle rapporte. L'état ou l'action dont il est question dans la phrase sont exprimés différemment selon le mode du verbe. Les principaux modes sont :

- l'**indicatif**, qui exprime des faits réels ; c'est le mode le plus courant
- le **subjonctif**, qui est employé pour exprimer un souhait, une incertitude ou une possibilité, etc.
- le **conditionnel**, qui présente l'action comme une éventualité ou exprime le résultat d'une condition
- l'**impératif**, qui permet de donner des ordres ou de faire des suggestions

Pour la formation et l'emploi de l'impératif, du conditionnel et du subjonctif, voir respectivement les chapitres 14, 15 et 16.

Les temps et les aspects

a) Le **temps** d'un verbe indique le moment de l'action. Les temps de base sont le présent, le passé et le futur (pour l'emploi des temps, voir chapitres 10-12).

En anglais, la plupart des verbes prennent la même terminaison à toutes les personnes d'un même temps. Par exemple au prétérit :

I/you/he/she/it/we/they went

L'exception majeure concerne la troisième personne du singulier au présent. Elle prend **-s** ou **-es** (voir les verbes modèles page 16). Par exemple :

	SINGULIER	PLURIEL
1ère	I watch	we watch
2ème	you watch	you watch
3ème	he/she/it watches	they watch

b) La plupart des temps peuvent avoir différents aspects. L'aspect correspond à la manière dont l'action est envisagée : dans sa durée, son déroulement, son achèvement, etc. On distingue en anglais l'aspect simple, l'aspect progressif (ou continu) et le "perfect" (ou passé).

La forme progressive, qui exprime l'action dans sa durée, se construit avec **to be** + participe présent.

Le perfect, qui exprime une action accomplie ou une action du passé ayant des conséquences au moment de l'énonciation, se forme avec **to have** + participe passé.

c) Les temps des verbes se forment de la manière suivante :

infinitif	(to) watch *(regarder)*
infinitif progressif	(to) be watching *(être en train de regarder)*
infinitif passé	(to) have watched *(avoir regardé)*
infinitif passé progressif	(to) have been watching
présent simple	(I/you/he, etc.) watch(es)
présent progressif	" am/are/is watching
futur simple	" will watch
futur progressif	" will be watching
prétérit simple	" watched
prétérit progressif	" was/were watching
present perfect	" have/has watched
present perfect progressif	" have/has been watching
plus-que-parfait (ou past perfect)	" had watched
plus-que-parfait progressif	" had been watching
futur antérieur	" will have watched

futur antérieur progressif	" will have been watching
conditionnel présent	" would watch
conditionnel présent progressif	" would be watching
conditionnel passé	" would have watched
conditionnel passé progressif	" would have been watching

Pour le passif, voir chapitre 5.

4 Les verbes modèles

On propose dans cette section une classification des verbes en différents modèles selon les variations orthographiques qu'ils subissent. Les verbes qui figurent dans l'index de ce livre sont codés et renvoient à un verbe modèle.

M1

	ajouter
he/she/it au présent	-s
participe présent	-ing
participe passé	-ed

Par exemple : look : looks - looking - looked

M2

	ajouter
he/she/it au présent	-es
participe présent	-ing
participe passé	-ed

Par exemple : watch : watches - watching - watched

Remarque :

On ajoute -es aux verbes qui se terminent en -s, -z, -ch et -sh.

M3

	ajouter
he/she/it au présent	-s
participe présent	-ing
participe passé	-d

Par exemple : agree : agrees - agreeing - agreed

M4

	enlever	*ajouter*
he/she/it au présent		-s
participe présent	-e final	-ing
participe passé		-d

Par exemple : hate : hates - hating - hated

M5

	changer	*ajouter*
he/she/it au présent		-s
participe présent	doubler la consonne finale	-ing
participe passé	doubler la consonne finale	-ed

Par exemple : grab : grabs - grabbing - grabbed
occur : occurs - occurring - occurred

Remarque :

Le redoublement de la consonne finale a lieu après une voyelle courte accentuée, comme dans les exemples donnés ci-dessus. Mais il ne se produit pas dans le cas suivant :

keep : keeps - keeping

où la voyelle est longue. Ni dans :

vomit : vomits - vomiting - vomited

où la voyelle précédant la consonne finale n'est pas accentuée (l'accent tonique se trouve sur la première voyelle).

En **anglais britannique**, le redoublement de la consonne se produit parfois même après une voyelle courte non accentuée comme dans :

kidnap : kidnaps - kidnapping - kidnapped
travel : travels - travelling - travelled

Mais en anglais américain, on écrit ces formes verbales avec une seule consonne :

kidnap - kidnaping - kidnaped
travel - traveling - traveled

(Am) dans l'index indique les verbes qui se construisent sur le modèle américain.

M6

	changer	*ajouter*
he/she/it au présent	le -y final en -ies	
participe présent		-ing
participe passé	le -y en -ied	

Par exemple : accompany : accompanies - accompanying - accompanied
cry : cries - crying - cried

M7

	changer	*ajouter*
he/she/it au présent		-s
participe présent	le -ie final en -y	-ing
participe passé		-d

Par exemple : die : dies - dying - died

M8

	changer	*ajouter*
he/she/it au présent		-s
participe présent	le -c final en -ck	-ing
participe passé	le -c final en -ck	-ed

Par exemple : picnic : picnics - picnicking - picnicked

M9

Ce code est employé pour indiquer les verbes dont le participe passé est irrégulier (voir page 22) :

choose : chooses - choosing - chosen

Ces verbes portent deux codes. Dans le cas de choose, on trouvera les codes suivants : M4M9. Le code M9 signifie que le verbe est irrégulier et que les formes irrégulières, étant fixes, ne subissent pas de changement orthographique. Pour les autres formes, le verbe suit le modèle M4.

5 Le passif

Dans la phrase **our new partner signed the contract** (*notre nouvel associé a signé le contrat*), le verbe **signed** est à la voix active : le sujet accomplit l'action. Mais dans la phrase **the contract was signed by our new partner** (*le contrat a été signé par notre nouvel associé*), le verbe **was signed** a un sens passif : le sujet subit l'action. La voix passive est plus courante en anglais qu'en français.

a) Le passif se forme avec l'auxiliaire **be** + participe passé. Prenons, par exemple, le verbe **watch** (les traductions sont données à titre indicatif) :

infinitif	**(to) be watched** *(être regardé)*
infinitif passé	**(to) have been watched** *(avoir été regardé)*
infinitif progressif	**(to) be being watched** *(être en train d'être regardé)*
présent simple	**am/are/is watched** *(suis/es/est, etc. regardé)*
présent progressif	**am/are/is being watched** *(suis/es/est, etc. en train d'être regardé)*
futur simple	**will be watched** *(serai/seras, etc. regardé)*
futur progressif	**will be being watched** *(serai/seras, etc. en train d'être regardé)*
prétérit simple	**was/were watched** *(étais/était, etc. regardé)*
prétérit progressif	**was/were being watched** *(étais/était, etc. en train d'être regardé)*
present perfect	**have/has been watched** *(ai/as/a, etc. été regardé)*
present perfect progressif	**have/has been being watched** *(ai/as/a, etc. été en train d'être regardé)*
plus-que-parfait (ou past perfect)	**had been watched** *(avais/avait, etc. été regardé)*

plus-que-parfait progressif	had been being watched *(avais/avait, etc. été en train d'être regardé)*
futur antérieur	will have been watched *(aurai/auras, etc. été regardé)*
conditionnel présent	would be watched *(serais/serait, etc. regardé)*
conditionnel présent progressif	would be being watched *(serais/serait, etc. en train d'être regardé)*
conditionnel passé	would have been watched *(aurais/aurait, etc. été regardé)*

Quelques exemples avec différents verbes :

it was hidden under some old papers
il était caché sous de vieux papiers

it had deliberately been hidden by his assistant
il avait délibérément été caché par son assistant

it was thought to have been hidden by the Romans
on pensait qu'il avait été caché par les Romains

he objected to this information being hidden away at the bottom of the form
il s'est plaint que l'information, située en bas du formulaire, n'était pas mise en évidence

you'll be closely watched
tu seras surveillé de près

the programme will have been watched by ten million viewers in total
l'émission aura été regardée en tout par dix millions de téléspectateurs

if he were a suspect, he would be being asked a lot of questions by now
s'il était suspect, on lui poserait un certain nombre de questions à l'heure qu'il est

if he had made any comment, it would have been ignored
s'il avait fait des commentaires, ils n'en auraient pas tenu compte

b) Remarquez que la phrase active :

they sent him the wrong letter
ils lui ont envoyé la mauvaise lettre

peut se dire de deux façons différentes au passif :

the wrong letter **was sent to him**
la mauvaise lettre lui a été envoyée

he was sent the wrong letter
on lui a envoyé la mauvaise lettre

c) Les verbes intransitifs peuvent souvent être employés avec un sens passif :

it **opens** at the front
elle s'ouvre sur le devant

her article **reads** well
son article est bien écrit

this material won't **wash** very well
ce tissu ne se lave pas très bien

6 LISTE DES VERBES IRRÉGULIERS

Les américanismes sont indiqués par *. Les formes peu courantes, archaïques ou littéraires sont données entre parenthèses. Les traductions ne sont pas restrictives et ne donnent qu'un des sens de base.

INFINITIF		PRÉTÉRIT	PARTICIPE PASSÉ
abide	*supporter*	(abode) [1]	abided
arise	*surgir*	arose	arisen
awake	*s'éveiller*	awoke, awaked	awoken, (awaked)
bear	*porter*	bore	borne [2]
beat	*battre*	beat	beaten [3]
become	*devenir*	became	become
befall	*arriver*	befell	befallen
beget	*engendrer*	begot	begotten
begin	*commencer*	began	begun
behold	*apercevoir*	beheld	beheld
bend	*courber*	bent	bent [4]
bereave	*priver*	bereaved	bereft [5]
beseech	*implorer*	besought	besought
bestride	*chevaucher*	bestrode	bestridden
bet	*parier*	bet, betted	bet, betted
bid	*offrir*	bid	bid
bid	*commander*	bade	bidden

1 Régulier dans la construction **abide by** *se conformer à, suivre* : they **abided by** the rules.

2 Mais **born** au passif ou comme adjectif = "né": he was **born** in France; a **born** gentleman.

3 Remarquez la forme familière this has me **beat**/you have me **beat** there *cela me dépasse/tu m'as posé une colle* et **beat** dans le sens de "très fatigué, épuisé" : I'm (dead) **beat**.

4 Remarquez l'expression on one's **bended** knees *à genoux*.

5 Mais **bereaved** dans le sens de "endeuillé", comme dans the **bereaved** received no compensation *la famille du disparu ne reçut aucune indemnité*. Comparez : he was **bereft** of speech *il en perdit la parole*.

INFINITIF		PRÉTÉRIT	PARTICIPE PASSÉ
bind	*attacher*	bound	bound
bite	*mordre*	bit	bitten
bleed	*saigner*	bled	bled
blow	*souffler*	blew	blown
break	*casser*	broke	broken [6]
breed	*élever*	bred	bred
bring	*apporter*	brought	brought
broadcast	*diffuser*	broadcast	broadcast
build	*construire*	built	built
burn	*brûler*	burnt, burned	burnt, burned
burst	*éclater*	burst	burst
buy	*acheter*	bought	bought
cast	*jeter*	cast	cast
catch	*attraper*	caught	caught
chide	*gronder*	chid, chided	chid, (chidden), chided
choose	*choisir*	chose	chosen
cleave	*fendre*	clove, cleft	cloven, cleft [7]
cleave	*adhérer*	cleaved, (clave)	cleaved
cling	*s'accrocher à*	clung	clung
clothe	*habiller*	clothed, (clad)	clothed, (clad)
come	*venir*	came	come
cost	*coûter*	cost	cost
creep	*ramper*	crept	crept
crow	*chanter*	crowed, (crew)	crowed
cut	*couper*	cut	cut
dare	*oser*	dared, (durst)	dared, (durst)
deal	*traiter*	dealt	dealt
dig	*fouiller*	dug	dug
dive	*plonger*	dived, dove*	dived
draw	*dessiner, tirer*	drew	drawn
dream	*rêver*	dreamt, dreamed	dreamt, dreamed

6 Mais **broke** quand il s'agit d'un adjectif = "fauché" : I'm **broke**.

7 **Cleft** n'est employé que dans le sens de "coupé en deux".
Remarquez **cleft** palate *palais fendu* et to be caught in a **cleft** stick *être dans une impasse*, mais **cloven** foot/hoof *sabot fendu.*

INFINITIF		PRÉTÉRIT	PARTICIPE PASSÉ
drink	*boire*	drank	drunk [8]
drive	*conduire*	drove	driven
dwell	*demeurer*	dwelt, dwelled	dwelt, dwelled
eat	*manger*	ate	eaten
fall	*tomber*	fell	fallen
feed	*nourrir*	fed	fed
feel	*sentir*	felt	felt
fight	*battre*	fought	fought
find	*trouver*	found	found
fit	*aller à*	fit*, fitted	fit*, fitted
flee	*s'envoler*	fled	fled
fling	*lancer*	flung	flung
fly	*voler*	flew	flown
forbear	*s'abstenir*	forbore	forborne
forbid	*interdire*	forbad(e)	forbidden
forget	*oublier*	forgot	forgotten
forgive	*pardonner*	forgave	forgiven
forsake	*abandonner*	forsook	forsaken
freeze	*geler*	froze	frozen
get	*obtenir*	got	got, gotten* [9]
gild	*dorer*	gilt, gilded	gilt, gilded [10]
gird	*ceindre*	girt, girded	girt, girded [10]
give	*donner*	gave	given
go	*aller*	went	gone
grind	*grincer*	ground	ground
grow	*pousser*	grew	grown

8 Quand il s'agit d'un adjectif épithète (placé devant le nom) désignant une personne, il est possible d'employer drunken (a lot of drunk(en) people *beaucoup de gens ivres*). Mais il doit toujours être employé devant les noms de choses, d'objets inanimés, etc. (drunken parties *des soirées bien arrosées*).

9 Mais have got to se dit aussi en américain avec le sens de "devoir, être obligé de" : I've got to go *je dois y aller*. Comparez avec : she has gotten into a bit of a mess *elle s'est fourrée dans le pétrin*.

10 Les formes du participe passé gilt et girt s'emploient comme adjectifs épithètes : gilt mirrors *des miroirs dorés*, a flower-girt grave *une tombe entourée de fleurs* (mais toujours gilded youth *la jeunesse dorée*, où gilded est employé au sens figuré).

INFINITIF		PRÉTÉRIT	PARTICIPE PASSÉ
hang	*accrocher, suspendre*	hung, hanged [11]	hung, hanged [11]
hear	*entendre*	heard	heard
heave	*lever*	hove, heaved [12]	hove, heaved [12]
hew	*tailler*	hewed	hewn, hewed
hide	*cacher*	hid	hidden
hit	*frapper*	hit	hit
hold	*tenir*	held	held
hurt	*blesser*	hurt	hurt
keep	*garder*	kept	kept
kneel	*s'agenouiller*	knelt, kneeled	knelt, kneeled
knit	*tricoter*	knit, knitted [13]	knit, knitted [13]
know	*savoir, connaître*	knew	known
lay	*coucher*	laid	laid
lead	*mener*	led	led
lean	*s'appuyer*	leant, leaned	leant, leaned
leap	*sauter*	leapt, leaped	leapt, leaped
learn	*apprendre*	learnt, learned	learnt, learned
leave	*laisser*	left	left
lend	*prêter*	lent	lent
let	*laisser*	let	let
lie	*coucher*	lay	lain
light	*allumer*	lit, lighted	lit, lighted [14]

11 Régulier quand il signifie "pendre quelqu'un".

12 **Hove** est utilisé dans le domaine nautique, comme dans l'expression **heave into sight** (*poindre à l'horizon*), également employée au sens figuré : and suddenly, she **hove** into sight *et tout à coup, elle apparut.*

13 Irrégulier quand il a le sens de "unir" (a close-**knit** family *une famille unie*), mais régulier lorsqu'il a le sens de "fabriquer en laine" et quand il fait référence aux os = "se souder".

14 Lorsque le participe passé est employé comme adjectif épithète, on préfère souvent **lighted** à **lit** : a **lighted** candle *une bougie allumée* (mais : the candle is **lit** *la bougie est allumée*, she has **lit** a candle *elle a allumé une bougie*). Dans les noms composés, on emploie généralement **lit** : well-**lit** streets *des rues bien éclairées.* Au sens figuré (avec **up**), c'est uniquement **lit** qui est employé au prétérit et au participe passé : her face **lit** up when she saw me *son visage s'illumina lorsqu'elle me vit.*

INFINITIF		PRÉTÉRIT	PARTICIPE PASSÉ
lose	*perdre*	lost	lost
make	*faire*	made	made
mean	*signifier*	meant	meant
meet	*rencontrer*	met	met
melt	*fondre*	melted	melted, molten [15]
mow	*faucher*	mowed	mown, mowed
pay	*payer*	paid	paid
plead	*plaider*	pled*, pleaded	pled*, pleaded [16]
put	*poser*	put	put
quit	*quitter*	quit, (quitted)	quit, (quitted) [17]
read	*lire*	read	read
rend	*déchirer*	rent	rent
rid	*débarrasser*	rid, (ridded)	rid
ride	*monter à*	rode	ridden
ring	*sonner*	rang	rung
rise	*se lever*	rose	risen
run	*courir*	ran	run
saw	*scier*	sawed	sawn, sawed
say	*dire*	said	said
see	*voir*	saw	seen
seek	*chercher*	sought	sought
sell	*vendre*	sold	sold
send	*envoyer*	sent	sent
set	*mettre*	set	set
sew	*coudre*	sewed	sewn, sewed
shake	*secouer*	shook	shaken
shear	*tondre*	sheared	shorn, sheared [18]

15 On emploie **molten** uniquement comme adjectif épithète, et seulement lorsqu'il signifie “fondu à très haute température”, par exemple : **molten** lead *du plomb fondu* (mais **melted** butter *du beurre fondu*).

16 En anglais d'Écosse et en américain, on emploie **pled** au passé et au participe passé.

17 En américain, les formes régulières ne sont pas employées, et elles sont de plus en plus rares en anglais britannique.

18 Le participe passé est normalement **shorn** devant un nom (newly-**shorn** lambs *des agneaux tout juste tondus*) et toujours dans l'expression to be **shorn** of *être privé de* : **shorn** of his riches he was nothing *privé de ses richesses, il n'était plus rien.*

INFINITIF		PRÉTÉRIT	PARTICIPE PASSÉ
shed	*perdre, verser*	shed	shed
shine	*briller*	shone [19]	shone [19]
shoe	*chausser*	shod, shoed	shod, shoed [20]
shoot	*abattre, tirer*	shot	shot
show	*montrer*	showed	shown, showed
shrink	*rétrécir*	shrank, shrunk	shrunk, shrunken [21]
shut	*fermer*	shut	shut
sing	*chanter*	sang	sung
sink	*couler*	sank	sunk, sunken [22]
sit	*s'asseoir*	sat	sat
slay	*tuer*	slew	slain
sleep	*dormir*	slept	slept
slide	*glisser*	slid	slid
sling	*lancer*	slung	slung
slink	*se glisser furtivement*	slunk	slunk
slit	*fendre*	slit	slit
smell	*sentir*	smelt, smelled	smelt, smelled
smite	*frapper*	smote	smitten [23]
sneak	*se faufiler, se glisser*	snuck*, sneaked	snuck*, sneaked
sow	*semer*	sowed	sown, sowed
speak	*parler*	spoke	spoken
speed	*aller vite*	sped, speeded	sped, speeded
spell	*écrire*	spelt, spelled	spelt, spelled
spend	*dépenser*	spent	spent
spill	*renverser*	spilt, spilled	spilt, spilled

19 Mais régulier quand il a le sens de "cirer, astiquer" en américain.

20 Quand il est adjectif, on n'emploie que **shod** : a well-**shod** foot *un pied bien chaussé.*

21 **Shrunken** n'est employé que lorsqu'il est adjectif : **shrunken** limbs/her face was **shrunken** *des membres rabougris/elle avait le visage flétri.*

22 **Sunken** ne s'emploie que comme adjectif : **sunken** eyes *des yeux enfoncés.*

23 Verbe archaïque dont le participe passé **smitten** s'emploie encore comme adjectif : he's completely **smitten** with her *il est complètement fou d'elle.*

INFINITIF		PRÉTÉRIT	PARTICIPE PASSÉ
spin	*filer*	spun	spun
spit	*cracher*	spat, spit*	spat, spit*
split	*se briser*	split	split
spoil	*abîmer*	spoilt, spoiled	spoilt, spoiled
spread	*étendre*	spread	spread
spring	*bondir*	sprang	sprung
stand	*se tenir*	stood	stood
steal	*voler*	stole	stolen
stick	*enfoncer, coller*	stuck	stuck
sting	*piquer*	stung	stung
stink	*puer*	stank	stunk
strew	*répandre*	strewed	strewn, strewed
stride	*marcher à grands pas*	strode	stridden
strike	*frapper*	struck	struck, stricken [24]
string	*enfiler*	strung	strung
strive	*s'efforcer*	strove	striven
swear	*jurer*	swore	sworn
sweat	*suer*	sweat*, sweated	sweat*, sweated
sweep	*balayer*	swept	swept
swell	*gonfler*	swelled	swollen, swelled [25]
swim	*nager*	swam	swum
swing	*se balancer*	swung	swung
take	*prendre*	took	taken
teach	*enseigner*	taught	taught
tear	*déchirer*	tore	torn
tell	*dire*	told	told

24 **Stricken** n'est utilisé qu'au sens figuré (**stricken** with grief *accablé par le chagrin*). Il est très courant dans les noms composés (*accablé par*) : **poverty-stricken**, **fever-stricken**, **grief-stricken**, **horror-stricken** (aussi **horror-struck**), **terror-stricken** (aussi **terror-struck**), mais on dit toujours **thunderstruck** *abasourdi*.

C'est aussi un emploi américain : the remark was **stricken** from the record *la remarque a été rayée du procès-verbal*.

25 **Swollen** est plus courant que **swelled** comme verbe (her face has **swollen** *son visage a gonflé*) et comme adjectif (her face is **swollen**/a **swollen** face). To have a **swollen** head (*avoir la grosse tête*) devient to have a **swelled** head en américain.

INFINITIF		PRÉTÉRIT	PARTICIPE PASSÉ
think	*penser*	thought	thought
thrive	*fleurir*	thrived, (throve)	thrived, (thriven)
throw	*jeter*	threw	thrown
thrust	*pousser*	thrust	thrust
tread	*marcher*	trod	trodden
understand	*comprendre*	understood	understood
undertake	*s'engager*	undertook	undertaken
wake	*se réveiller*	woke, waked	woken, waked
wear	*porter*	wore	worn
weave	*tisser*	wove [26]	woven [26]
weep	*pleurer*	wept	wept
wet	*mouiller*	wet*, wetted [27]	wet*, wetted [27]
win	*gagner*	won	won
wind	*remonter*	wound	wound
wring	*tordre*	wrung	wrung
write	*écrire*	wrote	written

[26] Mais il est régulier lorsqu'il a le sens de "se faufiler" : the motorbike **weaved** through the traffic *la moto se faufila entre les voitures.*

[27] Mais irrégulier aussi en anglais britannique lorsqu'il a le sens suivant : he **wet** his bed *il a fait pipi au lit.*

7 Les contractions

Les formes contractées sont très courantes dans l'anglais parlé d'aujourd'hui et dans l'anglais écrit non officiel :

BE

I am	I'm
you are	you're
he/she/it is	he's/she's/it's
we/they are	we're/they're
I am not	I'm not
you are not	you're not, you aren't
he/she/it is not	he's/she's/it's not, he/she/it isn't
we/they are not	we/they aren't
am I not?	aren't I?
are you not?	aren't you?
is he/she/it not?	isn't he/she/it?
are we/they not?	aren't we/they?

DO

I/you/we/they do not	I/you/we/they don't
he/she/it does not	he/she/it doesn't
do I/you/we/they not?	don't I/you/we/they?
does he/she/it not?	doesn't he/she/it?

HAVE

I have	I've
you/we/they have	you've/we've/ they've
he/she/it has	he's/she's/it's (plus courant avec le "present perfect" comme dans : I've seen, etc.)
I/you/we/they have not	I/you/we/they haven't
he/she/it/has not	he/she/it hasn't
have I/you/we/they not?	haven't I/you/we/ they?
has he/she/it not?	hasn't he/she/it?
I/he/she/it was not	I/he/she/it wasn't
you/we/they were not	you/we/they weren't
I, etc. did not	I, etc. didn't
I/you, etc. will	I'll/you'll, etc.
I/he, etc. will not	I/he, etc. won't
I shall	I'll
I shall not	I shan't
I/you, etc. would	I'd/you'd, etc.
I/you, etc. would not	I/you, etc. wouldn't
I/he, etc. would have	I'd've/ he'd've, etc.
I/he, etc. would not have	I/he, etc. wouldn't have

Les contractions ne sont pas seulement utilisées avec les pronoms personnels :

> **that'll** be the day!
> **Mummy's** just gone out

Voir aussi Les auxiliaires modaux, page 63.

8 Les questions

1 En l'absence d'auxiliaire, on forme les questions avec l'auxiliaire **do** :

do you like whisky?
vous aimez le whisky ?

how **do** you spell it?
comment ça s'écrit ?

doesn't she expect you home?
est-ce qu'elle ne vous attend pas à la maison ?

did you talk to him?
tu lui as parlé ?

didn't I tell you so?
ne vous l'avais-je pas dit ?

2 Si un autre auxiliaire est utilisé (**be**, **have**, **will**, etc.), on inverse alors le sujet et le verbe. Attention à l'ordre des mots :

he is Welsh
il est gallois

is he Welsh?
est-ce qu'il est gallois ?

they're going home tomorrow
ils rentrent chez eux demain

are they going home tomorrow?
est-ce qu'ils rentrent chez eux demain ?

Daphne will be there too
Daphne y sera aussi

will Daphne be there too?
est-ce que Daphne y sera aussi ?

I can't understand
je ne comprends pas

why **can't I** understand?
pourquoi est-ce que je ne comprends pas ?

Remarquez que dans les propositions interrogatives indirectes, l'ordre des mots est le même que celui d'une phrase affirmative :

when is she leaving?
quand est-ce qu'elle part ?

she is leaving tomorrow
elle part demain

he asked me **when she was leaving**
il m'a demandé quand elle partait

3 Si le sujet est un pronom interrogatif, il n'y a pas d'auxiliaire :

who made that noise?
qui a fait ce bruit ?

what happened?
qu'est-ce qui s'est passé ?

4 Les question-tags :

Le question-tag, équivalent du "n'est-ce pas ?" français, est une tournure interrogative très courante en anglais qui se place en fin de phrase et qui permet généralement de demander confirmation. Il se compose d'un pronom personnel et d'un auxiliaire.

a) Une phrase affirmative est suivie d'un question-tag négatif, et vice versa :

you **can** see it, **can't** you?
tu peux le voir, n'est-ce pas ?

you **can't** see it, **can** you?
tu ne peux pas le voir, si ?

Si le question-tag ne s'emploie pas pour poser une question mais sert à renforcer le sens de la phrase principale, alors un question-tag positif suit une phrase affirmative :

so **you've** seen a ghost, **have you**? *(incrédulité, sarcasme)*
alors comme ça vous avez vu un fantôme ?

he's got married again, **has he**? *(surprise, intérêt)*
alors comme ça il s'est remarié ?

Remarquez, dans ce dernier exemple, qu'il est important de pouvoir distinguer **be** et **have** à la forme contractée pour former le question-tag.

b) Le question-tag reprend le temps de la phrase principale. Si la proposition précédente est au présent simple ou au prétérit, et donc sans auxiliaire, on utilise **do** dans le question-tag :

you want to meet him, **don't you**?
tu veux le rencontrer, n'est-ce pas ?

you wanted to meet him, **didn't you**?
tu voulais le rencontrer, n'est-ce pas ?

you'll want to meet him, **won't you**?
tu voudras le rencontrer, n'est-ce pas ?

c) Si la proposition précédente est régie par un auxiliaire, c'est-à-dire s'il s'agit d'un temps composé, on répète l'auxiliaire dans le question-tag :

Peter has been here before, **hasn't he**?
Peter est déjà venu ici, n'est-ce pas ?

they aren't stopping, **are they**?
ils ne s'arrêtent pas, si ?

you will sign it, **won't you**?
tu le signeras, n'est-ce pas ?

d) Si le question-tag suit un impératif, on emploie le plus souvent **will/would**. Ces question-tags permettent d'adoucir la phrase, d'éviter un ton abrupt :

leave the cat alone, **will you**?
laisse donc ce chat tranquille

take this to Mrs Brown, **would you**?
tu veux bien apporter ça à Mme Brown ?

Dans le cas suivant, la forme négative **won't** indique une invitation :

help yourselves to drinks, **won't you**?
servez-vous à boire, je vous en prie

9 LA FORME NÉGATIVE

1 En l'absence d'auxiliaire (**be**, **will**, etc.), on emploie **do** suivi de **not** (voir aussi Les contractions, page 30) :

I like it *ça me plaît*	I **do not** (**don't**) like it *ça ne me plaît pas*
she agrees with them *elle est d'accord avec eux*	she **does not** (**doesn't**) agree with them *elle n'est pas d'accord avec eux*
I expected him to say that *je m'attendais à ce qu'il dise ça*	I **did not** (**didn't**) expect him to say that *je ne m'attendais pas à ce qu'il dise ça*

2 S'il y a un autre auxiliaire, on emploie seulement **not** :

I will (I'll) take them with me with *je les prendrai avec moi*	I **will not** (I **won't**) take them me *je ne les prendrai pas avec moi*
they are just what I'm looking for *c'est exactement ce que je cherche*	they **are not** (they **aren't**/they'**re not**) really what I'm looking for *ce n'est pas vraiment ce que je cherche*

3 **Not** s'emploie aussi avec les infinitifs et les gérondifs :

to be or **not** to be *être ou ne pas être*	try **not** to think about it *évite d'y penser*

it would have been better **not** to have mentioned it at all
il aurait mieux valu ne pas en parler du tout

he's worried about **not** having enough money
il a peur de ne pas avoir assez d'argent

Voir aussi L'impératif, page 55.

10 Le présent

Le présent simple et le présent progressif (ou présent continu) sont deux façons différentes d'exprimer le présent en anglais. Ils ne s'emploient pas de la même manière.

Le présent simple est employé

a) Pour exprimer des événements généraux ou habituels, ou des vérités universelles :

I **get up** at seven o'clock every morning
je me lève à sept heures tous les matins

she **works** for an insurance company
elle travaille dans une compagnie d'assurances

where **do** you buy your shoes?
où est-ce que tu achètes tes chaussures ?

where **do** you come from?
d'où viens-tu ?

the earth **revolves** round the sun
la Terre tourne autour du Soleil

b) Avec des verbes qui expriment un état d'esprit, une humeur, une opinion, etc., ou des verbes qui font référence aux sens (odorat, goût, toucher, vue, ouïe) :

I **(dis)like/love/hate/want** that girl
j'aime (je n'aime pas)/j'adore/je déteste/je veux cette fille

I **believe/suppose/think/imagine** he's right
je crois/je suppose/je pense/j'imagine qu'il a raison

we **hear/see/feel/perceive** the world around us
nous entendons/voyons/sentons/percevons le monde qui nous entoure

it **tastes** good/it **smells** good
c'est bon/ça sent bon

Le présent progressif est employé

a) Pour exprimer des événements ou des états qui se déroulent ou ont lieu au moment où l'on parle :

what **are** you **doing** up there?
qu'est-ce que tu fais là-haut ?

I**'m trying** to find my old passport
j'essaie de trouver mon ancien passeport

at the moment it**'s being** used as a bedroom
en ce moment, on s'en sert comme chambre

what **are** you **thinking** about?
à quoi penses-tu ?

b) Avec des adverbes de fréquence (normalement employés avec le présent simple), pour exprimer une action (ou un fait) qui se produit souvent, mais de manière non intentionnelle ou inattendue :

he**'s** always **mixing** our names up
il confond toujours nos noms

he**'s** forever **forgetting** his car keys
il oublie toujours ses clés de voiture

Les différences entre le présent simple et le présent progressif

I **live** in London (*simple*)
je vis à Londres

I**'m living** in London (*progressif*)
je vis (actuellement) à Londres

La seconde phrase implique que le locuteur n'habite pas d'une façon définitive à Londres, mais qu'il y est installé temporairement. La première phrase exprime un état de choses.

I **have** a shower every morning (*simple*)
je prends une douche tous les matins

I**'m having** a shower every morning (these days) (*progressif*)
je prends une douche tous les matins (en ce moment)

La seconde phrase implique que prendre une douche régulièrement le matin n'est qu'un fait temporaire, quelque chose que l'on fait à un certain moment (et qui peut ne pas durer). La première phrase, au présent simple, n'implique pas ces restrictions temporelles.

she **works** for an insurance company
elle travaille pour une compagnie d'assurances

she**'s working** for an insurance company
elle travaille (actuellement) pour une compagnie d'assurances

La différence est moins apparente dans cet exemple. Mais la première phrase ne pourrait pas faire référence à une situation temporaire. La seconde phrase peut faire référence à une situation temporaire ou définitive.

On trouve des cas dans lesquels il n'existe pas de différence entre le présent simple et le présent progressif :

how **are you feeling** this morning?
how **do you feel** this morning?
comment te sens-tu ce matin ?

11 LE PASSÉ

Le prétérit simple

Il est employé pour exprimer des situations ou des faits accomplis à un moment précis du passé :

he **got up** and left the room
il s'est levé et a quitté la pièce

he **caught** the train yesterday
il a pris le train hier

in what year **did** the Rolling Stones **have** their first hit?
en quelle année les Rolling Stones ont-ils eu leur premier succès ?

Used to/would

Ces deux formes sont employées pour faire référence à des événements habituels ou réguliers du passé :

on Fridays we always **used to have** fish
on Fridays we **would have** fish
le vendredi, on mangeait toujours du poisson

Le prétérit progressif

Ce temps se forme avec l'auxiliaire **be** au passé + verbe en **-ing**. Il permet d'insister sur la continuité, la durée d'une action ou d'une situation :

I **was living** in Germany when that happened
j'habitais alors en Allemagne quand ça s'est passé

sorry, could you say that again? I **wasn't listening**
pardon, est-ce que tu peux répéter ? je n'écoutais pas

what **were** you **doing** out in the garden last night?
que faisiez-vous dans le jardin hier soir ?

I **was having** dinner when he came home
j'étais en train de dîner quand il est arrivé à la maison

Le prétérit simple et le prétérit progressif sont souvent employés pour mettre en valeur le lien qui existe entre deux faits du passé ou la façon dont le locuteur veut les présenter. Dans le dernier exemple ci-dessus, une action ponctuelle (**he came home**) est opposée à une action qui dure (**I was having dinner**). Comparez cet exemple avec celui-ci :

I had dinner when he **was coming** home
j'ai dîné pendant qu'il rentrait à la maison

Le sens de cette phrase est très différent. L'action qui dure se trouve dans la proposition subordonnée (**he was coming home**). La proposition principale (**I had dinner**) fait référence à quelque chose qui a lieu à un moment précis pendant le déroulement d'une action plus longue (**coming home**). Comparez aussi :

I **was having** dinner while he **was coming** home
j'étais en train de dîner alors qu'il rentrait à la maison

Dans cette phrase, les deux événements se déroulent en parallèle.

Le "present perfect"

a) Ce temps est employé pour faire référence à des situations ou des actions du passé ayant un rapport avec le présent :

I **have read** nearly all of Somerset Maugham's books
j'ai lu presque tous les livres de Somerset Maugham

I **have** never **read** any of Somerset Maugham's books
je n'ai lu aucun des livres de Somerset Maugham

Dans ces deux exemples, on décrit ce qu'on a lu jusqu'à maintenant des œuvres de Somerset Maugham.

Comparez ces exemples avec :

I **read** one of Maugham's novels on holiday last year
j'ai lu un roman de Maugham quand j'étais en vacances l'année dernière

Cette phrase décrit un événement totalement accompli dans le passé, d'où l'emploi du passé simple.

Quelques comparaisons utiles :

have you **seen** him this morning?
(*la question est posée alors que c'est encore le matin*)
did you **see** him this morning?
(*la question est posée dans l'après-midi ou dans la soirée*)
est-ce que tu l'as vu ce matin ?

b) La forme progressive du "present perfect" peut être employée pour insister sur la durée :

what **have** you **been reading** recently?
qu'est-ce que tu as lu récemment ?

we haven't seen you for ages, what **have** you **been doing** with yourself?
ça fait une éternité qu'on ne vous a pas vu, qu'est-ce que vous devenez ?

what **have** you **been saying** to him to make him cry?
qu'est-ce que tu lui as dit pour le faire pleurer ?

I**'ve been meaning** to ask you something, doctor
cela fait un certain temps que je veux vous poser une question, docteur

Cependant, il y a parfois peu de différence de sens entre la forme simple et la forme progressive du "present perfect" :

I**'ve been living** here for 15 years (*progressif*)
I**'ve lived** here for 15 years (*simple*)
je vis ici depuis 15 ans

Remarquez que "depuis" se traduit par **for** lorsqu'il est suivi d'un nombre et par **since** lorsqu'il est suivi d'une date, c'est-à-dire lorsqu'on fait référence à un moment précis du passé :

I**'ve been living** here since 1972
I**'ve lived** here since 1972
je vis ici depuis 1972

Le plus-que-parfait ("past perfect")

a) Ce temps se forme avec l'auxiliaire **have** au passé + participe passé du verbe. On l'emploie pour décrire des actions ou des faits survenus avant d'autres événements du passé. Il fait référence à un moment du passé en relation à un autre moment du passé :

the fire **had** already **been put out** when they got there (*passif*)
l'incendie avait déjà été éteint quand ils sont arrivés sur place

he searched the directory but the file **had been erased** the day before *(passif)*
il a cherché dans le répertoire, mais le fichier avait été effacé la veille

had you **heard** of him before you came here?
tu avais déjà entendu parler de lui avant de venir ici ?

they **hadn't left** anything in the fridge so I went out to eat
ils n'avaient rien laissé dans le réfrigérateur, alors je suis allé manger en ville

Il peut aussi s'employer pour indiquer la fin d'un état de choses (d'un état d'esprit, d'une humeur, etc.) :

I **had hoped** to speak to him this morning
j'avais espéré lui parler ce matin

Ceci implique que la probabilité de pouvoir lui parler semble maintenant très faible ou nulle.

b) Le plus-que-parfait progressif peut être employé pour insister davantage sur la durée :

I'**d been wanting** to ask that question myself
je voulais moi aussi poser cette question

had you **been waiting** long before they arrived?
est-ce que tu as attendu longtemps avant qu'ils arrivent ?

Pour le plus-que-parfait dans les propositions qui expriment la condition, voir page 59.

12 Le futur

Will et shall

a) Pour exprimer le futur à la 1ère personne du singulier ou du pluriel, on emploie **will** ou **shall** (**shall** étant beaucoup plus fréquent en anglais britannique), qui peuvent se contracter en **'ll**. La forme contractée de **will not** est **won't** et celle de **shall not** est **shan't** :

I **will**/I'**ll**/I **shall let** you know as soon as I can
je vous le ferai savoir aussi vite que possible

we **won't**/**shan't need** that many
nous n'en aurons pas besoin d'autant

b) On emploie **will** pour les autres personnes :

will you **be** there?
tu seras là ?

lunch **will take** about another ten minutes
le déjeuner sera prêt dans environ dix minutes

they'**ll** just **have** to wait
ils n'auront qu'à attendre

c) Si le locuteur exprime une intention à la 2ème ou 3ème personne (par exemple une promesse ou une menace), on trouve parfois **shall**, mais cet emploi est aujourd'hui bien moins courant que **will** :

you **shall be treated** just like the others
tu seras traité comme les autres

they **shall pay** for this!
ils vont me le payer !

Si l'intention ou la volonté ne dépend pas du locuteur, on emploie **will** (**'ll**) :

he **will**/he'**ll do** it, I'm sure
il le fera, j'en suis sûr

d) **Shall** est employé pour faire des propositions, des suggestions :

shall we **go**?
on y va ?

e) **Will** peut être employé pour demander à quelqu'un de faire quelque chose :

will you **come** with me, please?
veuillez venir avec moi, s'il vous plaît

f) Pour exprimer le futur immédiat :

Dans les exemples suivants, **will** est plus employé que **shall** (la forme contractée **'ll** demeurant la plus fréquente) :

leave it, I'**ll do** it myself
laisse, je vais le faire

I'**ll have** a beer, please
je prendrai une bière, s'il vous plaît

that's the doorbell – ok, I'**ll get** it
on sonne à la porte – d'accord, j'y vais

Le futur simple et le futur progressif

a) **Will** et **shall** suivis de la forme progressive peuvent être employés pour insister sur la continuité de l'action :

what **will** you **be doing** this time next year?
qu'est-ce que tu feras l'année prochaine à cette époque ?

b) Comparez les exemples suivants :

will you **speak** to him about it? *(simple)*
tu lui en parleras ?

will you **be speaking** to him about it? *(progressif)*
tu comptes lui en parler ?

L'emploi de la forme progressive dans le second exemple indique que le locuteur ne fait pas une demande directe (comme dans le premier exemple), mais qu'il demande simplement et objectivement si la personne à laquelle il s'adresse a l'intention de "lui en parler".

Be going to

a) Cette forme s'emploie souvent de la même manière que **will** :

will it ever stop raining?
is it ever **going to** stop raining?
est-ce qu'il va s'arrêter de pleuvoir un jour ?

b) **Be going to** est plus courant que **will** ou **shall** pour exprimer une intention :

I'm going to take them to court
je vais les poursuivre en justice

they**'re going to** buy a new car
ils vont acheter une nouvelle voiture

c) On préfère **be going to** à **will** lorsque les raisons justifiant les prévisions sont directement liées au présent :

it**'s going to** rain (look at those clouds)
il va pleuvoir (tu as vu les nuages)

I know what he**'s going to** say (it's written all over his face)
je sais ce qu'il va dire (ça se lit sur son visage)

Le présent simple

a) Ce temps peut exprimer le futur lorsque l'on fait référence à un programme établi, un horaire, etc. :

when **does** the race **start**?
à quelle heure commence la course ?

the match **kicks off** at 2 o'clock
le match commence à 14 heures

Comme le montre ce dernier exemple, il est très courant d'employer le présent simple lorsque l'on précise le temps ou l'heure par un adverbe ou autre expression temporelle :

we **go** on holiday tomorrow
nous partons en vacances demain

the plane **leaves** at 7 a.m.
l'avion décolle à 7 heures

b) On emploie généralement le présent simple dans les propositions temporelles ou conditionnelles :

you'll be surprised **when** you **see** her
vous serez surpris quand vous la verrez

if he **turns up**, will you speak to him?
tu lui en parleras s'il vient ?

Remarque :

Les propositions commençant par **when** ou **if** ne doivent pas être confondues avec des propositions interrogatives indirectes dans lesquelles il est possible d'employer le futur :

does he know when they**'ll arrive**? (when will they arrive?)
est-ce qu'il sait quand ils vont arriver ? (quand est-ce qu'ils vont arriver ?)

I don't know if he**'ll agree** (will he agree?)
je ne sais pas s'il sera d'accord (est-ce qu'il sera d'accord ?)

Le présent progressif

a) Le présent progressif est souvent employé de façon semblable à **be going to** pour exprimer l'intention :

I'm putting you in charge of the investigation (= I'm going to put you in charge of...)
je vous confie la responsabilité de l'enquête (= je vais vous confier...)

what **are** you **doing** over Christmas? (= what are you going to do...?)
qu'est-ce que tu fais à Noël ? (= qu'est-ce que tu vas faire...?)

Mais remarquez une différence subtile entre les deux exemples suivants :

I'm taking him to court
je lui fais un procès

I'm going to take him to court
je vais lui faire un procès

L'intention est plus forte dans le premier exemple ; elle est moins définitive dans le second.

b) Le présent progressif peut aussi être employé pour faire référence à un événement organisé ou prévu dans le futur, son emploi étant alors similaire à celui du futur progressif ou à celui du présent simple :

he**'s giving** a concert tomorrow
il donne un concert demain

when **are** they **coming**?
quand est-ce qu'ils viennent ?

they**'re arriving** at Heathrow at midnight
ils arrivent à Heathrow à minuit

Be to

Be to est souvent employé, dans un style soutenu, pour faire référence à des projets d'avenir spécifiques, en particulier des projets qui dépendent de la décision d'autres personnes :

we **are to** be there by ten o'clock
nous devons y être pour dix heures

I**'m to** report to a Mr Glover on Tuesday
je dois me présenter mardi à un certain M. Glover

Be about to

Cette forme est employée pour exprimer le futur immédiat :

please take your seats, the play **is about to** begin
veuillez vous asseoir, la pièce va maintenant commencer

you **are about to** meet a great artist
vous êtes sur le point de rencontrer un grand artiste

Cette forme peut aussi s'employer pour exprimer les intentions futures d'une personne :

I'm not about to sign a contract like that!
je ne signerai pas un tel contrat !

En anglais britannique, on aurait davantage tendance à employer **be going to**.

Le futur antérieur

a) Le futur antérieur, c'est-à-dire **will have** + participe passé, s'emploie pour faire référence à une action qui sera accomplie avant une autre action dans le futur :

by the time you get there we **will have finished** dinner
le temps que vous arriviez, nous aurons fini de dîner

b) Il est aussi employé pour faire des suppositions, des hypothèses quant au présent ou au passé, comme dans l'exemple suivant à la forme progressive :

I expect you**'ll have been wondering** why I asked you here
je suppose que vous vous êtes demandé pourquoi je vous ai convoqué

13 L'INFINITIF ET LE GÉRONDIF

L'infinitif

1 Employé sans **to**

a) Après **do** (**I don't know**), après les auxiliaires modaux tels que **might**, **must**, etc. (voir chapitre 17) et après **dare** et **need** lorsqu'ils sont employés comme auxiliaires (voir page 74)

b) Après **had better** :

you**'d better apologize**
tu ferais mieux de t'excuser

c) Après **why** ou **why not** :

why stay indoors in this lovely weather?
pourquoi rester à l'intérieur par ce beau temps ?

d) Dans la construction complément d'objet direct : nom/pronom + infinitif (comparez avec 2 b) ci-dessous) :

- après **let** (*laisser*), **make** (*faire*) et **have** (*faire*):

we **let him smoke**
nous l'avons laissé fumer

I **made him turn** round
je l'ai fait se retourner

we **had him say** a few words
nous lui avons fait dire quelques mots

- après les verbes de perception **feel** (*sentir*), **hear** (*entendre*), **see** (*voir*), **watch** (*regarder*) :

I **felt the woman touch** my back
j'ai senti la femme me toucher le dos

Ces verbes peuvent aussi être suivis du participe présent pour mettre l'accent sur la durée de l'action :

I **felt her creeping** up behind me
je sentais qu'elle s'approchait de moi à pas de loup

- on peut trouver les deux formes de l'infinitif après help :

  we helped him (to) move house
  nous l'avons aidé à déménager

2 Employé avec to

a) L'infinitif avec to peut s'employer comme sujet, comme attribut ou comme complément d'objet direct dans une phrase. La phrase suivante contient les trois emplois (dans cet ordre) :

   to die is to cease to exist
   mourir, c'est cesser d'exister

b) Comme complément d'objet direct (comparez avec 1 d) ci-dessus) :

- après des verbes exprimant un désir ou une antipathie, en particulier want (*vouloir*), wish (*souhaiter*), like (*aimer*), prefer (*préférer*), hate (*détester/haïr*) :

  I want you to remember this
  je veux que tu t'en souviennes

- dans un langage assez soutenu, après des verbes exprimant un point de vue, un jugement, une supposition ou une affirmation :

  we believe this to be a mistake
  nous pensons que c'est une erreur

  Dans un langage moins soutenu, on préférera une proposition introduite par that :

  we believe (that) this is a mistake

- dans la construction passive correspondante, on garde to :

  this was believed to be a mistake
  on pensait que c'était une erreur

- la forme to + infinitif doit aussi être employée dans des constructions passives avec les verbes mentionnés dans 1 d) ci-dessus :

  she was made to do it
  on l'a forcée à le faire

c) À la suite de noms, de pronoms et d'adjectifs :
   there are things to be done
   il y a des choses à faire

glad to meet you!
heureux de faire votre connaissance !

d) Correspondant à une proposition subordonnée :

- exprimant un but ou une conséquence, parfois accompagné de **in order** ou **so as** (but) ou **only** (conséquence) :

he left early **to/in order to/so as to get** a good seat for the performance
il est parti tôt pour/afin d'être bien placé au spectacle

they arrived **(only) to find** an empty house
à leur arrivée, la maison était vide

- dans des propositions interrogatives indirectes :

we didn't know **who to ask**
nous ne savions pas à qui demander

- pour exprimer le temps, la proposition infinitive équivalant alors à un complément circonstanciel commençant par **when** (**when one hears him speak...**) :

to hear him speak, one would think he positively hates women
à l'entendre parler, on dirait vraiment qu'il déteste les femmes

e) Dans la construction **for** + nom/pronom + infinitif :

he waited **for her to finish**
il attendit qu'elle ait fini

f) La césure de l'infinitif :

On dit que l'infinitif “se coupe” lorsqu'un adverbe est placé entre **to** et le radical :

they then decided **to definitely leave**
ils ont alors décidé de partir pour de bon

Cette forme est devenue courante, mais elle est souvent peu appréciée. On lui préfère la forme :

they then decided **definitely to leave**

Le gérondif

Le gérondif, appelé aussi verbe substantivé, possède des caractéristiques propres aux noms et aux verbes. Il a la même forme que le participe présent (terminaison en **-ing**), mais son champ d'application est différent.

1 Caractéristiques nominales

a) Un gérondif peut être sujet, attribut ou complément d'objet :

smoking is not good for you (*sujet*)
fumer n'est pas bon pour la santé

that's cheating (*attribut*)
c'est de la triche

I love reading (*complément*)
j'adore lire

b) Il peut être placé après une préposition :

he's thought of leaving
il a pensé partir

c) Il peut être modifié par un article, un adjectif ou un possessif :

the timing of his remarks was unfortunate
il a mal choisi son moment pour faire des remarques

careless writing leaves a bad impression
une écriture peu soignée donne une mauvaise impression

do you remember his trying to persuade her?
tu te souviens qu'il a essayé de la persuader ?

Remarque :

Dans ce dernier exemple, nous aurions pu avoir le pronom him à la place de l'adjectif possessif his. Les deux formes sont possibles lorsque le gérondif est complément du verbe ou lorsqu'il est placé après une préposition. L'emploi de l'adjectif possessif est plus courant à l'écrit (style soutenu) qu'à l'oral :

we were surprised about you/your not being chosen
nous avons été surpris que vous n'ayez pas été sélectionnés

2 Caractéristiques verbales

a) Un gérondif peut avoir un sujet :

the thought of Douglas doing that is absurd
penser que Douglas ait pu faire ça est absurde

b) Il peut être suivi d'un complément d'objet ou d'un attribut :

writing this letter took me ages
j'ai mis un temps fou à écrire cette lettre

being left-handed has never been a problem
être gaucher n'a jamais été un problème

c) Il peut être modifié par un adverbe :

it's a question of **precisely defining** our needs
il s'agit de définir précisément quels sont nos besoins

Comparaison entre l'infinitif et le gérondif

On peut parfois employer l'un ou l'autre après un verbe quand ils sont compléments d'objet direct :

I can't **stand seeing** him like this
I can't **stand to see** him like this
je ne supporte pas de le voir comme ça

Mais il y a parfois une différence de sens importante :

we **stopped smoking** *nous avons arrêté de fumer*	we **stopped to smoke** *nous nous sommes arrêtés pour fumer*
he was too **busy talking** to her *il était trop occupé à lui parler*	he was too **busy to talk** to her *il était trop occupé pour lui parler*

Dans ces exemples, le gérondif est employé comme complément d'objet direct tandis que l'infinitif fonctionne comme un complément circonstanciel de but, ce qui explique la différence de sens.

Voici des verbes fréquemment employés qui ne sont suivis que de l'infinitif :

demand	*exiger*
deserve	*mériter*
expect	*s'attendre à*
hope	*espérer*
want	*vouloir*
wish	*souhaiter*

et des verbes fréquemment employés qui ne sont suivis que du gérondif :

avoid	*éviter*
consider	*considérer*
dislike	*ne pas aimer*
enjoy	*apprécier*
finish	*finir*
keep	*garder*
practise	*pratiquer, faire*
risk	*risquer*

14 L'IMPÉRATIF

Le mode impératif s'emploie pour donner des ordres ou faire des suggestions. À la forme négative, il permet d'exprimer l'interdiction.

1 Pour exprimer l'impératif, on emploie le verbe à l'infinitif (sans **to**) :

stop that!
arrête ça !

well, just **look** at him!
eh bien, regarde-le, celui-là !

somebody **do** something!
que quelqu'un fasse quelque chose !

have another
prenez-en un autre

try mine
essayez le mien

2 Pour faire une suggestion ou une proposition à la 1ère personne du pluriel, on emploie **let's** + infinitif sans **to** :

let's leave it at that for today
restons-en là pour aujourd'hui

let's just **agree** to differ
acceptons tout simplement de ne pas être du même avis

3 L'interdiction ou la commande négative :

Pour exprimer l'interdiction ou la commande négative, on emploie **do not** ou **don't** placés devant l'infinitif. En anglais courant et parlé, **don't** est la forme la plus fréquente, à moins de vouloir donner plus d'emphase à la phrase :

don't listen to what he says
n'écoute pas ce qu'il dit

please **don't feel** you have to accept
je t'en prie, ne te sens pas obligé d'accepter

look, I've told you before, **do not put** your hands near the hotplate!
écoute, je te l'ai déjà dit, ne mets pas tes mains près de la plaque chauffante !

Avec la forme **let's**, on place **not** entre **let's** et le verbe. On peut aussi employer la forme plus rare **don't let's** :

let's not go just yet
don't let's go just yet
ne partons pas encore

4 **Do not** s'emploie beaucoup sur les panneaux d'indication :

please **do not feed** the animals
prière de ne pas donner à manger aux animaux

5 Pour renforcer un impératif, il est possible d'employer l'auxiliaire **do** :

oh, **do be** quiet!
oh, reste tranquille !

15 LE CONDITIONNEL

La phrase :

if you don't hurry, you'll miss your train
si tu ne te dépêches pas, tu vas manquer ton train

est une phrase conditionnelle. La condition est exprimée dans la proposition subordonnée (commençant par **if**) qui peut être placée avant ou après la proposition principale (**you'll miss your train**).

La forme des verbes varie selon le temps auquel ils font référence et selon le degré de probabilité de la condition.

Pour faire référence au présent/futur

a) Possibilité vraisemblable :

Le verbe de la proposition commençant par **if** est au présent ou au "present perfect" ; le verbe de la proposition principale est **will** + infinitif (parfois **shall** + infinitif, à la 1ère personne) :

if I **see** her, **I'll tell** her
si je la vois, je le lui dirai

if you **have completed** the forms, I **will send** them off
si vous avez rempli les formulaires, je les enverrai

Il y a trois exceptions majeures :

- Si le verbe de la proposition principale est aussi au présent, on s'attend à une conséquence logique, par automatisme ou habitude. Dans ce cas, **if** a le sens de **when(ever)** (*chaque fois, quand*) :

if the sun shines, people **look** happier
quand le soleil brille, les gens ont l'air plus heureux

if you're happy, then I**'m** happy
si ça te va, ça me va

- Quand **will** est employé dans la proposition qui commence par **if**, le locuteur fait allusion à la volonté ou à l'intention de quelqu'un de faire quelque chose :

  if you **will** kindly **look** this way, I'll try to explain the painter's method
  si vous voulez bien regarder par ici, je vais vous expliquer la méthode utilisée par le peintre

  well if you **will mix** your drinks, what can you expect!
  si tu tiens absolument à faire des mélanges d'alcool, que veux-tu qu'il arrive ?!

  Quand on emploie cette forme pour faire une demande, on peut rendre la phrase plus polie en employant **would** :

  if you **would be** kind enough to look this way...
  si vous voulez bien regarder par ici...

- Lorsque **should** est employé dans la proposition commençant par **if** (à n'importe quelle personne), la condition semble avoir moins de chance de se réaliser. Ces propositions avec **should** sont souvent suivies de l'impératif, comme dans le premier exemple :

  if you **should see** him, please ask him to ring me
  si vous deviez le rencontrer, pourriez-vous lui demander de me téléphoner ?

  if they **should not be** there, you will have to manage by yourself
  si par hasard ils ne sont pas là, il faudra bien que vous vous débrouilliez tout seul

  Dans un style plus soutenu, **if** peut être omis et la phrase peut commencer avec une proposition subordonnée employant **should** :

  should the matter **arise** again, telephone me at once
  si le problème devait se présenter à nouveau, téléphonez-moi immédiatement

b) Possibilité peu probable ou irréelle :

Si la condition n'est pas supposée se réaliser, si elle présente un caractère de doute ou si elle s'oppose à des faits connus, le verbe de la proposition commençant par **if** est au passé ; le verbe de la proposition principale est **would** (ou aussi **should** à la 1ère personne) + infinitif :

if I **saw** her, I **would** (I'**d**) **tell** her
si je la voyais, je le lui dirais

if she **had** a car, she **would visit** you more often
si elle avait une voiture, elle viendrait te voir plus souvent

Remarque :

Remarquez que ce type de phrase n'exprime pas nécessairement une possibilité peu probable ou irréelle. Il y a souvent très peu de différence entre ce type de phrase et celui décrit en a) :

if you **worked** harder, you **would pass** the exam
if you **work** harder, you **will pass** the exam
si tu travaillais davantage, tu réussirais ton examen

L'emploi du passé peut donner à la phrase un ton plus amical ou plus poli.

Pour faire référence au passé

a) La condition ne s'est pas réalisée. Le verbe de la proposition subordonnée est au plus-que-parfait ; on trouve **would** (ou aussi **should** à la 1ère personne) + infinitif passé dans la proposition principale :

if I **had seen** her, I **would have told** her
si je l'avais vue, je le lui aurais dit

if you **had finished** that one, I **would have given** you another one
si tu avais fini celui-ci, je t'en aurais donné un autre

Dans un style légèrement plus soutenu, **if** peut être omis et la proposition subordonnée peut commencer par **had**. Attention à l'inversement du pronom personnel et de **had** :

had I seen her, I would/should have told her
si je l'avais vue, je le lui aurais dit

b) Exceptions :

- Si la proposition principale fait référence à la non-réalisation dans le présent d'une condition passée, on peut aussi employer **would** + infinitif (présent) :

if I had studied harder, I **would be** an engineer today (= if I had

studied harder, I **would have been** an engineer today)
si j'avais étudié davantage, je serais ingénieur maintenant

- Le passé est employé dans les deux propositions si, comme nous l'avons vu page 57), une conséquence automatique ou habituelle est sous-entendue (**if** = **when(ever)**, *chaque fois, quand*) :

  if people **got** ill in those days, they often **died**
  si les gens tombaient malades à cette époque-là, ils mouraient souvent

- Si la condition est censée avoir eu lieu, les restrictions sur les formes verbales ne sont plus valables. En effet dans ce cas, **if** signifie souvent "comme" ou "puisque" :

  if he **was** rude to you, why **did** you not **walk** out?
  puisqu'il était impoli avec toi, pourquoi n'es-tu pas sorti ?

  if he **was** rude to you, why **have** you still **kept** in touch?
  puisqu'il était impoli avec toi, pourquoi es-tu resté en contact avec lui ?

  if he **was** rude to you, why **do** you still **keep** in touch?
  puisqu'il était impoli avec toi, pourquoi restes-tu en contact avec lui ?

16 Le subjonctif

Par opposition à l'indicatif, qui est le mode du réel, le subjonctif est le mode du non-réel et exprime le souhait, l'espoir, la possibilité, etc.

On reconnaît le subjonctif à l'omission du **-s** à la 3ème personne du singulier et à l'emploi de **be** au lieu de **is** au présent, et de **were** au lieu de **was** au passé. Le mode subjonctif n'est pas aussi courant en anglais qu'en français. Principaux emplois :

1 Dans des locutions fixes qui expriment le souhait :

long **live** the King!
vive le Roi !

God **rest** his soul
Dieu ait son âme

Heaven **be praised**
Dieu soit loué

2 Dans l'expression **if need be** (*si besoin est, s'il le faut*) :

well, **if need be**, you could always hire a car
eh bien, s'il le faut, vous pouvez toujours louer une voiture

3 Dans des propositions comme :

it is vital that he **understand** this
il est très important qu'il comprenne cela

they recommended she **sell** the house
ils lui ont conseillé de vendre la maison

we propose that this new ruling **be adopted**
nous proposons que cette nouvelle loi soit adoptée

On trouve cet emploi du subjonctif dans un style plus soutenu. Dans la langue parlée, il est plus fréquent en anglais américain qu'en anglais britannique.

4 Après **if only** et dans les propositions qui suivent **wish** et **had rather** :

if only we **had** a bigger house...
si seulement nous avions une maison plus grande...

where's your passport? – I **wish** I **knew**!
où est ton passeport ? – si je le savais !

do you want me to tell you? – I'**d rather** you **didn't**
tu veux que je te le dise ? – je ne préfère pas !

Remarque :

Dans ces propositions qui expriment le souhait et le désir, on emploiera toujours le subjonctif passé. Il se construit comme le prétérit sauf pour **to be** dont le subjonctif est **were** à toutes les personnes du passé.

5 Après **it's time** (emploi du subjonctif passé) :

it'**s (high) time** we **spoke** to him
il est (grand) temps que nous lui parlions

Comparez avec l'emploi de l'infinitif qui ne fait qu'exprimer l'opportunité du moment :

it'**s time to speak** to him about it
c'est le moment de lui en parler

6 **if I was/if I were** :

Comparez :

(a) **if I was** in the wrong, it wasn't intentional
si je me suis trompé, je ne l'ai pas fait exprès

(b) **if I were** in the wrong, I would admit it
si je m'étais trompé, je le reconnaîtrais

Dans l'exemple (a), le locuteur n'émet aucun doute sur le fait qu'il se soit trompé, mais précise l'absence d'intention malveillante. Dans l'exemple (b), par contre, le locuteur n'accepte pas qu'il se soit trompé ; pour le locuteur, un doute persiste concernant ce point. D'où l'emploi du subjonctif **were**.

Dans la phrase (b), on pourrait aussi employer **was** tout en conservant le même sens. **Was** serait d'un style plus familier que **were**.

17 LES AUXILIAIRES MODAUX

Les auxiliaires modaux, qui comme tout auxiliaire modifient le verbe principal de la phrase, sont appelés ainsi car ils remplacent le mode du subjonctif dans de nombreux cas. Une de leurs caractéristiques est qu'ils se construisent sans **do** aux formes interrogative et négative.

Can-Could

Les formes contractées négatives sont **can't-couldn't**. La forme négative non contractée du présent est **cannot**.

a) Pour exprimer la capacité, le fait de pouvoir faire quelque chose :

I **can't** afford it
je ne peux pas me le permettre

I **can** swim
je sais nager

when I was a student, I **could** explain this theory easily
quand j'étais étudiant, je pouvais expliquer cette théorie sans aucun problème

Dans ce dernier exemple au passé, il est possible d'employer **be able to** (*pouvoir, être capable de*). Cette tournure permet d'exprimer la capacité à tous les autres temps :

I **used to be able to** explain this theory easily
avant je pouvais expliquer cette théorie sans aucun problème

I'll be able to tell you the answer tomorrow
je pourrai te donner la réponse demain

I've never been able to understand her
je n'ai jamais pu la comprendre

Remarque :

Dans une proposition conditionnelle, **could** + infinitif fait référence au présent ou au futur (comparez avec **would** dans Le conditionnel, page 58) :

you **could** do a lot better if you'd only try
tu pourrais faire bien mieux si seulement tu faisais un effort

b) Pour exprimer la permission :

can/could I have a look at your photos?
est-ce que je peux/pourrais voir vos photos ?

Remarque :

Could fait autant référence au présent et au futur que **can**. La seule différence réside dans le fait que **could** est un peu plus poli ou moins affirmatif. Par exemple, un enfant ne dira pas :

could I go out to play?
pourrais-je aller jouer ?

On peut parfois employer **could** pour exprimer une permission dans le passé, lorsqu'il est évident qu'il s'agit d'un contexte au passé :

for some reason we **couldn't** smoke in the lounge before; but now we can
pour une raison que j'ignore, nous ne pouvions pas fumer avant dans le salon ; mais maintenant nous pouvons

Dans ce dernier exemple, il est possible d'employer **be allowed to** (*pouvoir, être autorisé à*). Cette tournure permet d'exprimer la permission à tous les autres temps :

we **weren't allowed to** see him, he was so ill
nous ne pouvions pas le voir, il était trop souffrant

will they **be allowed to** change the rules?
est-ce qu'ils auront le droit de changer les règles ?

c) Pour exprimer la possibilité :

that **can't** be right
ça ne peut pas être ça

what shall I do? – you **can** always talk to a lawyer/you **could** talk to a lawyer
qu'est-ce que je vais faire ? – vous pouvez toujours vous adresser à un avocat/vous pourriez vous adresser à un avocat

Là encore, remarquez que could ne fait pas référence au passé, mais au présent ou au futur. Si l'on souhaite faire référence au passé, could doit être suivi de l'infinitif passé :

you **could have talked** to a lawyer
vous auriez pu vous adresser à un avocat

I know I **could have**, but I didn't want to
je sais que j'aurais pu, mais je ne voulais pas

Could et **may** sont parfois interchangeables lorsqu'ils expriment la possibilité, l'éventualité :

you **could/may** be right
vous avez peut-être raison

Mais il existe parfois une différence importante entre **can** et **may** dans leur rapport à la possibilité, à l'éventualité :

(a) your comments **can** be overheard
on peut entendre vos remarques

(b) your comments **may** be overheard
on pourrait entendre vos remarques

(a) signifie qu'il est possible que l'on entende les remarques (parce qu'elles sont faites à voix haute, par exemple) sans spécifier si quelqu'un les entendra véritablement ou non. (b) signifie qu'il existe une probabilité, une chance que les remarques soient réellement entendues.

La différence existe aussi à la forme négative :

don't worry, he **can't** have heard us
ne t'inquiète pas, il ne peut pas nous avoir entendus (il est impossible qu'il nous ait entendus)

because of all the noise, he **may not** have heard us
avec ce bruit, il se peut qu'il ne nous ait pas entendus

d) Pour exprimer la suggestion (could uniquement) :

you could try a supermarket
tu peux essayer d'aller voir au supermarché

they could always sell their second house if they need money
ils peuvent toujours vendre leur maison secondaire s'ils ont besoin d'argent

e) Pour exprimer le reproche, l'ennui, l'agacement (could uniquement) :

you could have told me I had paint on my face!
tu aurais pu me dire que j'avais de la peinture sur la figure !

May-Might

La forme contractée négative mayn't n'est pas courante dans le sens de "permission" de may. On emploie à la place may not ou must not/mustn't. La forme négative contractée de might est mightn't, mais elle ne s'emploie pas pour exprimer l'interdiction.

a) Pour exprimer la permission ou l'interdiction :

may I open a window? – no, you may not!
est-ce que je peux ouvrir la fenêtre ? – non, pas question !

L'emploi de may donne une forme légèrement plus polie que can. Un locuteur qui emploie might pour demander une permission se montrerait extrêmement poli :

I wonder if I might have another of those cakes
pourrais-je reprendre un autre gâteau, s'il vous plaît ?

might I suggest we stop there for today?
puis-je suggérer que nous nous arrêtions là pour aujourd'hui ?

Remarque :

Remarquez que **might** exprime le présent ou le futur. Il fait très rarement référence au passé quand il est employé dans une proposition principale. Comparez :

he then asked if he **might** smoke (**might** *dans la proposition subordonnée)*
he then asked if he was allowed to smoke
il a alors demandé s'il pouvait fumer

et

he wasn't allowed to smoke
il ne pouvait pas fumer/il n'avait pas le droit de fumer

On ne peut pas employer **might** dans le dernier exemple ; on a recours aux formes de **be allowed to** à la place.

b) Pour exprimer la possibilité :

it **may/might** still be possible
c'est peut-être encore possible

they **may/might** change their minds
il se peut qu'ils changent d'avis

it **may not/mightn't** be necessary after all
ça ne sera peut-être pas nécessaire après tout

she **may/might** have left a note upstairs
elle a peut-être laissé un mot en haut

c) Pour exprimer la surprise, l'agacement (**might** habituellement) :

and who **may/might** you be to give out orders?
pour qui est-ce que tu te prends pour donner des ordres ?

and what **might** that be supposed to mean?
et qu'est-ce que c'est censé vouloir dire ?

d) Pour exprimer la suggestion (**might** uniquement) :

they **might** at least apologize
ils pourraient au moins s'excuser

you **might** like to try one of these cigars
vous voulez peut-être essayer un de ces cigares

Remarque :

Remarquez que, dans cet usage, on a presque un ordre :

you **might** take this down the road to your Gran
tu veux bien apporter ça à ta grand-mère

you **might** like to read the next chapter for Monday
vous voudrez bien lire le chapitre suivant pour lundi

e) Pour exprimer le **reproche** (**might** uniquement) :

you **might** have told me he was deaf!
tu aurais pu me dire qu'il était sourd !

they **might** have written back to us at least!
ils auraient pu au moins nous répondre !

f) Pour exprimer le **souhait** (attention à l'ordre des mots) :

may you have a very happy retirement
je vous souhaite une très heureuse retraite

may all your dreams come true!
je souhaite que tous vos rêves se réalisent !

may/might you be forgiven for telling such lies!
que le bon Dieu te pardonne de tels mensonges !

Cet usage est normalement limité aux locutions fixes ou à un style rhétorique ou littéraire.

Must-Had to

La forme contractée négative de **must** est **mustn't** (pour **have**, voir page 31).

a) Pour exprimer l'**obligation** :

you have no choice, you **must** do what he wants
tu n'as pas le choix, tu dois faire ce qu'il veut

must you go already?
faut-il que tu partes déjà ?

Le style de ce dernier exemple est très soutenu. On peut aussi employer au présent **have to** ou, dans un style plus familier, **have got to** :

you have no choice, you have (got) to do what he says
tu n'as pas le choix, tu dois faire ce qu'il dit

do you have to go already/have you got to go already?
tu dois déjà partir ?

Le sens est souvent le même, mais on distingue parfois une légère différence. Must exprime des sentiments personnels d'obligation ou de contrainte, tandis que have to est plus souvent employé lorsqu'une obligation extérieure est sous-entendue (c.-à-d. quelqu'un vous a dit de faire quelque chose). Comparez :

I must go to the dentist (= I have toothache, etc.)
il faut que j'aille chez le dentiste (= j'ai mal aux dents, etc.)

I have (got) to go to the dentist (= I have an appointement)
je dois aller chez le dentiste (= j'ai rendez-vous)

Pour le passé et le futur, on emploie have to :

we had to do what he wanted
nous devions faire ce qu'il voulait

I'll have to finish it tomorrow
il faudra que je le finisse demain

b) Pour exprimer l'interdiction ou l'absence d'obligation (forme négative) :

- Must not est employé pour signifier l'interdiction :

  you mustn't drink and drive
  il ne faut pas boire et conduire

  Au passé, on emploie not to be allowed to :

  when we were children we weren't allowed to...
  quand nous étions petits, nous n'avions pas le droit de...

- Don't have to ou haven't got to sont employés pour signifier une absence d'obligation :

  we don't have to drive all night, we could always stop at a hotel
  nous ne sommes pas obligés de conduire toute la nuit, nous pouvons nous arrêter à l'hôtel

  La forme passée suit la conjugaison de **have** :

  you **didn't have to** buy one, you could have used mine
  tu n'avais pas besoin d'en acheter un, tu aurais pu prendre le mien

c) Pour exprimer la probabilité, la déduction :

hello, you must be Susan
bonjour, vous devez être Susan

that must be my mistake
ça doit être une erreur de ma part

she must have been surprised to see you
elle a dû être surprise de te voir

Have to est aussi souvent employé dans ce sens :

you have to be kidding!
tu veux rire !

de même que have got to, surtout en anglais britannique :

well if she said so, it's got to be true (it's = it has)
si elle l'a dit, c'est que c'est vrai

Ought to

La forme contractée négative est oughtn't to. L'infinitif après ought est précédé de to, à la différence des autres auxiliaires modaux.

a) Pour exprimer l'obligation :

Ought to a le même sens que should quand il exprime l'obligation :

you oughtn't even to think things like that
tu ne devrais même pas penser à des choses pareilles

and he ought to know!
et il est bien placé pour le savoir !

Mais ought to est moins fort que must dans ce sens. Comparez :

I must/have to avoid fatty foods (*obligation ferme ou nécessité*)
je dois éviter les matières grasses

et

I ought to avoid fatty foods (*obligation moins stricte*)
je devrais éviter les matières grasses

Must ou have (got) to remplacent normalement ought to dans les questions :

must you/do you have to/have you got to visit your mother every Sunday?
est-ce que tu dois aller voir ta mère tous les dimanches ?

b) Pour exprimer la probabilité :

they ought to have reached the summit by now
ils devraient avoir atteint le sommet maintenant

£50, that ought to be enough
50 livres, ça devrait suffire

Shall-Should

Les formes contractées négatives sont shan't-shouldn't. Pour le conditionnel, voir page 57. Pour exprimer le futur, voir page 43.

a) Pour exprimer l'**obligation**, souvent morale (should uniquement) :

you should take more exercise
tu devrais faire plus d'exercice

you shouldn't talk to her like that
tu ne devrais pas lui parler comme ça

what do you think I should do?
à ton avis, qu'est-ce que je devrais faire ?

with a new fuse fitted it should work
avec un nouveau fusible, ça devrait marcher

b) Pour exprimer la **probabilité**, la **déduction** (should uniquement) :

it's after ten, they should be in Paris by now
il est plus de dix heures, ils doivent être arrivés à Paris maintenant

if doing one took you two hours, then three shouldn't take longer than six hours, should it?
si tu en fais un en deux heures, tu dois pouvoir en faire trois en six heures, non ?

is it there? – well, it should be because that's where I left it
il est là ? – eh bien il devrait, parce que c'est là que je l'ai laissé

c) Pour exprimer son **avis de manière hésitante**, should étant légèrement plus poli que would (should uniquement) :

I should just like to say that...
j'aimerais simplement dire que...

I should hardly call him a great intellectual but...
je ne dirais pas vraiment que c'est un grand intellectuel, mais...

d) Pour exprimer la **surprise**, l'**agacement**, l'**ennui** :

there was a knock at the door, and who should it be but...
on frappe à la porte, et qui c'est ?...

where have I put my glasses? – how should I know?
où est-ce que j'ai mis mes lunettes ? – comment veux-tu que je le sache ?

e) shall est employé dans le **langage juridique** ou **officiel** :

the committee shall consist of no more than six members
le comité sera constitué de six membres au plus

the contract shall be subject to English law
le contrat sera régi par la loi anglaise

Will-Would

Les formes négatives contractées sont won't-wouldn't. Pour les phrases au conditionnel, voir page 57. Pour exprimer le futur, voir page 43.

a) Will est employé pour insister sur la notion de **capacité**, d'**inclination naturelle**, d'**habitude** ou de **comportement caractéristique** :

cork will float on water
le liège flotte sur l'eau

the car won't start
la voiture ne veut pas démarrer

the tank will hold about 50 litres
ce réservoir a une contenance d'environ 50 litres

he will sit playing quietly on his own for hours
il peut rester tranquillement assis à jouer tout seul pendant des heures

it's so annoying, he **will** keep interrupting!
c'est énervant, il n'arrête pas de m'interrompre !

On emploie **would** pour faire référence au passé :

when he was little, he would sit playing quietly on his own for hours
quand il était petit, il restait tranquillement assis à jouer tout seul pendant des heures

they would insist on calling me "Jacko"
ils tenaient absolument à m'appeler "Jacko"

she created a scene in public – she would!
elle a fait une scène en public – c'est bien elle !/ça ne m'étonne pas d'elle !

b) Pour exprimer des ordres, ou pour renforcer une affirmation, plutôt qu'un simple futur :

you will do as you are told!
tu feras ce qu'on te dit !

will you stop that right now!
arrête ça tout de suite !

I will not tolerate this!
je ne tolérerai pas ça !

c) Pour faire appel, sur un ton plutôt cérémonieux, aux souvenirs ou aux connaissances de quelqu'un :

you will recall last week's discussion about the purchase of a computer
vous vous souvenez certainement de notre discussion de la semaine dernière concernant l'achat d'un ordinateur

as you will all know, there have been rumours recently about...
comme vous le savez certainement tous, il y a des rumeurs qui courent au sujet de...

d) Pour faire des suppositions :

there's someone at the door – that'll be Graham
il y a quelqu'un à la porte – ça doit être Graham

how old is he now? – he'll be about 45
quel âge a-t-il maintenant ? – il doit avoir à peu près 45 ans

e) Pour poser des questions ou faire des propositions de manière légèrement soutenue :

will you have another cup of tea? – thank you, I **will**
voulez-vous une autre tasse de thé ? – oui, merci, je veux bien

won't you try one of these?
vous ne voulez pas y goûter ?

did they ask you if you **would** like to try one?
est-ce qu'ils t'ont demandé si tu voulais en prendre un ?

f) Pour formuler des demandes :

will/would you move your car, please?
est-ce que vous pourriez déplacer votre voiture, s'il vous plaît ?

La forme **would** est plus polie, moins directe.

AUTRES AUXILIAIRES

Used to

Used to (pour exprimer une action habituelle dans le passé) peut être considéré comme une sorte de semi-auxiliaire, puisque l'emploi de **do** est facultatif dans les phrases interrogatives et négatives :

he **used** not **to** smoke so much
he didn't **use to** smoke so much
il ne fumait pas tant avant

used you **to** know him?
did you **use to** know him?
est-ce que vous le connaissiez ?

Cependant, la forme sans **do** est très rare et appartient davantage au langage écrit.

Dare, need

Ces verbes peuvent se comporter comme des verbes ordinaires ou comme des auxiliaires modaux. Lorsqu'ils sont auxiliaires, ils ne prennent pas de **-s** à la 3ème personne du singulier du présent ; **do** n'est pas employé dans les phrases interrogatives et négatives ; et s'ils sont suivis d'un infinitif, on ne met pas **to** devant le radical.

a) Comme **verbes ordinaires** :

I **don't dare** to say anything
je n'ose rien dire

does he **dare** talk openly about it?
est-ce qu'il ose en parler ouvertement ?

you **don't need** to ask first
tu n'as pas besoin de demander

do I **need** to sign it?
est-ce qu'il faut que je le signe ?

b) Comme auxiliaires modaux :

I daren't say anything
je n'ose rien dire

dare he talk openly about it?
ose-t-il en parler ouvertement ?

you needn't ask first
tu n'as pas besoin de demander

need I sign it?
faut-il que je le signe ?

L'emploi de dare et de need comme auxiliaires modaux appartient à un niveau de langue plus soutenu.

- Dare peut aussi fonctionner comme un verbe ordinaire aux formes interrogative et négative (c'est-à-dire avec do) et, comme les auxiliaires, être suivi d'un infinitif sans to :

I don't dare say anything
je n'ose rien dire

- Dans les propositions principales qui ne sont ni interrogatives ni négatives, need se comporte toujours comme un verbe ordinaire :

I need to go to the toilet
il faut que j'aille aux toilettes

Have, Get

Have ou get peuvent être employés dans des constructions du type "faire faire quelque chose à quelqu'un" (have/get + complément d'objet direct + participe passé) :

we're going to have/get the car resprayed
nous allons faire repeindre la voiture

I can't do it myself but I can have/get it done for you
je ne peux pas le faire moi-même, mais je peux le faire faire pour vous

Quand have/get sont suivis d'un infinitif à la voix active, le to est omis après have, mais il est maintenu après get :

I'll have the porter bring them up for you
I'll get the porter to bring them up for you
je les ferai monter par le portier

18 LES PARTICULES DES VERBES COMPOSÉS

Dans cette section, on s'intéresse aux particules des verbes composés. Le sens de ces verbes, appelés en anglais "phrasal verbs", n'équivaut pas forcément à la somme du sens des deux éléments qui les composent. Par exemple, run up peut avoir le sens de "monter en courant" ou de "laisser s'accumuler" (I've run up a huge overdraft *j'ai un découvert énorme*). Les verbes composés forment donc un tout ; la particule est indispensable, elle permet de modifier le sens du verbe principal.

Vous trouverez ici une liste de particules avec leurs principaux emplois et des exemples correspondant à chaque sens.

Voir aussi le Dictionnaire des verbes composés, page 107.

About

1 mouvement désordonné, qui part dans tous les sens :

I felt about for the light switch
je cherchais l'interrupteur à tâtons

I was rushing about trying to get ready when the phone rang
je courais dans tous les sens pour être prête à l'heure lorsque le téléphone sonna

people milled about in the streets
les rues fourmillaient de monde

2 immobilité, inaction, oisiveté :

I hate standing about at street corners, so make sure you're on time
je déteste rester planté au coin d'une rue, alors essaie d'être à l'heure

she always keeps me hanging about when we arrange to meet
elle me fait toujours poireauter quand on a rendez-vous

3 autour de soi, dans les alentours :

he looked about for a taxi
il chercha un taxi des yeux

4 au sujet de :

what do you think about his latest film?
que penses-tu de son dernier film ?

Across

communiquer, faire passer ou faire comprendre quelque chose :

he finds it hard to put his ideas across
il a du mal à exprimer clairement ses idées

how can I get it across to them that it's important to keep copies of all your files?
comment est-ce que je peux leur faire comprendre qu'il est important de faire une copie de tous les fichiers ?

After

1 en suivant, derrière :

he was running after his ball and dashed out into the road
il courait après son ballon et surgit sur la route

she tore after him, determined to catch him
elle se lança à sa poursuite, voulant à tout prix l'attraper

2 au sujet de :

she always remembers to ask after them
elle n'oublie jamais de demander de leurs nouvelles

3 lien ou ressemblance entre les membres d'une famille :

my niece takes after me
ma nièce me ressemble

he's called after his grandfather
il a le même nom que son grand-père

Against

1 protection contre quelque chose :

fluoride is said to guard against tooth decay
on dit que le fluor protège des caries

2 être préjudiciable à quelqu'un :

will the fact that he has a previous conviction go against him?
est-ce que le fait qu'il ait déjà été condamné peut jouer en sa défaveur ?

Ahead

1 en face, devant :

the favourite has got ahead now and looks likely to win
le favori est maintenant en tête et semble bien parti pour la victoire

2 notion de succès, de progrès :

you will never get ahead unless you are conscientious
tu n'arriveras jamais à rien si tu n'es pas consciencieux

3 dans l'avenir :

let's look ahead to the next month's meeting
pensons à la réunion du mois prochain

it is essential to plan ahead for your retirement
il est très important de préparer sa retraite

Along

1 action en cours, progression :

we were driving along when suddenly...
on roulait tranquillement quand soudain...

they were tearing along, so that they would arrive first
ils couraient à toute allure pour arriver les premiers

things are coming along nicely
les choses ne se présentent pas trop mal

2 partir ou faire partir :

I'll have to hurry along if I want to catch my train
j'ai intérêt à me dépêcher si je ne veux pas rater mon train

it's time for me to be getting along
il faut que j'y aille

the police told the crowd to move along
la police a demandé à la foule de se disperser

3 avec :

why not bring your sister along?
tu devrais venir avec ta sœur

4 vers un endroit proche, souvent dans la même rue :

my mother sent me along to see how you were
ma mère m'a dit de venir prendre de tes nouvelles

Apart

1 séparation :

the two fighters had to be pulled apart
ils ont dû séparer les deux combattants

I saw them draw apart as I entered the room
je les ai vus s'éloigner l'un de l'autre quand je suis entré dans la pièce

I can't get these two pieces apart
je n'arrive pas à détacher ces deux morceaux

2 en morceaux, en différentes parties :

he says it just came apart in his hands
il dit que ça s'est cassé quand il l'a pris dans ses mains

3 se distinguer des autres :

her talent sets her apart from all the other children in my class
elle se distingue par son talent des autres enfants de ma classe

Around (voir aussi round)

1 en différents endroits, autour de soi :

you have to search around for that kind of information
il faut que tu cherches autour de toi pour trouver ce genre d'information

I'm hunting around for a new flatmate
je suis à la recherche d'un nouveau colocataire

2 dans les alentours :

where's that umbrella? – it must be lying around somewhere
où est ce parapluie ? – il doit traîner quelque part

3 n'avoir rien à faire :

how much longer do we have to wait around before he arrives?
on doit rester là à attendre encore combien de temps avant qu'il arrive ?

Aside

1 de côté, sur le côté :

please step aside and let us pass
s'il vous plaît, écartez-vous et laissez-nous passer

2 à l'écart d'un groupe :

the teacher drew him aside to ask how his father was
la maîtresse l'a pris à part pour lui demander comment allait son père

3 mettre quelque chose de côté pour y revenir ou s'en servir plus tard :

leaving that question aside for the moment...
laissons cette question de côté pour le moment...

could you put that aside and work on this instead?
est-ce que tu peux laisser ça de côté et travailler sur ça à la place ?

I have some money set aside for emergencies
j'ai de l'argent de côté en cas d'urgence

At

vers, en direction de :

the explorers worked their way through the jungle, chopping at the undergrowth with their machetes
les explorateurs se frayèrent un chemin à travers la jungle à coups de machette

the birds were picking at the crumbs
les oiseaux picoraient les miettes

he hinted at the possibility of my getting a promotion
il a laissé entendre que je pourrais obtenir de l'avancement

Away

1 s'absenter ou partir :

I'm sorry but he has been called away on business
je suis désolé mais il a dû s'absenter pour affaires

he ran away into the crowd
il partit dans la foule en courant

2 prendre de la distance ou s'éloigner :

she backed away from the dog
elle recula devant le chien

why do you move away whenever I approach you?
pourquoi est-ce que tu t'éloignes à chaque fois que j'approche ?

3 continuer quelque chose pendant un certain temps :

they just sat there giggling away
elles étaient assises là, à ricaner sans arrêt

she was in the bath, singing away to herself
elle fredonnait dans son bain

he lay groaning away on the ground
il était étendu par terre et poussait de longs gémissements

he's working away on his novel
il travaille d'arrache-pied à son roman

4 enlever ou se débarrasser de quelque chose :

maybe someone with a van could take the wardrobe away
quelqu'un avec une camionnette pourrait peut-être emporter l'armoire

if you don't want it, throw it away
si tu n'en veux pas, jette-le

5 mettre à l'abri, en réserve :

lock it away where it'll be safe
mets-le sous clé dans un endroit sûr

he keeps it stored away in the attic
il le garde dans le grenier

I wouldn't be surprised if he had salted away a lot of money
cela ne m'étonnerait pas qu'il ait mis beaucoup d'argent de côté

6 jusqu'à disparaître :

the water has all boiled away
l'eau s'est évaporée

he is wasting away with grief
le chagrin le ronge petit à petit

the water trickled away down the plughole
l'eau s'écoulait lentement dans le trou de l'évier

7 épuiser quelque chose :

he has drunk his entire inheritance away
il a dépensé tout l'argent de son héritage en alcool

8 début d'une action :

could I ask some questions? – sure, fire away
puis-je vous poser quelques questions ? – je vous en prie, allez-y

Back

1 en arrière, vers l'arrière :

she flung back her hair
elle rejeta ses cheveux en arrière

thinking back...
quand on y repense...

2 idée de retour :

flood waters are receding and people are beginning to filter back to their homes
les inondations diminuent et les gens commencent petit à petit à rentrer chez eux

it's so cold I think I'll head back
il fait tellement froid que je crois que je vais rentrer

she's being moved back to the personnel department
ils l'ont renvoyée travailler au service du personnel

bring it back once you've finished with it
rapporte-le-moi quand tu auras fini

3 de nouveau :

we've bought back our old house
on a racheté notre ancienne maison

stop the tape and play the last ten frames back
arrêtez la cassette et repassez les dix dernières images

4 battre en retraite, perdre sa vitalité, etc. :

the intense heat forced them back
la chaleur intense les a obligés à reculer

the plant will die back in autumn
la plante va dépérir en automne

5 ralentir :

rein your horse back
fais ralentir ton cheval

the pilot throttled the engines back and came in to land
le pilote coupa les gaz et amorça son atterrissage

6 couper ou réduire quelque chose :

this old rose bush needs to be cut back
ce vieux rosier a besoin d'être taillé

we'll have to cut back on our expenses
nous allons devoir rogner sur les dépenses

7 retenir, réprimer ou cacher quelque chose :

I forced back my tears
j'ai retenu mes larmes

what are you keeping back from us?
qu'est-ce que tu nous caches ?

Behind

1 en retard :

the landlady says we're getting behind with the rent
la propriétaire dit qu'on est en retard pour le loyer

if you're slipping behind with your work...
si vous prenez du retard dans votre travail...

2 être laissé en arrière, rester en arrière :

do you mind being left behind to look after the children?
ça ne te fait rien de rester et de garder les enfants ?

you go on ahead, I'll stay behind
allez-y, moi je vais rester

By

1 mouvement, passage :

we had to push by a lot of people
on a dû bousculer beaucoup de monde

the cars raced by
les voitures sont passées à toute allure

time goes by so fast
le temps passe si vite

2 se référer à quelque chose :

my mother swears by castor oil
ma mère ne jure que par l'huile de ricin

which theory do you go by?
sur quelle théorie vous appuyez-vous ?

3 faire une visite ou un arrêt rapide :

we'll drop by to see you one day
on passera vous voir un de ces jours

I stopped by at the chemist's on the way home
je suis passé à la pharmacie en rentrant

Down

1 mouvement de haut en bas, vers le bas ou vers le sol :

call Tom down for tea
appelle Tom et dis-lui de descendre prendre le thé

pass me down that big plate from the top shelf
passe-moi la grande assiette qui est sur l'étagère du haut

I bent down to pick up the old man's stick
je me suis baissé pour ramasser la canne du vieil homme

the hurricane blew down hundreds of mature trees
l'ouragan a fait tomber des centaines de vieux arbres

pull the blinds down
baisse les stores

2 prendre en note, pour s'y référer plus tard :

could someone note down the main points?
est-ce que quelqu'un peut prendre en note les points principaux ?

I've written it down in my notebook
je l'ai noté dans mon calepin

I could see him scribbling something down
je l'ai vu griffonner rapidement quelque chose

3 rejeter ou mettre fin à quelque chose :

the bill was voted down
le projet de loi a été rejeté

they all shouted the speaker down
ils ont hué l'intervenant, si bien qu'il n'a pas pu s'exprimer

4 attacher ou serrer quelque chose :

nail it down or the wind will blow it away
cloue-le ou le vent va l'emporter

screw the lid down properly
visse bien le couvercle

glue it down
fais-le tenir avec de la colle

5 arrêter un véhicule :

we flagged a taxi down
on a hélé un taxi

6 transmettre quelque chose d'une génération à une autre :

the necklace came down to her from her great-aunt
elle tient ce collier de sa grand-tante

the song was passed down from generation to generation
cette chanson a été transmise de génération en génération

7 réduction, diminution :

everything in the shop has been marked down
tous les articles du magasin sont vendus à prix réduit

thin the sauce down with a little milk if necessary
allongez la sauce avec un peu de lait si nécessaire

you're going too fast, slow down
tu vas trop vite, ralentis

8 ne pas marcher, ne pas être en forme, etc. :

the car has broken down
la voiture est en panne

she broke down and wept
elle a craqué et s'est mise à pleurer

9 action punitive imposée par une autorité :

the police are clamping down on illegal parking
la police sévit contre les automobilistes en stationnement interdit

the teacher really came down on me for not having learnt the dates properly
le prof m'a passé un savon parce que je n'avais pas bien appris les dates

10 avaler de la nourriture, etc. :

if you don't force some food down you'll collapse
si tu ne te forces pas à avaler quelque chose, tu ne vas pas tenir le coup

the dog gobbled it down in a second
le chien n'en a fait qu'une bouchée

she absolutely wolfed her dinner down
elle a littéralement englouti son dîner

For

1 le but, l'objectif :

she felt in her bag for the keys
elle chercha les clés dans son sac

stop fishing for compliments!
arrête de rechercher les compliments !

the qualities looked for in candidates are...
les qualités recherchées chez les candidats sont...

2 être en faveur de quelque chose :

the points of view argued for in this paper...
les points de vue défendus dans cet article...

Forth

1 en avant, surtout pour affronter un adversaire :

the army went forth into battle *(emploi vieilli ou littéraire)*
l'armée se mit en route pour la bataille

he sallied forth to face the waiting fans *(emploi littéraire ou humoristique)*
il sortit affronter tous les fans qui l'attendaient

2 idée de naissance ou de production :

Mary brought forth a son *(emploi vieilli ou soutenu)*
Mary mit au monde un fils

the tree puts forth the most gloriously scented blossom
cet arbre donne des fleurs aux parfums les plus exquis

3 parler longtemps et parfois d'une manière pompeuse :

he is always holding forth about something
il est toujours en train de disserter sur tout et n'importe quoi

she spouted forth about the benefits of free enterprise
elle a dégoisé d'interminables discours sur les avantages de la libre entreprise

Forward

1 en avant, droit devant :

please come forward one by one as I call your names
veuillez avancer un par un au fur et à mesure que je vous appelle

she leaned forward to hear what they were talking about
elle se pencha en avant pour entendre de quoi ils parlaient

pull your chair forward
avance ta chaise

2 parler du futur, anticiper :

we're really looking forward to seeing them again
nous avons vraiment hâte de les revoir

that's something I am definitely not looking forward to
c'est quelque chose qui ne m'enchante vraiment pas

looking forward to hearing from you *(dans une lettre)*
dans l'attente de vous lire

3 avancer un événement :

the board meeting has been brought forward a week
la réunion du conseil d'administration a été avancée d'une semaine

4 suggérer, proposer quelque chose :

does anyone have any other suggestions they wish to bring forward?
est-ce que quelqu'un souhaite faire d'autres suggestions ?

the theory that he puts forward in his book...
la théorie qu'il avance dans son livre...

Home

1 à la maison, chez soi :

who is taking you home?
qui est-ce qui te ramène chez toi ?

I'll see you home
je te raccompagne chez toi

2 enfoncer correctement quelque chose :

make sure you hammer the nails home
veillez à enfoncer les clous à fond

is the plug pushed home properly?
est-ce que la bonde est bien enfoncée ?

3 faire comprendre ou faire apprécier quelque chose à quelqu'un :

did you drive it home to them that they must be back by midnight?
est-ce que tu leur as bien fait comprendre qu'ils doivent rentrer avant minuit ?

the recent accident brought home to them the need for insurance
avec l'accident qu'ils ont eu récemment, ils se sont rendu compte à quel point il est nécessaire d'être assuré

that comment really hit home
cette remarque a fait mouche

In

1 mouvement de l'extérieur vers l'intérieur :

there's no need to burst in like that
tu n'as pas besoin d'entrer à toute vitesse comme ça

we crept in so as not to disturb you
nous sommes entrés à pas de loup pour ne pas te déranger

don't stand so close to the edge of the pool, you might fall in
ne te mets pas si près de la piscine, tu pourrais tomber dedans

2 quelque part, à un endroit ou dans un lieu :

you shouldn't have left this paragraph in
tu n'aurais pas dû laisser ce paragraphe

I'm going to the bank to pay in these cheques
je vais à la banque déposer ces chèques sur mon compte

fold in the flour
incorporez la farine

the car's pretty full but we could squeeze one more in
la voiture est presque pleine mais on peut encore faire entrer une personne

3 être enfermé ou ne pas pouvoir sortir :

when the police arrived they found he had barricaded himself in
à son arrivée, la police a vu qu'il s'était barricadé à l'intérieur

the man next door has blocked me in
la voiture de mon voisin m'empêche de sortir la mienne

help, I'm locked in!
au secours, je suis enfermé !

4 entrer, s'approcher en direction de quelque chose :

members of the orchestra began to filter in
les membres de l'orchestre ont commencé à entrer les uns après les autres

when the train pulled in...
quand le train est entré en gare...

as I looked out of the window I saw a car drive in
je regardais par la fenêtre et j'ai vu une voiture entrer

5 compléter ou remplir quelque chose :

fill in this form
remplissez ce formulaire

the artist then drew in the remaining features
l'artiste a ensuite ébauché le reste des traits du visage

6 chez soi ou chez quelqu'un :

I'm staying in this evening to wash my hair
ce soir, je reste chez moi pour me laver les cheveux

let's invite the people next door in for a coffee
invitons les voisins à venir prendre le café

7 action de rendre ou de se rendre :

the wanted man handed himself in to the police
l'homme recherché par la police s'est rendu

hand your essays in tomorrow
rendez-moi vos dissertations demain

8 arrêter ou s'arrêter :

I've jacked my job in
j'ai plaqué mon boulot

pack that noise in!
arrête ce boucan !

the engine's packed in
le moteur a lâché

9 céder, s'affaisser, etc. :

they had to beat the door in since nobody had a key
ils ont dû enfoncer la porte puisque personne n'avait la clé

the roof fell in, showering the firemen with debris
le toit s'est effondré et une pluie de débris s'est abattue sur les pompiers

10 diminuer ou rétrécir quelque chose :

I asked the dressmaker to take in the sleeves
j'ai demandé à la couturière de raccourcir les manches

pull the rope in a bit to get rid of the slack
tire un peu la corde vers toi pour qu'elle soit bien tendue

the nights are drawing in
les nuits raccourcissent

hold your stomach in
rentre ton ventre

Into

1 mouvement de l'extérieur vers l'intérieur :

don't just barge into the room, knock first
ne fais pas irruption comme ça dans la pièce, frappe avant d'entrer

the operator cut into our conversation
l'opératrice a brusquement interrompu notre conversation

the Fraud Squad is looking into the affair
la brigade de répression des fraudes examine l'affaire

2 utiliser une partie de quelque chose, le plus souvent à contrecœur :

we're going to have to break into our savings to pay for the repairs to the roof
nous allons devoir entamer nos économies pour payer les réparations du toit

it cuts into our free time too much
cela empiète trop sur notre temps libre

3 contact physique, rentrer dans quelqu'un ou quelque chose :

if you looked where you were going, you wouldn't keep running into people
si tu regardais un peu devant toi, tu ne rentrerais pas dans les gens sans arrêt

some idiot running for a train barged into me
une espèce d'imbécile qui courait pour attraper son train m'est rentré dedans

Off

1 enlever quelque chose, emmener quelqu'un :

don't bite it off, use the scissors
ne l'arrache pas avec les dents, prends des ciseaux

it took ages to scrape the paint off
on a mis un temps fou à gratter toute la peinture

he was taken off in a police car
il a été emmené dans une voiture de police

2 partir :

the car slowly moved off
la voiture s'éloigna lentement

they rushed off when they saw the policeman approaching
ils ont déguerpi quand ils ont vu le policier arriver

don't hurry off, stay and have some tea
ne pars pas si vite, tu prendras bien une tasse de thé ?

3 commencer quelque chose :

let me start off by saying...
permettez-moi de commencer en disant...

who's going to lead off with the first question?
qui va entamer le débat en posant la première question ?

4 quitter un moyen de transport :

as the bus slowed, he jumped off
quand le bus a ralenti, il a sauté

the doors opened and everyone got off
les portes se sont ouvertes et tout le monde est descendu

she doesn't like riding because she keeps falling off
elle n'aime pas le vélo parce qu'elle n'arrête pas de tomber

5 éteindre, arrêter quelque chose :

turn the lights off, please
éteins les lumières, s'il te plaît

he has sworn off alcohol
il a arrêté de boire

6 changement, dégradation de quelque chose :

the meat has gone off
la viande est avariée

attendances have fallen off
la fréquentation a baissé

7 pour intensifier le sens d'un verbe :

the scriptwriters have decided to kill off this character
les scénaristes ont décidé de faire mourir ce personnage

the detective was bought off
le détective a été acheté

most of the land has been sold off
la plupart des terres ont été vendues

8 pour un congé :

take a few days off
prenez quelques jours de vacances

9 être inutilisable, condamné ou inaccessible :

for reasons of safety, that part of the road has been closed off
pour des raisons de sécurité, ce tronçon de route est fermé à la circulation

this part has been partitioned off from the rest of the room
on a séparé cette partie de la pièce par une cloison

On

1 continuer quelque chose :

read on to the end of the chapter
continuez la lecture jusqu'à la fin du chapitre

they chatted on for hours
ils ont parlé pendant des heures

she worked on into the night
elle a travaillé jusque tard dans la nuit

2 mettre ou enfiler quelque chose :

she threw a dressing gown on and went to answer the door
elle a enfilé une robe de chambre et est allée ouvrir

what did he have on?
qu'est-ce qu'il portait ?

I couldn't get it on
je ne rentrais pas dedans

3 allumer, en parlant d'un appareil électrique, etc. :

turn the TV on, would you?
allume la télé, s'il te plaît

do you know that you've left the headlights on?
tu sais que tu as laissé tes phares allumés ?

4 utiliser quelque chose pour fonctionner, survivre, etc. :

what do the animals feed on in winter?
de quoi se nourrissent ces animaux en hiver ?

all cars should run on unleaded petrol
toutes les voitures devraient rouler au sans-plomb

5 à bord d'un moyen de transport :

the train stopped and everybody got on
le train s'est arrêté et tout le monde est monté

they couldn't get any more passengers on
ils n'ont pas pu faire monter d'autres passagers à bord

6 s'adapter sur quelque chose, s'emboîter, etc. :

the lid bolts on
le couvercle se fixe à l'aide de boulons

where does this bit fit on?
où va ce bout-là ?

7 accepter quelque chose :

it seemed like an excellent idea and we seized (up)on it immediately
cette idée nous a paru excellente et nous l'avons aussitôt adoptée

8 faire avancer :

the crowd is cheering her on as she reaches the last mile
alors qu'elle arrive dans le dernier kilomètre, elle est acclamée et encouragée par la foule

he wanted to look in the car showroom but I hurried him on
il voulait regarder les voitures en exposition mais je lui ai fait hâter le pas

9 prévu, programmé :

I've got something on every night next week
j'ai quelque chose de prévu tous les soirs de la semaine prochaine

10 transmettre ou passer quelque chose à quelqu'un :

she passed your book on to me
elle m'a passé ton livre

could you pass the news on?
est-ce que tu peux faire passer la nouvelle ?

Out

1 sortir d'un endroit, partir :

they bolted out of the door
ils sont sortis à toute allure

she drove out of the garage
elle a sorti la voiture du garage

I'm popping out to the library
je vais faire un saut à la bibliothèque

the train had only just pulled out of the station when...
le train venait tout juste de partir quand...

he walked out on his wife and kids
il a quitté sa femme et ses enfants

2 indique une privation ou une exclusion :

that tree is blocking out all the sun
cet arbre empêche le soleil d'entrer

heavy floods have driven thousands of people out of their homes
des milliers de personnes ont dû évacuer leur maison à cause d'importantes inondations

I've thrown out your old jacket
j'ai jeté ta vieille veste

I feel a bit left out
je me sens un peu exclu

they have a habit of freezing out people they don't like
ils ont pour habitude de snober tous ceux qu'ils n'aiment pas

3 distribuer :

we need volunteers to hand out leaflets
on a besoin de volontaires pour distribuer les prospectus

4 tendre quelque chose :

he held out his hand in a pleading gesture
il a tendu la main d'un geste suppliant

hold out your glass
tends ton verre

5 enlever ou faire sortir :

it's time to take the cake out
il est temps de sortir le gâteau du four

don't push me out of the way
ne me pousse pas comme ça

a lot of the pages have been ripped out
il y a beaucoup de pages arrachées

6 résoudre un problème, arranger une situation :

things just didn't work out between us
ça n'a tout simplement pas marché entre nous

it all came out right in the end
tout s'est arrangé au bout du compte

7 se tirer d'une situation difficile ou échapper à quelque chose :

how did you get out of doing your maths homework?
comment as-tu réussi à échapper à tes devoirs de maths ?

I wish I could wriggle out of this visit to my in-laws
si seulement je pouvais trouver une excuse pour ne pas aller chez mes beaux-parents !

8 indique un bruit fort :

stop barking out orders like a sergeant-major
arrête d'aboyer des ordres comme un sergent-chef

the loudspeakers were blaring out the candidate's message
les haut-parleurs diffusaient le message du candidat à plein volume

she cried out in pain
elle poussa un cri de douleur

9 s'éteindre :

the fire has gone out
le feu s'est éteint

he stubbed his cigar out in the ashtray
il écrasa son cigare dans le cendrier

switch the garage light out
éteins la lumière du garage

the boxer was knocked out in the first round
le boxeur a été mis K.-O. au premier round

10 à l'extérieur, hors de la maison :

the soldiers camped out in the fields
les soldats ont campé dans les champs

I've been invited out for lunch
on m'a invité au restaurant à midi

11 élargir ou rallonger quelque chose :

my dress needs to be let out at the seams
ma robe a besoin d'être élargie au niveau des coutures

your essay needs to be fleshed out
tu dois étoffer un peu plus ta dissertation

Over

1 aller d'un côté à l'autre, traverser :

she walked over the railway bridge
elle traversa le pont ferroviaire

he saw me on the other side of the road and hurried over
il m'a vu de l'autre côté de la route et s'est dépêché de traverser

hey, move over, there's room for two in this bed!
eh, pousse-toi, il y a de la place pour deux dans ce lit !

2 en parcourant une courte distance :

I'll drive over and see you soon
je viendrai te voir bientôt en voiture

our neighbours are having us over for dinner on Saturday night
nos voisins nous ont invités à manger chez eux samedi soir

3 passer d'une chose à une autre :

I don't like this programme, could you change over?
je n'aime pas cette émission, est-ce que tu peux changer de chaîne ?

4 retourner quelque chose :

he folded over the letter so that I couldn't see the signature
il a plié la lettre pour que je ne voie pas la signature

fork the ground over thoroughly before planting
retournez bien la terre avant de planter

5 transmettre un sentiment, une intention, une impression, etc. :

they need to find a better way of putting their company image over
il leur faut trouver un meilleur moyen de communiquer l'image de leur entreprise

they come over as being rather arrogant
ils donnent l'impression d'être arrogants

6 au-dessus de :

he leaned over the balcony for a better look
il s'est penché sur le balcon pour avoir une meilleure vue

with this threat hanging over him...
avec cette menace qui plane sur lui...

7 idée de couvrir :

skies are expected to cloud over in the afternoon
le ciel devrait se couvrir dans l'après-midi

the lake rarely freezes over
le lac gèle rarement

the door was papered over many years ago
il y a des années qu'on a recouvert la porte de papier peint

8 rester, en parlant de quelque chose :

there's quite a lot left over
il en reste pas mal

9 finir ou faire complètement quelque chose :

be sure to read over your essay before handing it in
pensez à relire vos dissertations avant de les rendre

10 déborder, se répandre :

the milk has boiled over
le lait a débordé de la casserole

the river flooded over into the streets
la rivière est sortie de son lit et a inondé les rues

11 être renversé, tomber :

she was knocked over by a bus
elle a été renversée par un bus

she fell over
elle est tombée par terre

Past

indique le passage :

he brushed past me in the street
il m'a frôlé dans la rue

we had just gone past the shop when...
on venait juste de passer devant le magasin quand...

cars raced past
des voitures sont passées à toute vitesse

he just casually strolled past
il est passé tranquillement, sans se presser

Round (surtout en anglais britannique)

1 mouvement circulaire :

thoughts were spinning round in her head
tout se bousculait dans sa tête

pass your sweets round
fais passer tes bonbons

2 en formant un rond :

a crowd gathered round to watch
les gens se sont regroupés autour pour regarder

they all crowded round
ils se sont tous pressés autour

3 faire le tour de quelque chose, voir autour de soi :

we went round the art gallery
on a fait le tour du musée des beaux-arts

would you like to see round the house?
est-ce que vous voulez visiter la maison ?

I'll phone round and see if anyone else knows about it
je vais passer des coups de fil et voir si quelqu'un d'autre est au courant

4 changer de place ou de direction :

I've been bumping into things ever since your mother changed all the furniture round
je n'arrête pas de me cogner partout depuis que ta mère a changé les meubles de place

he turned the car round and went home
il a fait demi-tour et il est rentré chez lui

5 venir chez quelqu'un qui n'habite pas très loin :

could you call round tomorrow morning, doctor?
est-ce que vous pouvez passer demain matin, docteur ?

they always go out when their son has his friends round
ils sortent toujours quand leur fils invite ses amis

drop round some time
passe nous voir un de ces jours

let's invite them round for dinner
invitons-les à manger un soir

Through

1 à travers, indique le passage :

we're not stopping here, just passing through
on ne s'arrête pas ici, on ne fait que passer

he looked through me as if I didn't exist
il m'a regardé comme si je n'existais pas

2 pénétrer à l'intérieur de quelque chose :

the crowd broke through the barriers
la foule a enfoncé les barrières

the sun didn't break through until the afternoon
pas un rayon de soleil n'a percé avant l'après-midi

the soles of my boots are almost worn through
les semelles de mes bottes sont presque trouées

3 indique le succès :

we'll just have to muddle through without her
il va falloir qu'on se débrouille sans elle

he was very ill but he's pulled through now
il a été très malade mais il est tiré d'affaire maintenant

4 faire quelque chose correctement, de fond en comble, du début à la fin :

they went through everyone's hand luggage
ils ont fouillé tous les bagages à main

will you read through my speech and give me your opinion?
tu veux bien lire mon discours et me dire ce que tu en penses ?

the plan hasn't been properly thought through
le projet n'a pas été pensé suffisamment en détail

To

1 en arriver ou en venir à quelque chose :

it got to the point where she could no longer look after him
il est arrivé un moment où elle ne pouvait plus s'occuper de lui

I never thought it would come to this
je ne me doutais pas qu'on en arriverait là

2 se mettre à faire quelque chose :

we fell to work
nous nous sommes mis à l'œuvre

she took to wearing black every day
elle s'est mise à s'habiller en noir tous les jours

3 s'occuper de quelqu'un ou de quelque chose :

are you being attended to, madam?
est-ce que l'on s'occupe de vous, madame?

I'll see to the dinner
je vais m'occuper du dîner

it fell to me to break the bad news to everyone
ce fut à moi d'annoncer la mauvaise nouvelle à tout le monde

4 s'élever à :

profits amounted to several million dollars
les bénéfices se sont chiffrés à plusieurs millions de dollars

how much did the dinner come to?
combien le dîner a-t-il coûté ?

5 rester quelque part :

he's taken to his bed with the flu
il est cloué au lit par la grippe

you should keep to the main roads when it's icy
tu devrais rester sur les grandes routes quand il y a du verglas

6 reprendre connaissance :

when he came to, he had no recollection of the accident
quand il est revenu à lui, il n'avait aucun souvenir de l'accident

Together

ensemble, pour former un tout :

we always gathered together for morning prayers
on se rassemblait toujours pour la prière du matin

you must keep the group together and not let people wander off on their own
vous devez rester ensemble et ne laisser personne s'écarter du groupe

what were just vague ideas are coming together into a definite proposal
ce qui a commencé avec de vagues idées est en train de prendre forme pour aboutir à un projet bien défini

Under

1 sous :

when the sirens sounded, we always used to get under the table
lorsque les sirènes retentissaient, on se mettait toujours sous la table

fold the edges under
repliez les bords en dessous

2 en vertu de, relever de quelque chose :

that information comes under the Official Secrets Act
cette information relève de la loi sur le secret défense

3 réprimer, contenir :

a military government held the country under for many years
le pays est resté pendant des années sous l'emprise d'un gouvernement militaire

the government is doing its best to keep the rebels under
le gouvernement fait tout ce qu'il peut pour contenir les rebelles

4 désigner une certaine catégorie :

I'm looking for books on landscape gardening; what subject do they come under in the catalogue?
je cherche des livres sur le paysagisme ; sous quelle rubrique sont-ils classés dans le catalogue ?

what should I look under? vegetables or fruit?
à quel mot dois-je chercher ? légumes ou fruits ?

Up

1 mouvement vers le haut :

pass that hammer up so I don't have to get off the stepladder
passe-moi le marteau ; ça m'évitera de descendre de l'escabeau

she hitched up her skirt and started to run
elle remonta sa jupe et se mit à courir

I'll just finish pinning up the hem of this dress
je vais juste finir d'épingler l'ourlet de cette robe

hold your head up
redresse la tête

2 à l'étage supérieur :

carry this tray up to your father
monte ce plateau à ton père

let's invite our neighbours up for coffee
invitons les voisins du dessous à venir prendre le café

3 se lever ou redresser quelque chose :

I jumped up to protest
je me suis levé d'un bond pour protester

they all stood up
ils se sont tous levés

the old man sat up in bed with a start
le vieillard s'est redressé d'un seul coup dans son lit

4 s'approcher :

the dog ran up to me as soon as I went in
le chien a couru vers moi dès que je suis entré

he wandered up to us
il s'est approché tranquillement de nous

5 s'améliorer :

business is looking up
les affaires s'améliorent

the weather has cleared up
le temps s'est éclairci

6 augmenter, en parlant d'un prix, d'une quantité, d'un volume, etc. :

this has forced prices up
ça a fait monter les prix

the fire blazed up
le feu a pris très rapidement

turn the television up, I must be going deaf
mets la télé plus fort, je crois que je deviens sourd

let me plump up your pillows
laisse-moi retaper tes oreillers

7 rassembler ou chercher quelque chose :

she bundled up her clothes and left hurriedly
elle fit un ballot de ses vêtements et s'en alla en vitesse

do you think you can rake up enough money for the deposit?
est-ce que tu crois que tu peux rassembler assez d'argent pour la caution ?

where did you dig up that story?
où es-tu allé chercher une histoire pareille ?

8 soutenir :

it's held up by a central beam
il est soutenu pour une poutre centrale

can anyone back your story up?
est-ce que quelqu'un peut confirmer ce que vous dites ?

9 la fin d'une action :

that wraps up our programme for today
et c'est tout pour notre émission d'aujourd'hui

come on, drink up
allez, finis ton verre

they ate up and left
ils ont fini de manger et sont partis

10 faire quelque chose à fond ou complètement :

she's in big trouble for smashing up the company car
elle est vraiment dans le pétrin parce qu'elle a démoli la voiture de fonction

you've messed our plans up
tu as fichu nos projets en l'air

tighten this screw up
resserre cette vis

11 finir par arriver quelque part, après une suite d'actions :

we ended up in the pub, of course
on a fini au pub, évidemment

we're going to land up in hospital if you don't slow down
on va se retrouver à l'hôpital si tu ne ralentis pas

12 être enfermé ou retenu à l'intérieur :

he'll be locked up for several years
il va rester sous les verrous pendant plusieurs années

why don't you talk about your problems instead of bottling things up?
pourquoi est-ce que tu ne parles pas de tes problèmes au lieu de tout garder pour toi ?

they've bricked up the old doorway
ils ont muré l'ancienne porte

13 être coupé en morceaux :

chop the meat up
coupez la viande en morceaux

break it up into four pieces
partage-le en quatre

14 sortir quelque chose :

you owe me money, so pay up
tu me dois de l'argent, alors allonge

he has been coughing up blood
il crache du sang

Upon

parfois interchangeable avec **on** (voir **On**) mais d'un usage souvent plus soutenu

With

utiliser ou se servir de quelque chose :

you can have the ones I've finished with
tu peux prendre ceux dont je n'ai plus besoin

Dictionnaire des verbes composés

Les abréviations suivantes sont utilisées dans le Dictionnaire des verbes composés :

AM	anglais américain
BR	anglais britannique
FAM	style familier
FIG	sens figuré
QCH	quelque chose
QN	quelqu'un

Les abréviations des types de verbes sont :

VI	verbe intransitif (1)
VT INSÉP	verbe transitif à particule inséparable (2)
VT SÉP	verbe transitif à particule séparable (3)

1 **VI** : verbe intransitif, c'est-à-dire un verbe qui n'appelle pas de complément d'objet direct.

get off : he **got off** at Victoria Station
il descendit à la gare Victoria

listen in : do you mind if I **listen in** while you talk?
ça vous dérange si j'écoute votre conversation ?

2 **VT INSÉP** : verbe transitif à particule inséparable. Le complément d'objet direct vient après la particule ; il ne peut jamais séparer le verbe de la particule.

look after : she **looks after** children
elle garde des enfants

3 **VT SÉP** : verbe transitif à particule séparable. Le complément d'objet direct peut se placer entre le verbe et la particule, ou après la particule.

send back : he **sent back** the letter
il a renvoyé la lettre

ou

he **sent** the letter **back**
il a renvoyé la lettre

A

abide by VT INSÉP *(se conformer à, suivre)* you'll have to abide by the rules

account for VT INSÉP (a) *(rendre compte de, expliquer)* how did they account for their absence?; there's no accounting for taste, I suppose, but have you seen what they've done with their living room? (b) *(retrouver, localiser)* the firemen did not need to enter the building since all the occupants were accounted for (c) *(représenter)* wine accounts for 5% of all exports; *(être la source de, la cause de)* shoplifting accounts for most of the store's losses (d) *(détruire, éliminer)* in recent action, the rebels have accounted for a great many government troops

act (up)on VT INSÉP (a) *(agir sur)* rust is caused by salt acting on metal (b) *(suivre, pour un conseil, etc.)* acting on her lawyer's advice, she has decided not to sue

act out VT SÉP *(concrétiser, réaliser)* he treats his patients for neuroses by having them act out their fantasies; *(reconstituer)* local people act out scenes from the town's history

act up VI FAM *(faire des siennes)* that child acts up every time her mother goes out without her; *(marcher mal)* the photocopier is acting up again

add in VT SÉP *(ajouter)* add in a little salt and the mixture is complete

add on VT SÉP *(ajouter)* we're thinking about adding on a conservatory; should we add something on as a tip?

add up 1 VI (a) *(compter)* I'd have thought that at your age you could add up by now! (b) *(s'expliquer)* it's all beginning to add up; it's a mystery, it just doesn't add up
2 VT SÉP *(additionner)* if you add all the figures up the total is surprisingly large

add up to VT INSÉP (a) *(s'élever à)* how much does it all add up to? (b) *(se résumer à, faire, constituer)* is that all you've done? – it doesn't add up to much, does it?; if you put all the facts together it adds up to quite an interesting case

adhere to VT INSÉP *(adhérer à)* I don't adhere to that philosophy at all

admit to VT INSÉP *(reconnaître, avouer)* he admitted to a slight feeling of apprehension

agree on VT INSÉP *(se mettre d'accord sur)* they cannot agree on a name for the baby

agree to VT INSÉP *(consentir, accepter)* she felt she could not agree to my terms; they agreed to their son taking the job

agree with VT INSÉP (a) *(être d'accord avec, approuver)* I'm afraid I cannot agree with you; she doesn't agree with all this psychoanalytic treatment for paedophiles (b) *(réussir à, convenir à)* seafood doesn't agree with me

allow for VT INSÉP *(prévoir, tenir compte de)* when calculating how much material you'll need, always allow for some wastage; I suppose I should allow for his inexperience; has that been allowed for in your figures?

allow out VT SÉP *(autoriser à sortir)* the curfew meant that nobody was allowed out after dark; some prisoners are allowed out at weekends

angle for VT INSÉP FIG *(chercher (à avoir))* he was angling for promotion so he developed a sudden interest in the boss's daughter; never angle for compliments

answer back 1 VI (a) *(répondre (avec insolence))* don't answer back, young man! (b) *(répliquer)* she's the boss, so I can't answer back
2 VT SÉP *(répondre (avec insolence) à)* that child will answer anyone back

answer for VT INSÉP *(répondre de)* if he keeps on at me like this, I won't answer for my actions; *(être responsable de)* the people who voted for him have a great deal to answer for

answer to VT INSÉP (a) *(être responsable envers, rendre compte à)* who do you answer to in your job?; *(avoir affaire à, rendre des comptes à)* if you lay one finger on him you'll have me to answer to (b) *(correspondre à, répondre à)* a woman answering to the description has been seen in the area

argue away 1 VT SÉP *(nier l'importance de)* you cannot argue the facts away: ozone depletion is a serious problem
2 VI *(se disputer)* they've been arguing away all morning

argue for/against VT INSÉP *(débattre le pour/le contre de)* the speakers will argue for and against unilateral disarmament

argue out VT SÉP *(régler, chercher une solution)* I'll leave you to argue it out between you

ask after VT INSÉP *(demander des nouvelles de)* let your grandfather know I was asking after him

ask around VI *(demander, se renseigner)* I'll ask around at work and see if anyone else is interested

ask back VT SÉP *(inviter chez soi, après une sortie ensemble)* do you want to ask them back for a drink after the theatre?

ask in VT SÉP *(inviter chez soi, quand la personne invitée se trouve tout près)* I would ask you in for tea but my husband's not very well

ask out VT SÉP *(inviter à sortir)* he's asked her out so many times she must be running out of excuses by now; he's finally summoned up the courage to ask her out

ask round VT SÉP *(inviter chez soi)* why don't we ask them round for dinner one night?

ask up VT SÉP *(inviter à monter chez soi)* don't get too excited if she asks you up for coffee, her mother lives with her!

attend to VT INSÉP **(a)** *(s'occuper de)* are you being attended to?; I'll attend to this **(b)** *(prêter attention à, observer)* now attend to the experiment very closely, I'll be asking you questions later

auction off VT SÉP *(vendre aux enchères)* they auctioned off all the family silver to raise some money

average out 1 VT SÉP *(faire la moyenne de)* I've averaged out how much I spend a week, and it's frightening
2 VI *(faire une moyenne)* over a full year it averages out quite differently

average out at VT INSÉP *(faire en moyenne)* how much does that average out at a year?

B

babble away/on VI *(bredouiller, parler)* you were babbling away in your sleep last night; *(raconter)* I have no idea what you're babbling on about

back down VI *(céder, s'incliner)* he takes pride in never backing down, however strong the opposition's case

back on to *ou* **onto** VT INSÉP *(donner sur (à l'arrière))* the house backs on to a lane

back out 1 VI (a) *(reculer, sortir en marche arrière)* he backed out of the drive (b) FIG *(se dérober, se retirer)* they can't back out from the deal now!
2 VT SÉP *(sortir en marche arrière)* I'm not very good at backing the car out, will you do it?

back up 1 VI (a) *(reculer, faire marche arrière)* all the cars had to back up to let the ambulance past
(b) *Informatique (sauvegarder)* remember to back up regularly
2 VT SÉP (a) *(faire reculer)* the driver had to back his lorry up all the way to the service station
(b) *(appuyer, soutenir)* he'll need to back up his claim to the estate with something stronger than that; I doubt if the electors will back them up
(c) *Informatique (sauvegarder)* you should back up all your files at the end of the day
(d) AM *(immobiliser)* the accident backed traffic up all the way to the turnpike

bail out VT SÉP (a) *(libérer sous caution)* their lawyer bailed them out
(b) *(aider, tirer d'affaire)* I'm not bailing you out again, you're on your own this time

balance out 1 VI *(s'équilibrer, correspondre)* the figures don't balance out
2 VT SÉP *(se compléter)* he cooks and she knows a lot about wine, so they balance each other out very nicely

bale out 1 VI (a) *(sauter en parachute (d'un avion en détresse))* Dad never tires of telling how he had to bale out over the Channel during a dogfight (b) *(écoper)* she's taking on a lot of water, start baling out
2 VT SÉP *(écoper)* we'll have to bale the water out first

band together VI *(s'unir)* if we band together we can do something about this problem

bandy about/around VT SÉP *(utiliser souvent, pour des mots, des noms, etc.)* "decentralization" is a word the government bandies about a lot; *(faire circuler, faire du bruit à propos de)* the newspapers have been bandying that story around for weeks now

bank (up)on VT INSÉP *(compter sur)* him turn up on time? I wouldn't bank on it if I were you

bargain for VT INSÉP *(s'attendre à)* if she marries him she'll get more than she bargained for

bargain on VT INSÉP *(compter sur)* I'm bargaining on it; I didn't bargain on your kid brother coming as well

bash about/around VT SÉP FAM *(tabasser)* her husband bashes her about something awful; *(mettre à rude épreuve)* you can always rely on baggage handlers bashing your suitcases about

bash on VI BR FAM *(continuer, malgré des difficultés, etc.)* the weather forecast was bad but they decided to bash on with their plans for a picnic

battle on VI *(continuer à lutter, à se battre, malgré des difficultés, etc.)* he has fallen very far behind the other runners but he's still battling on; just battle on as best you can in the circumstances

bawl out VT SÉP (a) *(hurler)* please don't bawl out my name in public like that (b) FAM *(passer un savon à, engueuler)* the boss really bawled us out for that mistake

bear down 1 VI (a) *(pousser, pour une femme en travail)* if that midwife had said "bear down, dear" one more time, I would have screamed (b) *(foncer sur, s'approcher d'une manière menaçante)* the crew of the fishing boat jumped overboard as they saw the liner bearing down on them; the boys scattered as the headmaster bore down on them

2 VT SÉP *habituellement au passif (accabler)* the Third World is borne down by the burden of poverty

bear out VT SÉP *(corroborer, confirmer)* onlookers bore out her statement to the police; he feels that the report bears him out in his estimates of radiation levels in the area

bear up VI *(tenir le coup)* she found it difficult to bear up when there was still no news after the second day; bear up! just one more day to the weekend

bear (up)on VT INSÉP *(concerner, avoir un rapport avec)* I don't see how that bears on what I am supposed to be doing

bear with VT INSÉP *(supporter patiemment, faire preuve de patience envers)* the old lady asked the salesman to bear with her while she looked for her glasses

beat back VT SÉP *(repousser)* they beat back the attackers three times but were eventually overrun

beat down 1 VI *(tomber à verse)* the rain was beating down so fast it was difficult to see the road; *(taper)* the sun was beating down
2 VT SÉP (a) *(détruire)* the drunk threatened to beat the door down if they didn't open up; hailstorms have beaten down the county's entire barley crop (b) *(faire baisser son prix à qn)* I felt quite proud of myself for beating him down so much

beat off VT SÉP *(repousser)* the tourists tried unsuccessfully to beat off all the people trying to sell them things

beat out VT SÉP (a) *(étouffer)* desperate sheep-farmers were beating out the brush fires with their bare hands (b) *(battre, marquer)* she beat out the rhythm on the table (c) *(débosseler)* the car door panel will have to be beaten out

beat up VT SÉP (a) FAM *(passer à tabac)* he got beaten up on his way home last night (b) *(battre, fouetter, pour de la crème, des œufs)* just beat up a few eggs for an omelette

beaver away VI FAM *(bosser, travailler d'arrache-pied)* he's still beavering away at his studies

belt out VT SÉP FAM *(gueuler, brailler)* he really belted that song out

belt up VI (a) BR FAM *(la boucler)* I wish you would belt up (b) *(attacher sa ceinture)* I'm not starting this car until you belt up

bind over VT SÉP *(relaxer sous condition de ne pas troubler l'ordre public)* the drunk was bound over for three months to keep the peace

black out 1 VI *(s'évanouir)* she was all right until she saw the blood and then she blacked out
2 VT SÉP (a) *(plonger dans l'obscurité)* the impact of the scene is heightened when they black the stage out (b) *(empêcher la retransmission de)* we regret that industrial action has blacked out this evening's programmes

blast off VI *(décoller, pour un engin spatial)* the latest space shuttle blasted off at 5 am local time today

blaze away VI (a) *(flamber, pour un feu)* the fire is blazing away merrily in the grate (b) *(maintenir un feu nourri, tirer sans cesse)* the troops blazed away at the target

blink at VT INSÉP FIG *(fermer les yeux sur)* his wife blinks at his affairs

blink away VT SÉP *(refouler)* I blinked my tears away

block in VT SÉP *(bloquer, pour une voiture, etc.)* that man next door has blocked me in again

block off VT SÉP *(bloquer, fermer)* the street will be blocked off until the wreckage is cleared

block up VT SÉP (a) *(boucher)* don't throw the tea leaves down the sink or you'll block it up; the worst thing about a cold is that your nose gets all blocked up (b) *(barrer)* they've blocked up the entry

blossom out VI FIG *(se métamorphoser)* she's blossoming out into quite a beautiful young woman

blot out VT SÉP *(effacer)* a word has been blotted out here; you must try to remember and come to terms with the past, not blot it out; *(cacher, masquer)* the mist has blotted out the view

blow in 1 VI (a) *(se briser)* all the windows blew in because of the explosion (b) *(entrer, sous la force du vent)* shut the door, the dust is blowing in (c) FAM *(débarquer (à l'improviste))* when did you blow in?
2 VT SÉP *(briser, enfoncer)* the blast blew all the windows in

blow off 1 VI *(s'envoler)* some of the roof tiles have blown off
2 VT SÉP (a) *(emporter (par le vent))* the high winds blew the tiles off the roof (b) *(emporter (par une explosion), faire sauter (par un coup de feu))* the gunman threatened to blow their heads off

blow out 1 VI (a) *(s'éteindre)* the candles have blown out (b) *(éclater)* the rear tyre blew out
2 VT SÉP (a) *(éteindre, souffler)* be sure to blow the match out properly (b) *(calmer)* the storm soon blew itself out (c) *(locution)* to blow someone's brains out *faire sauter la cervelle à qn*

blow over 1 VI (a) *(tomber, s'effondrer)* the garage must have blown over in the high winds last night (b) *(se calmer, passer)* the storm will blow over soon; FIG it will soon blow over and you'll be friends again
2 VT SÉP *(faire tomber, renverser)* did the wind blow anything over?

blow up 1 VI (a) *(sauter, exploser)* the ammunitions depot blew up (b) FAM *(exploser, se mettre en boule)* do you often blow up like that? (c) *(éclater, se déclencher)* the argument blew up out of nowhere
2 VT SÉP (a) *(faire sauter)* terrorists have blown up the presidential palace (b) *(gonfler)* do the tyres need blowing up? (c) *(agrandir)* I'd like this photograph blown up (d) *(exagérer)* you're blowing this up out of all proportion

bluff out VT SÉP *(se tirer d'affaire par le bluff, la ruse)* she can bluff her way out of anything; when the police get here we'll just have to bluff it out

board in/up VT SÉP *(barricader, obturer)* the windows and doors have all been boarded up to stop tramps getting in

bog down VT SÉP *habituellement au passif (embourber, enliser)* the car is bogged down in the mud; FIG *(se perdre)* the important thing is not to get bogged down in details

boil down to VI *(revenir à, se résumer à)* what his claim boils down to is...

boil up 1 VT SÉP *(faire bouillir)* boil up some water for the pasta
2 VI FAM *(monter)* I could feel the anger boiling up inside me

bolt down 1 VT INSÉP *(dévaler)* she bolted down the stairs and into the street
2 VT SÉP *(avaler, engloutir)* don't bolt your food down like that

bone up on VT INSÉP FAM *(potasser)* you'll have to bone up on your history if you want to pass that test next week

book in 1 VI BR *(se présenter à la réception (d'un hôtel))* do we have to book in by a certain time?
2 VT SÉP *(réserver une chambre pour)* I've booked them in to the best hotel in town

book out 1 VI *(quitter sa chambre d'hôtel, partir)* when do we have to book out by?

2 **VT SÉP** *(enregistrer le départ de)* the receptionist booked them out before noon

book up 1 **VI** *(réserver)* have you booked up for your holiday?
2 **VT SÉP** *habituellement au passif (être complet)* the hotel is all booked up

boot up *Informatique* 1 **VI** *(démarrer)* for some reason the computer is refusing to boot up
2 **VT SÉP** *(faire démarrer)* use this disk to boot up the computer

bottle up **VT SÉP** *(refouler, ne pas exprimer)* it does no good to bottle up your feelings

bottom out **VI** *(atteindre son niveau le plus bas)* the government hopes that unemployment has finally bottomed out

bow out **VI** *(tirer sa révérence)* when the company brought in computers, old Mr Parsons decided the time had come to bow out

bowl out **VT SÉP** *(mettre hors jeu, au cricket)* we bowled him out for ten

bowl over **VT SÉP** **(a)** *(renverser)* the old lady was bowled over by a boy on a bike **(b)** **FAM** *(stupéfier, sidérer)* I was bowled over when I won first prize

box in **VT SÉP** **(a)** *(coincer, encercler)* the defence seem to have him boxed in **(b)** *(enfermer)* don't you feel boxed in in such a small room? **(c)** *(encastrer)* we're boxing in the sink

branch off **VI** *(bifurquer)* the road branches off to the left

branch out **VI** *(se diversifier, se lancer)* the company intends to branch out into a new area of business

brazen out **VT SÉP** *(se montrer insolent, payer d'audace, d'effronterie) couramment "to brazen it out"* when they accused him of gatecrashing the party, he brazened it out and refused to admit he hadn't been invited

break away **VI** **(a)** *(échapper à)* she broke away from the guards who were escorting her to hospital **(b)** *(se séparer, rompre)* when did you break away from your family?; it was the year France broke away from NATO

break down 1 **VI** **(a)** *(tomber en panne)* the car broke down on the motorway

(b) *(échouer)* their marriage seems to be breaking down; talks between the two sides have broken down; *(ne pas tenir debout)* that's where your argument breaks down
(c) *(s'effondrer)* I broke down in tears
(d) *(se diviser)* the report breaks down into three parts
(e) *(se décomposer)* the compound breaks down into a number of components
2 **VT SÉP** **(a)** *(démolir, abattre, enfoncer)* the firemen had to break down the door to rescue the children
(b) *(vaincre)* she was unable to break down her parents' opposition to her plans
(c) *(détailler, décomposer)* we really need to break the figures down a bit further

break in 1 **VI** **(a)** *(entrer par effraction)* when did you realize that someone had broken in? **(b)** *(interrompre, pendant une conversation, etc.)* I really must break in at this point
2 **VT SÉP** **(a)** *(enfoncer)* the thieves broke the door in **(b)** *(dresser, pour un cheval)* she's good at breaking in horses; *(porter (pour user, assouplir))* I hate having to break new shoes in

break into **VT INSÉP** **(a)** *(entrer par effraction dans)* thieves broke into a number of houses on the street last night **(b)** *(entamer)* I'll have to break into my holiday money to pay for the repairs to my car **(c)** *(interrompre)* why did you break into the conversation like that? **(d)** *(se mettre à...)* I broke into a cold sweat when I realized how high up I was; he often breaks into song in the shower

break off 1 **VI** **(a)** *(se détacher, se casser)* it just broke off in my hand, honestly **(b)** *(s'interrompre)* he broke off when the chairman entered the room **(c)** *(s'arrêter)* can we break off for the rest of the day?
2 **VT SÉP** **(a)** *(détacher, casser)* break off two pieces of chocolate for you and your brother **(b)** *(suspendre, arrêter)* talks have been broken off **(c)** *(rompre, pour une relation amoureuse)* it wouldn't surprise me if they broke it off soon; they've broken off the engagement

break open **VT SÉP** **(a)** *(enfoncer (porte), forcer)* he broke the desk open **(b)** **FAM** *(ouvrir, déboucher)* let's break open another bottle

break out **VI** **(a)** *(éclater, se déclarer)* fires have broken out all over the city **(b)** *(avoir une éruption)* the baby is breaking out in a rash

(c) *(s'échapper, s'évader)* the prisoners broke out late last night

break up 1 VI (a) *(craquer, se briser)* the ice on the river is breaking up at last; *(se briser)* their marriage is breaking up; AM FAM *(locution)* I just broke up *j'ai éclaté de rire*
(b) *(se terminer)* when did the party finally break up?; the schools will be breaking up for summer soon
(c) *(rompre, se séparer)* I've heard that they're breaking up
2 VT SÉP (a) *(mettre fin à, arrêter)* the warder broke up the fight between the prisoners; *(détruire)* it was his drinking that broke the marriage up
(b) *(morceler, ameublir)* you'll have to break the earth up before you can plant anything

bring about VT SÉP *(entraîner, causer)* what brought this about?

bring back VT SÉP (a) *(ramener)* Mum told me to bring you back for supper (b) *(ramener à, pour un état)* a couple of days in bed will bring him back to normal; *(réélire)* it will be up to the electors to decide whether to bring back the previous government (c) *(rappeler, réveiller, pour des souvenirs, etc.)* that song brings back memories

bring down VT SÉP (a) *(faire crouler)* if that boy doesn't stop jumping up and down like that he's going to bring the house down about our ears; *(locution)* their jokes always bring the house down *leurs blagues connaissent toujours un succès triomphant*
(b) *(abattre)* the spy plane was brought down by a missile
(c) *(faire atterrir)* the badly damaged plane was brought down with no loss of life
(d) *(renverser, faire tomber)* it was really the students who brought down the government; he brought him down with a rugby tackle
(e) *(faire baisser)* this new drug will bring his temperature down; she would have brought the price down even further if you'd gone on bargaining
(f) *(attirer (l'attention))* stop making so much noise or you'll bring the headmaster down on us

bring in VT SÉP (a) *(faire entrer)* I've brought Mrs Jones in to see you
(b) *(introduire)* new tax legislation will be brought in next year
(c) *(faire appel à, faire intervenir)* the company is bringing consultants in to see if the problems can be solved; this

argument is between you two, why bring me in?
(d) *(fêter, pour le Nouvel An)* to bring in the New Year
(e) *(rapporter, gagner)* how much money is your eldest son bringing in?
(f) *(rendre, pour un jugement)* the jury brought in a verdict of not guilty

bring off VT SÉP (a) *(sauver ou récupérer d'un bateau, etc.)* the bodies are being brought off the ship today (b) *(réussir, pour une affaire)* did you bring the deal off?

bring on VT SÉP (a) *(faire entrer)* please bring on our next contestant (b) *(causer, provoquer)* damp days always bring on my arthritis; what brought this on? (c) *(faire pousser)* this mild weather will bring the roses on nicely (d) *(locution)* I brought it on myself *je n'ai personne à blâmer*

bring out VT SÉP (a) *(faire sortir)* they brought the man out under armed guard (b) *(faire sortir de sa réserve)* his granddaughter is about the only one who can bring him out (of himself)
(c) *(faire sortir, faire apparaître)* the sun has brought out all the bulbs; disasters bring out the best – and worst – in people; they're bringing out the new models very soon; *(provoquer chez, pour une allergie)* strawberries bring her out in a rash

bring round VT SÉP (a) *(amener, apporter)* I'll bring him round to meet you some time (b) *(persuader, convertir)* you'll never bring my dad round to that way of thinking (c) *(ranimer)* they brought her round quite quickly after she fainted (d) *(amener... sur)* I finally managed to bring the conversation round to what I wanted to talk about

bring up VT SÉP (a) *(élever)* we've brought four kids up (b) *(mentionner, soulever)* Madam Chairwoman, I wish to bring up the question of travel expenses (c) *(vomir)* everything she swallows she brings up ten minutes later

brush aside VT SÉP *(écarter, repousser)* the Minister brushed aside the reporters; she won't listen, she just brushes our objections aside

brush up VT SÉP (a) *(ramasser à la balayette)* I want all those crumbs brushed up off the floor (b) *(revoir, réviser)* he'll have to brush up his Spanish

buck up **FAM** 1 **VI** **(a)** *(se grouiller, se magner)* buck up or we'll be late **(b)** *(se secouer, reprendre courage)* I wish he would buck up a little
2 **VT SÉP** **(a)** *(remonter le moral à)* the good news bucked me up no end **(b)** *(locution)* to buck up one's ideas *se secouer, se remuer*

bucket down **VI BR FAM** *(pleuvoir des cordes)* it's bucketing down

buckle down/to **VI BR FAM** *(se mettre à, s'y mettre, en mettre un coup)* I suppose I'd better buckle down if I want to finish the housework this morning; if you don't buckle down to your piano practice you'll never pass the exam; he buckled to and finished cleaning the car

build on 1 **VT SÉP** *(ajouter)* they're building on a conservatory next door
2 **VT INSÉP** *(s'appuyer sur, consolider)* the company is building on its earlier success

build up 1 **VI** *(s'accumuler, augmenter)* pressure on the government is building up
2 **VT SÉP** **(a)** *(accumuler, augmenter)* I wouldn't build my hopes up if I were you; we're trying to build up our savings so we can buy a house soon
(b) *(donner de la force à)* the children need some vitamins to build them up
(c) *(établir, créer)* his father built that company up from nothing; you've built up quite a reputation for yourself
(d) *habituellement au passif (construire)* the area has become quite built up
(e) *(faire de la publicité pour)* the play has been so built up that it's impossible to get tickets for it

bump into **VT INSÉP** **(a)** *(rentrer dans, se cogner contre)* I was so engrossed in my thoughts that I bumped into a lamp post
(b) *(rencontrer par hasard, tomber sur)* he's always bumping into people he knows

bump off **VT SÉP FAM** *(tuer, liquider)* his job was bumping people off for a fee

bump up **VT SÉP FAM** *(augmenter)* they've bumped up the price of beer again

bundle off **VT SÉP** *(envoyer en toute hâte, expédier d'urgence)* the baby was bundled off to hospital in an ambulance

bundle up 1 VI *(s'emmitoufler)* you'd better bundle up, it's freezing out there
2 VT SÉP *(mettre en paquet, emmitoufler)* she bundled the baby up in a warm blanket

bung up VT SÉP FAM *(boucher)* who bunged the sink up?; I'm/my nose is all bunged up

burn down 1 VI *(être détruit par le feu, brûler complètement)* the theatre burned down; *(s'éteindre peu à peu)* the fire is burning down
2 VT SÉP *(incendier, brûler)* vandals have burned down a number of derelict buildings in the area

burn out 1 VI *(s'éteindre)* the fire is burning out; FIG *(s'épuiser, perdre son enthousiasme, etc.)* social workers frequently burn out at an early age
2 VT SÉP **(a)** *(être sans abri (en raison d'un incendie))* they were burned out **(b)** *(éteindre)* the fire has burnt itself out

burn up 1 VI *(se consumer)* the rocket burned up in the atmosphere
2 VT SÉP *(brûler, consommer)* children burn up a lot of energy playing; this stove burns up a lot of wood

burst into VT INSÉP **(a)** *(faire irruption dans)* she burst into the room **(b)** *(éclater en, se mettre à)* he burst into tears; then they all burst into song

burst out 1 VT INSÉP *(éclater de)* I burst out laughing; *(s'écrier)* "where were you last night?" he burst out
2 VI *(sortir précipitamment)* they all burst out of the room

butt in VI *(se mêler à la conversation, etc.)* we were just having a cosy chat when she butted in; is this a private argument or can anybody butt in?

buy into VT INSÉP *(acheter des actions ou une participation dans)* he has bought into his neighbour's business

buy off VT SÉP FAM *(acheter, verser des pots-de-vin à)* the councillor was bought off with an all-expenses-paid holiday in the south of France

buy out VT SÉP *(racheter les actions ou la part de)* all the other shareholders have been bought out

buy up VT SÉP *(dévaliser)* look at all those parcels, she must have bought up the entire store!; *(acheter en quantité)* because of the threatened shortage people have been buying up petrol

buzz off VI FAM *(dégager, se casser)* tell that kid brother of yours to buzz off; just buzz off and leave me alone

C

call back 1 VI (a) *(revenir, repasser)* I'll call back later to see her (b) *(rappeler, au téléphone)* if you'd like to call back in an hour...
2 VT SÉP (a) *(rappeler, au téléphone)* he said he would call you back (b) *(rappeler, faire revenir)* I know she's on holiday but she'll have to be called back to deal with this; I think the last pair should be called back for another audition

call for VT INSÉP (a) *(demander, réclamer)* the Opposition is calling for her resignation (b) *(passer prendre)* would it be too much of a rush if I called for you at seven? (c) *(exiger, demander)* this is the kind of job that calls for good interpersonal skills; that's wonderful news, it calls for a celebration

call in 1 VI (a) *(rendre visite, passer)* the social worker is going to call in later (b) *(appeler, téléphoner)* off-duty nurses called in and offered to help; prison officers are not actually on strike but a great many of them are calling in sick
2 VT SÉP (a) *(faire venir)* they've finally decided to call the doctor in (b) *(retirer de la circulation)* the bank has called in its loans

call off VT SÉP (a) *(annuler)* the meeting will have to be called off; does this mean we'll have to call our holiday off?; they've called it off *(c.-à-d. fiançailles ou mariage)* (b) *(rappeler)* call your dog off!

call out 1 VI *(crier, hurler)* don't call out in the street like that
2 VT SÉP (a) *(crier)* the master of ceremonies called out the names of the prizewinners (b) *(appeler, faire venir)* call out the guard!; I don't like calling the doctor out at this time of night (c) *(donner la consigne de grève)* the men were called out (on strike) halfway through the morning shift

call up VT SÉP (a) *(faire venir)* the situation looked dangerous and the lieutenant decided to call up reinforcements (b) *(appeler sous* *les drapeaux)* Dad was called up in 1940 (c) *(téléphoner à, appeler)* please don't call me up at midnight (d) *(évoquer)* the speech called up thoughts of the past

call (up)on VT INSÉP (a) *(demander, sommer)* the opposition called on the government to make its position clear (b) *(rendre visite à)* gentlemen used to ask permission to call on young ladies

calm down 1 VI *(se calmer)* getting hysterical won't help, just calm down; I want you all to calm down now, children
2 VT SÉP *(calmer)* leave it to Mum, she'll calm him down

care for VT INSÉP (a) *(soigner, s'occuper de)* she has spent years caring for her invalid mother (b) *(aimer)* you know I don't care for that kind of language; I don't believe he ever cared for you or he wouldn't have treated you the way he did

carry away VT SÉP *(emporter, pour des sentiments)* he let his enthusiasm carry him away; she gets carried away by the sound of her own voice; take it easy, don't get carried away! *(c.-à-d. ne t'emporte pas)*

carry forward VT SÉP (a) *(remettre, pour une date)* can I carry my leave forward and have six weeks next summer? (b) *(reporter, pour des chiffres)* this amount should have been carried forward to the next page

carry off VT SÉP (a) *(emporter, enlever)* the thieves carried off all their jewellery (b) *(réussir, mener à bien)* it wasn't the easiest of speeches to make but you carried it off very well
(c) *(remporter)* she carried off the prizes for Latin and French
(d) *(emporter, pour une épidémie)* tuberculosis carried off a great many people in the last century

carry on 1 VI (a) *(continuer)* just carry on with what you were doing
(b) FAM *(faire une scène ou des histoires)* he carried on just because his wife wanted an evening out; what a way to carry on!
(c) FAM *(avoir une liaison)* have you been carrying on behind my back?
2 VT SÉP *(continuer, poursuivre)* grandfather wants me to carry on the business after he dies; *(entretenir)* we have carried on a correspondence for years

carry out VT SÉP (a) *(porter à l'extérieur)* they had to carry him out since he couldn't walk (b) *(mener, pour une enquête)* the coastguard is carrying out a search for the missing crew members **(c)** *(tenir, pour une promesse)* never make a promise that you cannot carry out

carry through VT SÉP *(mener à bien)* the plan has to be carried through to the last detail

carve out VT SÉP **(a)** *(tailler, sculpter)* he has now carved out twenty or so statues **(b)** FIG *(se tailler)* the company plans to carve out its own niche in the market

carve up VT SÉP **(a)** *(découper, pour de la viande)* ask the butcher to carve the meat up for you **(b)** *(diviser, partager)* they just carved up the land among themselves with no regard for the native inhabitants **(c)** FAM *(faire une queue de poisson à)* did you see how that fool carved me up?

cash in 1 VT SÉP *(encaisser, se faire rembourser)* are you going to cash in your premium bonds?
2 VI FAM *(profiter de)* she's cashing in on the fact that her father knows a lot of influential people

cast away VT SÉP *(être naufragé)* Robinson Crusoe was cast away on his desert island for a great many years

cast back VT SÉP *(ramener dans le passé)* if you cast your mind back a week, you will recall that...

cast off 1 VT SÉP **(a)** *(rabattre, pour un tricot)* cast off the remaining stitches **(b)** *(larguer les amarres de)* we cast the launch off at dawn
2 VI **(a)** *(arrêter ou rabattre les mailles)* cast off when only four stitches remain **(b)** *(larguer les amarres)* they will cast off shortly

cast on 1 VI *(monter les mailles)* I usually cast on with my thumb
2 VT SÉP *(monter, pour un tricot)* cast on 80 stitches; have you cast the sleeve on yet?

catch at VT INSÉP *(essayer d'attraper)* she caught at his sleeve and asked for help

catch on VI **(a)** *(prendre, devenir populaire)* I remember you saying that the Beatles would never catch on **(b)** FAM *(piger)* she's so naive she didn't catch on

catch out VT SÉP **(a)** *(piéger, prendre en défaut)* the police caught him out by asking for a description of the programme he said he was watching (b) *(éliminer, au cricket)* he was caught out very early on

catch up 1 VI *(gagner du terrain, rattraper la distance)* the runners behind are catching up; *(rattraper (son retard))* I wish I could catch up with my work/sleep
2 VT SÉP (a) *(rattraper)* you go ahead and I'll catch you up (b) *(bloquer, coincer)* they were caught up in a traffic jam for hours

cave in VI *(s'effondrer)* the walls and roof caved in under the force of the blast

centre on VT INSÉP *(se concentrer sur)* the play centres on the idea of survivor guilt

chain up VT SÉP *(attacher, enchaîner)* I hope he chains that brute of a dog up at night; in those days people could be chained up in prison for years

chalk up VT SÉP FAM (a) *(remporter)* the team chalked up another win today (b) *(mettre sur son compte)* chalk it up, will you, and I'll pay next week (c) *(locution)* she'll just have to chalk it up to experience *elle n'aura qu'à le mettre sur le compte de l'expérience*

chance on VT INSÉP *(trouver par hasard, tomber sur)* I chanced on this piece of Meissen in a grubby little second-hand shop

change down VI *(rétrograder)* there are traffic lights coming up, so change down

change over VI (a) *(se convertir, passer à)* is it a good idea to change over entirely to electricity? (b) *(échanger)* let's change over and you wash while I dry; *(changer de chaîne)* as soon as opera or ballet comes on the TV, he changes over

change up VI *(passer la vitesse supérieure)* you have to change up faster than that

chase up VT SÉP BR (a) *(relancer, activer)* I had to chase him up for the £50 he owed me; I'll chase the matter up for you
(b) *(rechercher)* why not ask one of the big stores to chase up the pattern for you? (c) *(trouver)* we finally chased her up in the library

chat up VT SÉP FAM *(draguer, baratiner)* he's just chatting you up; I wish I could chat up men the way she does

cheat on VT INSÉP (a) *(tromper)* why didn't you tell me he was cheating on me? (b) *(tricher sur)* it's not a good idea to cheat on your expenses

check in 1 VI *(se présenter à l'enregistrement (aéroport), à la réception (hôtel))* have you checked in?
2 VT SÉP (a) *(enregistrer (aéroport), inscrire sur le registre (hôtel))* they must be here, I checked them in myself (b) *(réserver pour)* she checked me into a four-star hotel

check out 1 VI (a) *(quitter l'hôtel)* they checked out last night (b) FAM *(correspondre, coller)* it doesn't check out
2 VT SÉP (a) *(enregistrer le départ de)* the reception clerk will check you out (b) *(se renseigner sur)* we've checked her out and she's who she says she is (c) FAM *(essayer)* why don't we check out the restaurant that John told us about? (d) FAM *(mater, viser)* check this out

check through VT SÉP (a) *(examiner, fouiller)* they checked through everyone's hand luggage (b) *(faire envoyer par avion)* I have to change at Geneva, can my bags be checked right through to London?

cheer on VT SÉP *(encourager par des acclamations)* he's there every Saturday to cheer his team on

cheer up 1 VI *(retrouver le moral, se réjouir)* she soon cheered up when she heard she'd got the job
2 VT SÉP (a) *(remonter le moral à, réconforter)* a visit to the pub will cheer him up (b) *(égayer)* the new curtains really do cheer the room up

chew on VT INSÉP (a) *(mastiquer, mordiller, mâchonner)* he chewed on his pipe stem for a bit and then said... (b) *(ruminer)* how much longer do you need to chew on it?

chew over VT SÉP *(ruminer, tourner et retourner dans son esprit)* I've been chewing this problem over in my mind for some time

chew up VT SÉP (a) *(mâcher)* chew your food up well before swallowing (b) *(abîmer)* your machine has chewed up my bank card; it's those heavy lorries that are chewing up the road

chicken out VI FAM *(se dégonfler)* he had a date with my sister but he chickened out at the last minute; don't chicken out on us; *(se défiler)* he chickened out of his dental appointment

chip in FAM 1 VI (a) *(intervenir, dire son mot)* if I can chip in for a moment... (b) *(contribuer)* we've all chipped in for a present for her
2 VT SÉP *(contribuer)* how much is everyone else chipping in?

chip off 1 VI *(s'écailler)* the paint is chipping off
2 VT SÉP *(ébrécher)* be careful with those plates, I don't want any pieces chipped off; *(enlever)* we slowly chipped off the old paintwork

choke back VT SÉP *(refouler, contenir)* looking at these pictures, I find it hard to choke back my tears/anger

choke up VT SÉP (a) *(bloquer, boucher)* the drain is all choked up with leaves (b) FAM *habituellement au passif (émouvoir, toucher profondément)* she was all choked up

chuck in VT SÉP FAM *(laisser tomber, lâcher, plaquer)* you're surely not thinking of chucking in your job?; one day I'm going to chuck all this in and buy a farm; he's chucked his latest girlfriend in

chug along VI FAM *(se traîner)* Dad always chugs along at about 35, even on the motorway

clam up VI *(ne plus piper mot, se taire)* don't clam up, talk to me!

clamp down VI *(serrer la vis, devenir plus sévère)* the police are clamping down this Christmas so don't drink and drive

clamp down on VT INSÉP *(serrer la vis à, sévir contre)* the authorities are clamping down on misleading advertising

clean out VT SÉP (a) *(nettoyer à fond)* I'll clean out a few cupboards today, I think (b) FAM *(nettoyer, plumer)* the casino cleaned him out (c) FAM *(vider)* someone has cleaned the shop out of sugar

clean up 1 VT SÉP (a) *(nettoyer, laver)* when are you going to clean this place up? it's a mess; the kids need to be cleaned up before we go to your mother's (b) *(nettoyer, épurer)* I like those old cowboy films where the sheriff always says "I'm going to clean up this town"

2 **VI FAM** *(gagner gros)* she really cleaned up at the roulette table

clear away 1 **VT SÉP** *(enlever, débarrasser)* workmen were clearing away the debris; it's your turn to clear the dishes away
2 **VI** **(a)** *(débarrasser)* could you clear away, please? **(b)** *(se dissiper, disparaître)* the clouds have all cleared away

clear off 1 **VT SÉP** *(enlever)* clear all those papers off the table
2 **VI** *(filer, décamper)* clear off!; the boys cleared off when they saw the headmaster coming down the street

clear up 1 **VT SÉP** **(a)** *(éclaircir, résoudre)* I'd like to clear up a point or two; we have some problems that need to be cleared up
(b) *(ranger)* I can't come out, I have to clear up my room
(c) *(faire disparaître)* the doctor said this cream would clear up the acne
2 **VI** **(a)** *(se lever, s'éclaircir, pour la météo)* it's clearing up
(b) *(disparaître)* don't worry, that rash will soon clear up

climb down **VI** **(a)** *(descendre)* it took the climbers three hours to climb down **(b)** *(admettre qu'on a tort, céder)* she'll never climb down, however strong the arguments against her

clock in 1 **VI** **(a)** *(faire un temps de)* the last of the marathon runners clocked in at six hours **(b)** *(pointer (à l'arrivée))* I have to clock in; you clocked in 10 minutes late
2 **VT SÉP** *(pointer pour (à l'arrivée))* do you think just this once you could clock me in?

clock off 1 **VI** *(pointer (à la sortie))* when did you clock off?
2 **VT SÉP** *(pointer pour (à la sortie))* I'll clock you off if you like

clock up **VT SÉP** **(a)** *(faire, réaliser)* he clocked up a faster time than any of his rivals in the race **(b)** *(remporter)* the team has clocked up another victory

close down 1 **VI** **(a)** *(fermer définitivement)* the factory is closing down next month; we're closing down soon **(b)** *(terminer les émissions)* television used to close down at midnight
2 **VT SÉP** *(fermer définitivement)* they closed the restaurant down because of health code violations

close in 1 **VI** **(a)** *(raccourcir)* the days are closing in **(b)** *(approcher)* winter is closing in

2 **VT SÉP** *(boucher, fermer)* they're thinking of closing the porch in

close in on **VT INSÉP** *(cerner)* government troops are said to be closing in on the rebels

close up 1 **VI** *(se rapprocher, se serrer)* the photographer asked the people in the front line to close up so he could get them all in
2 **VT SÉP** *(fermer)* they must have gone away for some time, the house is all closed up; the opening in the fence has been closed up to prevent similar tragedies in the future

cloud over **VI** *(se couvrir, pour le ciel)* it clouded over this afternoon; **FIG** *(s'assombrir)* her face clouded over when she saw him

cloud up 1 **VI** *(se couvrir, pour le ciel)* it's clouding up; *(se couvrir de buée)* the mirror has clouded up
2 **VT SÉP** *(embuer, couvrir de buée)* the bathroom is poorly ventilated, steam always clouds the windows up

club together **VI** *(se cotiser)* if we club together, we can get one big present instead of lots of small ones

cobble together **VT SÉP** *(concocter à la hâte, bâcler)* my speech won't be very good, I'm afraid, I cobbled it together on the train

collect up **VT SÉP** *(rassembler, ramasser)* I began to collect up my parcels

comb through **VT INSÉP FIG** *(ratisser, passer au peigne fin)* I've combed through the entire book and haven't found any reference to him

come across 1 **VI** *(faire une impression, donner l'impression de)* how did her story come across?; they come across as (being) rather nice people
2 **VT INSÉP** *(trouver par hasard, tomber sur)* I came across this when I was tidying up, is it yours?

come across with **VT INSÉP FAM** *(donner, filer)* if we don't come across with the money, they say they'll kill him

come along **VI** (a) *(se dépêcher)* come along children, please!
(b) *(avancer, progresser)* my speech is coming along rather well (c) *(arriver)* everything was peaceful until you came along (d) *(venir)* can I come along?

come apart VI *(se casser)* honestly, I don't know how it happened, it just came apart in my hands; FIG *(s'écrouler)* she feels her life is coming apart at the seams

come at VT INSÉP *(attaquer, se jeter sur)* the pair of them came at me with a baseball bat; FIG *(assaillir)* questions came at me from all sides

come away VI (a) *(partir)* why not come away with me to Paris for the weekend?; *(s'éloigner)* come away from that cat, it's got fleas (b) *(se détacher)* the handle has come away from the knife

come back VI (a) *(revenir)* I've forgotten your name but it will come back to me eventually (b) *(répondre, répliquer)* then she came back with one of her usual cutting remarks (c) *(remonter, revenir)* we thought the fight was all over but he's coming back very strongly now (d) *(revenir à la mode)* short hair is coming back

come by 1 VT INSÉP *(se faire)* how did your brother come by all those bruises?; *(trouver, se procurer)* I wonder how he came by all that money

2 VI *(venir, passer)* I'll come by next week if that suits

come down VI (a) *(baisser)* oil prices have been coming down; her temperature came down overnight; *(baisser de)* he'll come down a few pounds if you bargain

(b) *(tomber)* rain was coming down in sheets; the ceiling came down

(c) *(descendre, atteindre)* the curtains should come right down to the floor

(d) *(être transmis, parvenir, par héritage)* the necklace came down to her from her great-aunt

(e) *(être décroché ou enlevé)* that disgusting poster is coming down right now, or else!

(f) *(se prononcer)* the majority came down in favour of/against abortion

come down on VT INSÉP (a) *(s'en prendre à, tomber sur le dos de)* one mistake and he'll come down on you like a ton of bricks

(b) *(se décider pour)* he'll wait and see what happens and then come down on the winning side

come down to VT INSÉP *(revenir au problème de, se résumer à)* it all comes down to money; *(en être réduit à)* this is what we've come down to – selling the house

come down with VT INSÉP *(attraper, pour un rhume, etc.)* I always come down with a cold at this time of year

come forward VI *(se présenter)* the police have appealed for witnesses to come forward

come in VI (a) *(arriver)* our new stock will not come in until next week (b) *(entrer, pour des sommes d'argent)* I don't have much coming in at the moment, can you wait a bit? (c) *(être, s'avérer)* an extra pair of hands always comes in useful (d) *(être impliqué, intervenir)* where does she come in in all this? *(c.-à-d. quel est son rôle dans tout ça ?)* (e) *(parler, par radio)* are you receiving me? come in, please

come in for VT INSÉP *(subir, être l'objet de)* the government is coming in for a lot of criticism over its latest proposals; he came in for a lot of adverse publicity when he was younger

come in on VT INSÉP *(prendre part à)* why should we let him come in on the deal?

come into VT INSÉP (a) *(hériter de)* she'll come into several hundred thousand pounds when her great-uncle dies (b) *(être concerné par, jouer un rôle dans)* wait a minute, when did I come into this crazy scheme?; *(avoir à voir)* ability doesn't come into it, it's who you know that matters (c) *(locutions)* to come into blossom *fleurir*; to come into effect *entrer en vigueur*; would you mind explaining how the car came into your possession, sir? *est-ce que vous pourriez me dire comment cette voiture est entrée en votre possession, monsieur ?*

come of VT INSÉP (a) *(résulter de)* nothing will come of it; this is what comes of being too self-confident (b) *(venir de)* the mare comes of good stock (c) *(locution)* she inherited a fortune when she came of age *elle a hérité d'une fortune lorsqu'elle a atteint sa majorité*

come off 1 VI (a) *(s'enlever, se détacher)* could you fix my bike? the chain has come off; my suede shoes are ruined, the mud won't come off
(b) *(s'en sortir, s'en tirer)* considering what he's done, he's come off very lightly; it could have been a serious accident,

but they all came off without a scratch; we came off very badly in the debate on capital punishment
(c) *(avoir lieu)* I shall be very surprised if that wedding ever comes off; the trip did eventually come off but several months later than planned
(d) **FAM** *(réussir)* yet another attempt to beat the record hasn't come off
2 **VT INSÉP** (a) *(se détacher de, partir de, s'enlever de)* the handle has come off the knife; that kind of mark never comes off silk
(b) **FAM** *(exclamation marquant l'impatience, l'incrédulité : allez, ça va !, arrête ton char !)* come off it! you can't expect me to believe that!

come on VI (a) *(se dépêcher)* come on, or we'll miss the start
(b) *(progresser, avancer)* how's the work coming on?
(c) *(commencer)* the rain came on about six; I have a sore throat coming on; when does that programme you want to watch come on? (d) *(entrer en scène)* the character he plays doesn't come on until halfway through the first act (e) **FAM** *(faire son/sa..., jouer les...)* he was coming on a bit too macho; she came on a bit strong *(c.-à-d. elle y est allée un peu fort)*

come out VI (a) *(paraître, sortir)* the magazine comes out on a Wednesday; when do you expect your latest film to come out?; now that the sun has come out maybe I'll get my washing dried; *(éclore)* next door's roses always come out early
(b) *(être connu ou annoncé)* the election results came out a few hours ago; the truth will come out eventually
(c) *(se mettre en grève)* nurses all over the country have come out in protest
(d) *(avoir, pour une éruption cutanée)* the baby has come out in a rash
(e) *(rendre, pour des photos)* they're pleased that their holiday photographs have come out so well
(f) *(partir, s'enlever, pour des taches, etc.)* I've had this coat cleaned three times and the stain still hasn't come out
(g) *(sortir de l'hôpital, de prison)* she'll be coming out soon
(h) *(se résoudre, pour un calcul)* of course the equation hasn't come out – you copied the figures down wrongly
(i) *(se déclarer, se prononcer)* we've come out against the idea of moving; the committee came out in her favour
(j) *(s'en sortir, se tirer d'affaire)* she came out of that looking rather silly, don't you think?

come out with VT INSÉP *(dire, sortir, pour quelque chose d'inattendu)* I'm always on the edge of my seat wondering what he'll come out with next; she finally came out with what was bothering her

come over 1 VI **(a)** *(se ranger à)* I doubt if I will ever come over to your way of thinking **(b)** *(donner l'impression de)* he comes over as (being) a bit pompous, but in fact he's rather shy **(c)** FAM *(se sentir, devenir)* Granny says she came over all funny in the supermarket
2 VT INSÉP *(envahir)* a feeling of fear came over her; *(prendre à, pour des sautes d'humeur)* I don't know what's come over her, she's usually so quiet

come round VI **(a)** *(retrouver une meilleure humeur)* give him time, he'll come round eventually; *(se ranger à)* I'm sure they'll come round to our point of view in the end **(b)** *(reprendre connaissance)* imagine that poor woman coming round and seeing all those faces staring at her **(c)** *(revenir périodiquement)* it's a good thing Christmas only comes round once a year

come through 1 VI **(a)** *(arriver, être obtenu, pour des documents officiels, etc.)* he's very annoyed because his visa is taking so long to come through **(b)** *(survivre, s'en tirer)* it must have been a terrifying experience but they have come through all right
2 VT INSÉP **(a)** *(réussir)* their daughter has come through her law exams with flying colours **(b)** *(survivre à, se sortir (indemne) de)* I am sure you will come through this ordeal; very few people came through the First World War unscarred either physically or mentally

come to 1 VI *(reprendre connaissance)* she came to in a hospital bed
2 VT INSÉP **(a)** *(s'élever à)* the bill came to much more than I could afford; *(arriver à)* that nephew of his will never come to anything; *(en être réduit à, en arriver à)* has it come to this, that we must leave a house our family has lived in for 400 years?
(b) *(être question de, s'agir de)* when it comes to buying a car, find yourself a reputable dealer
(c) *(aller jusqu'à)* if it comes to a malpractice suit, the surgeon is in trouble; when does the case come to trial? *(c.-à-d. être entendu)*; *(en venir à)* I do wish she would come to the point
(d) *(locution)* come to that, where were you last night? *à propos, où étais-tu hier soir ?*

come up VI (a) *(être entendu, pour des affaires juridiques)* when does her case come up (for trial)?; *(être soulevé)* he kept quiet when the subject of fee-paying schools came up; *(sortir, être posé)* do you think this question will come up in the exam? (b) *(être prochainement)* two other houses in our street are coming up for sale soon (c) *(sortir)* my number never comes up in the draw; the bulbs are starting to come up (d) *(arriver, se passer)* call me if anything comes up that you can't handle

come up against VT INSÉP *(rencontrer, pour des difficultés, un adversaire, etc.)* you realize that you'll come up against some pretty strong opposition on this?; who does she come up against in the next round?

come up to VT INSÉP (a) *(arriver à, atteindre)* she's so tall that I only come up to her shoulder; we're coming up to the halfway mark now (b) *(répondre à)* his latest play does not come up to expectations

come up with VT INSÉP *(trouver, concocter)* she's come up with a solution; he keeps coming up with these awful jokes; I'll let you know if I come up with anything that might help

conk out VI FAM (a) *(tomber en panne, lâcher)* the radio has conked out on us (b) *(tomber dans les pommes)* he's conked out, better send for a doctor (c) *(s'endormir, s'écrouler)* I conked out as soon as I lay down on the sofa

cool down 1 VI (a) *(se calmer)* we'll talk about it once you've cooled down (b) *(se rafraîchir, refroidir)* it has cooled down quite a bit since yesterday; let the soup cool down a bit; FIG things have cooled down between them *(c.-à-d. les relations se sont refroidies entre eux)*
2 VT SÉP (a) *(calmer)* I'll try to cool her down but I don't think I'll have much success (b) *(rafraîchir)* how about a beer to cool you down after all that hard work?

cotton on VI FAM *(piger)* I never did cotton on

cough up 1 VT SÉP (a) *(cracher, en toussant)* if you can cough the phlegm up, you'll soon feel better; people with tuberculosis cough up blood (b) FAM *(payer, allonger)* I've got to cough up another £50
2 VI FAM *(raquer, banquer)* he coughed up for the meal

count in VT SÉP *(compter, inclure)* have you counted the neighbours in?; anybody want to go out for lunch? – count me in! *(c.-à-d. je suis partant !)*

count on VT INSÉP *(compter sur)* we can always count on you to be late; he counted on me and I let him down

count out VT SÉP (a) *(compter)* count out the change and see if we have enough (b) *(faire le compte, déclarer K.O., en boxe)* his opponent is on the canvas and being counted out (c) *(exclure, ne pas compter sur)* he's teetotal, so count him out of the pub-crawl; a weekend camping out in the snow? no thanks, count me out!

count up VT SÉP *(additionner)* I've counted these figures up time and time again and get a different answer every time

cover up 1 VI *(cacher qch, étouffer l'affaire)* don't try to cover up, I know it was you; the government was accused of covering up
2 VT SÉP (a) *(couvrir)* that dress is much too low, cover yourself up a bit (b) *(cacher, dissimuler)* it's highly unlikely that he meant to cover things up

cover up for VT INSÉP *(couvrir, protéger)* the architects and builders are covering up for each other

crack down VI *(devenir plus strict, sévir)* in view of the increase in drunk driving the police are going to crack down

crack down on VT INSÉP *(sévir contre)* they're going to crack down on drunk drivers

crack up 1 VI (a) *(craquer, se fissurer)* the ice on the pond is cracking up (b) FAM *(s'effondrer, craquer)* if he doesn't take a holiday soon, he'll crack up; do you think their marriage is cracking up?; she cracked up under the pressure (c) FAM *(éclater de rire)* I cracked up when he said that
2 VT SÉP FAM *habituellement au passif* (a) *(faire rire)* it really cracked me up when I heard about it (b) *(locution)* he's not what he's cracked up to be *il n'est pas aussi fantastique qu'on le dit*; the play is everything it's cracked up to be *la pièce a toutes les qualités qu'on lui vante*

cream off VT SÉP *(s'accaparer, sélectionner)* the oldest universities cream off the best candidates

cross off VT SÉP *(barrer, rayer)* cross his name off the list

cross out VT SÉP *(barrer, rayer)* cross your mistakes out neatly, please

cry off VI *(se décommander)* I hate it when people cry off at the last minute

cry out VI (a) *(pousser un cri)* the pain made her cry out (b) FIG *(avoir grand besoin)* that room is just crying out for red velvet curtains

cuddle up VI *(se blottir, se pelotonner)* cuddle up if you're cold; the little girl cuddled up to her grandmother

curl up VI (a) *(se pelotonner, s'installer confortablement)* I like to curl up in bed with a good book (b) *(s'enrouler)* hedgehogs curl up into a ball for protection

cut across VT INSÉP (a) *(couper à travers)* we cut across the playing field (b) *(dépasser, transcender)* concern for the environment cuts across party lines (c) *(aller à l'encontre de)* it cuts across all my principles

cut back 1 VI *(économiser)* we're definitely going to have to cut back
2 VT SÉP (a) *(tailler)* now is the time to cut your raspberries back
(b) *(réduire)* the company is cutting back production until the seamen's strike is over

cut down VT SÉP (a) *(couper, abattre)* they're cutting down the trees that were damaged in the storm (b) *(tuer, abattre)* he was cut down by machine-gun fire (c) *(réduire)* we've been asked to cut down the amount of time we devote to sports; if you won't stop smoking then at least cut down

cut in 1 VI (a) *(interrompre)* the interviewer cut in to ask a question (b) *(faire une queue de poisson)* that idiot will cause an accident cutting in in front of people like that
2 VT SÉP *(faire participer)* can you cut me in on one of your deals?

cut off VT SÉP (a) *(découper, couper)* they had to cut his clothes off in the emergency room; cut off his head! (b) *(isoler)* the town has been cut off by floods; don't you feel cut off living in the country? (c) *(couper, pour l'électricité et le téléphone)* we'd hardly said hello before we were cut off; it's dreadful to think how many people have their electricity cut off because they can't afford to pay the bills (d) *(locution)* her family cut her off without a penny *sa famille l'a déshéritée*; he was cut off in his prime *il a été emporté à la fleur de l'âge*

cut out 1 VI *(caler, pour un moteur)* will you have a look at the engine, it keeps cutting out
2 VT SÉP (a) *(couper)* the hardest part is cutting the dress out
(b) *(découper)* I cut this magazine article out for you
(c) *(supprimer)* cut out starchy food for a couple of weeks; FAM *(arrêter)* I've told you already to cut out the silly jokes

cut out for VT SÉP FIG *toujours au passif (être fait pour)* I'm not cut out for all these late nights

cut up VT SÉP (a) *(couper)* cut the meat up quite small
(b) FAM *habituellement au passif (affecter, froisser)* he was definitely a bit cut up about not being invited

D

dash off 1 VI *(partir précipitamment)* she was sorry she missed you but she had to dash off
2 VT SÉP *(rédiger en vitesse)* I dashed off an answer yesterday; *(faire en un tour de main)* he says he dashes these paintings off in his spare time

deal with VT INSÉP (a) *(traiter avec, avoir affaire à)* we've been dealing with that company for years (b) *(s'occuper de, prendre en charge)* she dealt with that problem very well; the case wasn't very professionally dealt with (c) *(traiter de)* the play deals with euthanasia

die away VI *(s'affaiblir, s'éteindre, mourir)* the noise of the car engine died away

die down VI *(s'apaiser, diminuer)* he had to wait for the applause to die down

die off VI *(mourir les uns après les autres)* by the time he was in his twenties, his relatives had all died off; their livestock is dying off as the drought intensifies

die out VI *(s'éteindre, disparaître)* entire species are dying out as their habitat is destroyed

dig in 1 VI (a) *(creuser des tranchées)* the first thing the troops had to do when they got to the front was to dig in (b) FAM *(commencer à manger, attaquer)* dig in, there's plenty for everyone
2 VT SÉP *(mélanger à la terre, enterrer)* before planting, dig in a couple of handfuls of fertilizer

dig into VT INSÉP (a) FAM *(attaquer, entamer)* dig into that pie as much as you like, I made two (b) *(fouiller dans)* they want us to dig into her past

dig out VT SÉP (a) *(déterrer)* dig out the roots (b) *(dégager, pour des personnes ensevelies sous des décombres, etc.)* they hope to have the remaining survivors dug out by nightfall (c) FAM *(dénicher, trouver)* have you dug those files out yet?; we want more information on the company's early days, so see what you can dig out

dig up VT SÉP (a) *(arracher, déterrer)* this rose bush will have to be dug up and moved (b) FAM *(trouver, dénicher)* we're hoping to dig up some items to show that there was a Roman encampment here; I've dug something up that might prove he's been lying to us

dip into VT INSÉP (a) *(tremper rapidement dans)* she dipped her toes into the bath water to test it (b) *(puiser dans, entamer)* she doesn't want to dip into her savings if she can help it (c) *(feuilleter)* this is the kind of anthology to be dipped into rather than read all at once

dish out VT SÉP (a) *(servir)* Mum's dishing supper out now (b) FAM *(donner, prodiguer, pour des ordres ou des conseils non désirés)* you're always dishing out advice!

dish up 1 VT SÉP *(verser, servir)* somebody dish up the soup
2 VI *(servir)* when will you be dishing up?

dispense with VT INSÉP *(se passer de, se dispenser de)* let's dispense with formalities, call me Laura

dispose of VT INSÉP (a) *(se débarrasser de)* dispose of your waste paper here (b) *(régler)* let's just dispose of the matter now (c) FAM *(tuer, liquider)* we have to dispose of him before he talks (d) FAM *(se débarrasser de)* so far she has disposed of six opponents who want to take the title away from her

divide out VT SÉP *(distribuer, partager)* they divided the food out

divide up VT SÉP *(diviser, répartir)* contestants will be divided up into groups of four

do away with VT INSÉP (a) *(abolir)* they should do away with capital punishment (b) *(tuer, supprimer)* he has threatened to do away with himself

do by VT INSÉP FAM *(traiter)* the company did very badly by its employees; he'll feel very hard done by if you don't at least send him a birthday card; she did very well by her granddaughter at Christmas *(c.-à-d. sa grand-mère l'a gâtée pour Noël)*

do down VT SÉP BR FAM (a) *(avoir, rouler)* why did you let the salesman do you down? (b) *(dire du mal de)* there's always someone ready to do you down

do for VT INSÉP FAM (a) *(tuer)* if he keeps on treating her this way, she'll do for him (b) *(crever, épuiser)* it was that last hill that did for me (c) *(faire le ménage pour ou chez)* who does for you?

do in VT SÉP BR FAM (a) *(zigouiller, buter)* somebody on our street was done in last night (b) FIG *(épuiser, tuer, crever)* Christmas shopping always does me in

do out VT SÉP BR FAM *(nettoyer à fond, faire)* will you do the kitchen out tomorrow please, Mrs Jones?

do out of VT SÉP FAM *(escroquer de)* he always maintained that he had been done out of his inheritance; they did him out of his share of the money

do over VT SÉP (a) *(refaire, pour une pièce, etc.)* the whole house needs doing over (b) BR FAM *(tabasser, casser la gueule à)* the other gang did him over (c) AM *(refaire)* the teacher said I had to do my project over

do up 1 VI *(se fermer, se boutonner)* the dress does up at the back
2 VT SÉP (a) *(attacher, fermer, boutonner)* do your buttons up (b) *(emballer)* it seems a pity to open it when it's done up so nicely (c) FAM *(refaire, retaper)* they're doing up all the buildings on the street; *(se faire beau/belle, se mettre sur son trente et un)* you've really done yourself up, what's the occasion?

do with VT INSÉP (a) *après "could" (avoir besoin de)* you could do with a haircut; what I could be doing with right now is a hot bath (b) *(avoir un rapport avec)* he has something to do with computers; *(avoir à voir ou à faire dans)* it sounds very fishy to me and you should have nothing to do with it; my business has nothing to do with you; that's got nothing to do with it!; *(s'agir de, concerner)* it has to do with your mother, I'm afraid (c) *(finir de)* I've done with trying to help people; *(en finir avec)* he says it's all over, he's done with her (d) *(ne plus avoir besoin de)* if you've done with the hammer, put it back where it belongs

do without 1 VT INSÉP *(se passer de)* we can do without the sarcasm 2 VI *(faire sans)* if you don't find anything you like in here then you'll have to do without

double back 1 VI *(rebrousser chemin)* they decided to double back since they didn't recognize any landmarks 2 VT SÉP *(replier en deux)* double back the bedclothes and let the mattress air

double over/up VI *(se plier en deux, se tordre)* the pain struck again and she doubled over; the joke made me double up (with laughter)

double up VI *(partager un lit, une chambre, etc.)* with so many guests coming, some of them are going to have to double up; do you mind doubling up with me?

drag behind 1 VT SÉP *(tirer, traîner)* I ran for the bus, dragging my cases behind me 2 VI *(être à la traîne, être en retard)* you're dragging behind in maths

drag in VT SÉP (a) *(tirer à l'intérieur)* the trunk is too heavy to lift, let's just drag it in (b) *(mettre sur le tapis)* he insisted on dragging in the issue of customer satisfaction

drag on VI *(s'éterniser, ne pas en finir)* the play dragged on and on

drag out VT SÉP *(faire durer, faire traîner)* I had to drag my presentation out to fill the time allotted to me

drag up VT SÉP (a) *(monter, en tirant)* drag it up the stairs (b) FAM *(amener)* you dragged me up to London for this? (c) *(remettre sur le tapis)* there's no need to drag up the past (d) FAM *(élever,* *tant bien que mal)* those children are being dragged up, not brought up; where were you dragged up?

draw alongside 1 **VI** *(se mettre côte à côte ou à la même hauteur)* then this big Mercedes drew alongside...
2 **VT INSÉP** *(se mettre à côté ou à la hauteur de)* the Customs launch drew alongside the liner

draw apart **VI** *(se séparer)* they drew apart when I entered the room

draw away 1 **VI** (a) *(s'éloigner)* we waved as the car drew away (b) *(prendre de l'avance, se détacher)* the first half dozen runners are now beginning to draw away (c) *(s'écarter)* I can't help drawing away when he touches me
2 **VT SÉP** *(écarter, éloigner, mettre à part)* she drew us away from the other guests

draw back 1 **VI** *(reculer)* she drew back from the edge of the cliff
2 **VT SÉP** (a) *(ouvrir, tirer)* he drew back the curtains and light flooded into the room (b) *(pousser à revenir)* what drew you back to music?

draw in 1 **VI** (a) *(arriver)* the train will be drawing in soon; the car drew in to the drive (b) *(raccourcir, pour les jours et les nuits)* the days have started to draw in again
2 **VT SÉP** (a) *(rentrer, aspirer)* fresh air from outside is drawn in by these ventilators (b) *(impliquer, mêler)* they were arguing again and I left because I didn't want to be drawn in

draw on 1 **VI** *(avancer, pour le temps)* as the day gradually drew on; *(approcher)* summer is fast drawing on
2 **VT INSÉP** *(faire appel à)* for this essay, I want you to draw on your own childhood memories
3 **VT SÉP BR** *(enfiler)* she drew on a pair of long white gloves

draw out 1 **VI** (a) *(s'éloigner)* they waved as the train drew out (b) *(rallonger, pour les jours et les nuits)* after Christmas, the days start to draw out
2 **VT SÉP** (a) *(sortir)* she drew out a gun; *(retirer, pour de l'argent)* I've drawn out all my savings (b) *(prolonger)* they drew the meeting out on purpose (c) *(faire parler)* I managed to draw her out on her plans

draw up 1 **VI** *(s'arrêter, en voiture)* he drew up with a squeal of brakes
2 **VT SÉP** (a) *(approcher)* draw up a chair and join us

(b) *(établir, mettre au point)* I think we should draw up a plan of action; *(rédiger)* the old lady drew up a new will

dream away VT SÉP *(passer à rêver)* he'll dream his whole life away at this rate

dream up VT SÉP *(imaginer, inventer, concocter)* they've dreamed up some scheme that they say will make us all rich

dredge up VT SÉP (a) *(draguer)* the barges are dredging up silt (b) *(ressortir)* why did you dredge that old scandal up?

dress up 1 VI (a) *(bien s'habiller, se mettre sur son trente et un)* it's just an informal get-together, there's no need to dress up (b) *(se déguiser)* it's a Hallowe'en party and everybody has to dress up

2 VT SÉP (a) *(bien habiller, habiller avec élégance)* she dressed herself up for the wedding (b) *(déguiser)* you could dress yourself up as Pierrot

drink down VT SÉP *(avaler, boire d'un trait)* drink this down and you'll soon feel better

drink in VT SÉP (a) *(absorber, boire)* these plants will drink in plenty of water, even in winter (b) FIG *(boire, pour des paroles, etc.)* we drank in every word; *(s'imprégner de)* we stopped for a moment to drink in the atmosphere

drink up 1 VI *(finir son verre, etc.)* drink up and I'll get the next round

2 VT SÉP *(finir)* have you drunk up your tea?

drive at VT INSÉP *(vouloir dire, vouloir en venir)* I'm sorry, but I really don't see what you're driving at; did you think she was driving at something when she said she couldn't afford a holiday this year?

drive back 1 VI *(rentrer en voiture)* are you driving back or taking the train?

2 VT SÉP (a) *(ramener en voiture)* George will drive you back to your hotel (b) *(repousser)* the soldiers did not have the strength to drive back another attack

drive home VT SÉP (a) *(enfoncer à fond)* once you have driven the screws home... (b) *(faire comprendre)* I tried to drive it home to them that this was not an isolated incident

drive off 1 VI *(partir en voiture)* he drove off about an hour ago

2 **VT SÉP** (a) *(emmener en voiture)* all three of them were driven off in a police car (b) *(repousser, refouler)* the attackers were driven off when reinforcements arrived

drive on 1 **VI** *(poursuivre sa route)* he decided to drive on rather than stop there for the night
2 **VT SÉP** *(inciter, pousser)* her friends drove her on to sue

drive up **VI** *(arriver, pour une voiture)* a car has just driven up

drop back **VI** *(se laisser distancer)* he has dropped back and it looks as if he's given up the race

drop behind 1 **VI** *(prendre du retard, se laisser distancer)* you're dropping behind, do try to keep up
2 **VT INSÉP** *(se laisser distancer par)* that last lap exhausted her and now she's dropping behind the leaders

drop in 1 **VI** *(passer)* I'll drop in and see mother tomorrow; would you drop in at the supermarket on your way home?
2 **VT SÉP** *(déposer)* drop this in the night safe for me, will you?

drop off 1 **VI** (a) *(tomber)* with all this heavy shopping to carry, I feel as if my arms are going to drop off (b) *(s'endormir)* it was 4 a.m. before she dropped off; why don't you go to bed instead of dropping off in the chair? (c) *(diminuer)* church attendance has been dropping off for many years
2 **VT SÉP** *(déposer)* drop these books off at the library; *(déposer, en voiture)* where do you want to be dropped off?

drop out **VI** (a) *(tomber)* there's a hole in your pocket and the keys must have dropped out (b) **FAM** *(abandonner ou arrêter ses études, un cours, etc.)* he dropped out at the age of 14; so many have dropped out that the course may be cancelled (c) *(choisir de vivre en marge de la société)* in the sixties a lot of people dropped out (of society) and went off to places like India

drum into **VT SÉP** *(seriner à, répéter à)* drum it into the children that they mustn't take sweets from strangers

drum up **VT SÉP** *(trouver, décrocher)* how are you drumming up support for the campaign?; we must drum up some more business

dry off 1 **VI** *(sécher)* don't touch the varnish while it's drying off
2 **VT SÉP** *(sécher)* come and dry yourself off in front of the fire

dry out 1 VI (a) *(sécher)* leave your wet things in the bathroom to dry out (b) *(faire une cure de désintoxication, se faire désintoxiquer, pour un alcoolique)* I think she's somewhere drying out
2 VT SÉP *(assécher, rendre sec)* soap can dry your skin out

dry up VI (a) *(s'assécher, se tarir)* streams and rivers are drying up because of this long heat wave
(b) *(essuyer la vaisselle)* could you dry up, please?
(c) FAM *(avoir un trou de mémoire)* she was scared that she might dry up in the middle of her big speech in the second act
(d) FAM *(la fermer, la boucler)* why don't you dry up?

dwell (up)on VT INSÉP *(s'appesantir sur, penser sans cesse à)* get on with your life instead of dwelling on what might have been

E

ease off/up VI *(se calmer, ralentir)* he's been told to ease off if he doesn't want a heart attack; ease up, there's a 30-mile-an-hour limit here

eat away VT SÉP *(éroder, ronger)* the action of the waves is eating the coastline away

eat in VI *(manger chez soi)* I'm tired of eating in all the time

eat into VT INSÉP *(entamer)* it's silly to eat into your savings when you could get a bank loan; long-term unemployment eats into people's self-confidence

eat out 1 VI *(aller au restaurant)* let's eat out tonight
2 VT SÉP *(locution)* the child is eating her heart out for a pony *l'enfant meurt d'envie d'avoir un poney*

eat up 1 VT SÉP (a) *(finir)* eat up your spinach (b) FIG *(dévorer, ronger)* jealousy is eating him up
2 VI *(finir de manger)* eat up, the taxi's waiting; eat up, there's lots more *(c.-à-d. vas-y, mange ou régale-toi, il y en a plein)*

edge out 1 VI *(sortir lentement ou avec une extrême prudence)* I opened the window and cautiously edged out
2 VT SÉP (a) *(aller lentement ou avec une extrême prudence)* she edged her way out on to the ledge (b) *(écarter, évincer)* there's a move to edge him out of the chairmanship

egg on VT SÉP *(encourager, inciter)* it was sickening to hear the crowd egg the boxers on; I wish I hadn't let you egg me on to accept

end up VI *(finir)* no one ever thought she would end up in prison; *(finir par)* I ended up telling him in no uncertain terms what I thought

enter into VT INSÉP (a) *(conclure)* we entered into this contract with our eyes open (b) *(entrer en jeu dans, avoir à voir avec)* morality rarely enters into foreign policy

enter (up)on VT INSÉP *(commencer, débuter)* she has entered on a new career

even out 1 VI *(tourner autour de, pour des sommes, des quantités, etc.)* production figures are evening out at about 5,000 per week
2 VT SÉP *(répartir ou partager de façon égale)* we need to even out supplies over time

even up VT SÉP (a) *(égaliser)* that last goal evened up the score; if you pay for the meal, that will even things up (b) *(arrondir au chiffre supérieur)* just even it up to a pound

explain away VT SÉP *(justifier, d'une façon peu plausible)* he tried to explain away his absence from the last meeting; explain this away if you can

eye up VT SÉP FAM *(regarder, reluquer)* I passed the time eyeing up all the men; he eyed up every one of the women at the party

F

face up to VT INSÉP *(faire face à, affronter)* it might help if she faced up to her fears of rejection; *(accepter, pour un fait)* we'll have to face up to the fact that we're not getting any younger

fade away VI *(disparaître, s'effacer, s'éteindre)* the sound of the procession faded away; her smile faded away when she realized he hadn't been joking

fade in 1 VI *(monter, apparaître progressivement, dans un film)* the music faded in
2 VT SÉP *(faire apparaître en fondu, dans un film)* fade in the crowd scenes

fade out 1 VI *(diminuer, disparaître progressivement, dans un film)* the music fades out for the last few seconds
2 VT SÉP *(faire disparaître en fondu, dans un film)* fade out the crowd scenes

fall about VI BR FAM *(se tordre de rire)* her scripts always make me fall about

fall away VI (a) *(descendre en pente)* be careful, the ground falls away here (b) *(baisser, diminuer)* attendance at committee meetings has been falling away recently

fall back VI *(reculer)* the demonstrators fell back when they saw the water cannon

fall back on VT INSÉP *(avoir recours à)* I suppose we can always fall back on temporary staff

fall behind VI (a) *(se laisser distancer)* he began well but now seems to be falling behind (b) *(prendre du retard)* you mustn't fall behind with the payments

fall down VI (a) *(tomber par terre)* he fell down and bumped his head (b) *(s'écrouler)* why don't they demolish that old building instead of letting it fall down? (c) *(ne pas tenir debout)* that's where their argument falls down

fall down on VT INSÉP *(échouer à)* if you fall down on this, she won't give you another chance

fall for VT INSÉP (a) *(en pincer pour, tomber amoureux de)* he's fallen for the girl next door; *(être emballé ou attiré par)* I've really fallen for that Victorian chair in the antique shop (b) *(se laisser prendre par)* you didn't fall for that old story, did you?

fall in with VT INSÉP (a) *(finir par accepter)* I fell in with the plans for a picnic because the children were so keen (b) *(se mettre à fréquenter)* the teenager next door has fallen in with a bad crowd

fall off VI (a) *(tomber)* I was terrified of falling off and clung to the chimney for dear life (b) *(diminuer)* enrolment is falling off

fall on VT INSÉP (a) *(tomber ou retomber sur)* if anything goes wrong you can be sure that the blame will not fall on him
(b) *(attaquer, se jeter sur)* they fell on the meal as if they hadn't eaten for days

fall out VI (a) *(tomber)* the window is open so be careful you don't fall out (b) *(se brouiller, se disputer)* my sister and I have fallen out

fall over 1 VI *(tomber, se renverser)* the vase is top-heavy, that's why it keeps falling over
2 VT INSÉP (a) *(trébucher sur)* move your suitcase before someone falls over it (b) FAM *(se mettre en quatre ou faire tout son possible pour)* he was falling over himself to buy the woman a drink

fall through VI *(échouer)* their plans for a skiing holiday have fallen through

farm out VT SÉP *(donner en sous-traitance)* if deadlines are to be met then some of the work will have to be farmed out; *(confier la garde de)* those two next door are always farming their kids out

feed in VT SÉP *(entrer, dans un ordinateur)* feed the data in then let the computer perform the calculation

feed up VT SÉP *(faire manger plus que la normale, gaver)* Mum always wants to feed us up when we come home for the weekend

feel up VT SÉP FAM *(peloter, tripoter)* he's always feeling her up in public, it's so embarrassing

feel up to VT INSÉP *(se sentir capable de, se sentir le courage de)* he suggested a long walk but she didn't feel up to it; I don't feel up to cooking a big meal tonight, let's go out; do you feel up to a visit from my mother?

fetch up VI *(se retrouver)* we eventually fetched up in a tiny little village in the middle of nowhere; the road was very icy and they fetched up in a ditch

fiddle about/around VI FAM (a) *(bricoler)* he fiddled about for ages and still couldn't get the car to go (b) *(traînasser, perdre son temps)* why don't you stop fiddling about and get down to some work?

fight back 1 VI (a) *(se défendre)* everybody encounters a bully at some time – you must learn to fight back (b) *(recouvrer la santé, se rétablir)* he was critically ill but managed to fight back
2 VT SÉP *(refouler, contenir)* I fought back my anger and tried to answer calmly

fight down **VT SÉP** *(réprimer, vaincre)* you must fight down these fears

fight off **VT SÉP** *(repousser)* government troops have fought off a number of attacks; his bodyguards had to fight off over-eager fans

fight on **VI** *(continuer le combat)* she regards this as merely a setback and is determined to fight on

fight out **VT SÉP** *(régler, en se battant ou en se disputant)* you'll have to fight this one out; I left them to fight it out

figure on **VT INSÉP** *(compter (sur))* I didn't figure on your mother coming too; when are you figuring on leaving?

figure out **VT SÉP** (a) *((arriver à) comprendre)* she can't figure you out at all; the dog figured out how to open the door (b) *(calculer)* we figured out that they must be paying three times as much rent as we are

fill in 1 **VI** *(faire un remplacement)* this isn't her normal job, she's just filling in; who'll be filling in for you while you're on holiday? *(c.-à-d. qui va te remplacer... ?)*
2 **VT SÉP** (a) *(boucher, combler)* workmen are filling those potholes in at last (b) *(remplir, pour un formulaire)* there are several forms to fill in when you apply for a mortgage (c) *(informer, mettre au courant)* will someone please fill us in on what's been happening? (d) *(faire passer, pour le temps)* are you busy or just filling in time?

fill out 1 **VI** *(prendre du poids, s'étoffer)* he's beginning to fill out at last after his long illness
2 **VT SÉP** *(remplir, pour un formulaire)* will you fill out this form, please?

fill up 1 **VI** *(se remplir)* the room was filling up
2 **VT SÉP** (a) *(faire le plein d'essence)* fill it up, please; *(remplir, pour un récipient)* let me fill your glass up (b) *(remplir, pour un formulaire)* there are one or two forms to be filled up first

filter out 1 **VI** *(sortir petit à petit)* mourners filtered out of the church; *(filtrer)* the news was beginning to filter out that several arrests had been made
2 **VT SÉP** *(éliminer par filtrage, filtrer)* filter out the impurities

find out 1 **VT SÉP** *(trouver, découvrir)* I could have found that out for myself

2 **VI** *(découvrir ce qui était secret)* has your wife found out yet?

finish off 1 **VT SÉP** (a) *(finir)* let me just finish this chapter off; finish off your lunch; you can finish off the cream if you like (b) *(tuer, achever)* the men were finished off with a bullet through the skull (c) **FIG** *(épuiser, achever)* all that heavy digging has finished him off
2 **VI** *(finir)* what did you have to finish off with?

finish up 1 **VT SÉP** *(finir)* finish up your lunch; don't finish up the pie
2 **VI** *(se retrouver, finir)* we finished up in the pub down the road; he'll finish up in court; *(finir par devenir)* any more of this uncertainty and I'll finish up a nervous wreck

fire away **VI FAM** *(commencer, surtout à parler ou à poser des questions)* fire away, I'm all ears *(c.-à-d. allez-y, je suis tout ouïe)*

fish out **VT SÉP** (a) *(sortir, repêcher)* they fished him out of the river (b) **FIG** *(sortir)* just let me fish the keys out

fit in 1 **VT SÉP** (a) *(faire entrer)* could you fit this pair of shoes in the case? (b) *(prendre)* the hairdresser says she can fit me in tomorrow
2 **VI** (a) *(rentrer)* there's not enough room, the books won't fit in (b) *(concorder)* that doesn't fit in with what I was told (c) *(s'adapter, cadrer)* how does that fit in with your plans?; *(être à sa place, s'intégrer)* I hate parties like this, I never feel that I fit in

fix on 1 **VT SÉP** *(attacher)* he fixed the handle on for me
2 **VT INSÉP** *(choisir, décider de)* have you fixed on a date yet?

fix up 1 **VT SÉP** (a) *(installer, monter)* the marquee will be fixed up on their front lawn (b) *(fixer, prendre)* I've fixed up an interview for you (c) *(fournir)* our in-laws will fix us up with a bed (d) *(refaire, retaper)* they're busy fixing up the house; *(s'arranger)* if you're going out, don't you think you should fix yourself up a bit first?
2 **VI** *(prévoir)* I'm sorry but I've already fixed up to go out

fizzle out **VI** *(diminuer, tomber, pour des sentiments, etc.)* people's enthusiasm is starting to fizzle out; *(tomber à l'eau)* all those big plans we had have just fizzled out

flag down **VT SÉP** *(héler)* it's impossible to flag a taxi down when it's raining; *(faire signe de s'arrêter à)* I was cycling along when a policeman flagged me down

flake out VI FAM *(s'endormir, tomber comme une masse)* six late nights in succession, no wonder you flaked out; I just want to flake out on the couch

flare up VI (a) *(s'embraser, prendre)* the fire flared up, turning night into day (b) FIG *(éclater)* the argument flared up when she said something about favouritism; *(s'emporter)* he flares up at the least little thing

flip over 1 VT SÉP *(retourner)* do you want your egg flipped over?; *(tourner)* she was flipping over the pages of a magazine
2 VI *(se retourner)* the plane just seemed to flip over

float about/around VI FAM (a) *(circuler, courir)* rumours have been floating around about your resignation (b) *(traîner)* my keys must be floating about somewhere but I just can't find them; I spent a lazy weekend just floating around

flood in VI *(entrer (à flots))* when she opened the door water flooded in; light flooded in through the windows; *(entrer en masse, affluer)* the concert doesn't start for another hour but people are already flooding in

flood out 1 VT SÉP *habituellement au passif (être forcé à partir à cause des inondations)* thousands of people in Bangladesh have been flooded out
2 VI *(sortir en masse)* people flooded out of the cinema; *(s'échapper)* light flooded out of the open casement

fly in 1 VI *(arriver en avion)* the royal visitors will fly in tomorrow
2 VT SÉP *(envoyer en avion)* the army will fly troops in if necessary

fly off 1 VI (a) *(partir en avion, etc.)* they flew off in a helicopter (b) *(s'envoler)* his toupee flew off in the wind
2 VT SÉP (a) *(évacuer par avion, etc.)* the rescue team came to fly the oil rig workers off (b) *(emmener en avion)* the army flew the troops off to another country

fly out 1 VI *(partir en avion, prendre l'avion)* the President flew out this morning; which airport are you flying out of?
2 VT SÉP *(envoyer par avion, faire voyager en avion)* troops are being flown out as quickly as possible; the company is flying her out to be with her husband

fly past 1 VT INSÉP *(survoler)* the squadron will fly past the airfield at precisely two o'clock
2 VI *(passer à toute vitesse)* the weekend has just flown past

fold away 1 VI *(se plier)* does this table fold away?
2 VT SÉP *(plier et ranger)* fold your clothes away neatly; she folded the tablecloth away

fold in VT SÉP *(incorporer)* fold in the sugar

follow on VI (a) *(suivre)* you go ahead, we'll follow on (b) *(continuer)* how did the story follow on? (c) *(résulter)* it follows on from this that...

follow out VT SÉP AM *(suivre, exécuter)* he followed out his plans

follow through 1 VT SÉP *(poursuivre jusqu'au bout)* she firmly intends to follow the idea through
2 VI *(accompagner son coup, sa balle)* the problem is that you're not following through after you hit the ball

follow up 1 VT SÉP (a) *(poursuivre, suivre)* the police are following up a number of leads; I want you to follow the matter up
(b) *(appuyer, compléter)* he followed up his complaint to the shop with an angry letter to the manufacturer
2 VI *(poursuivre l'action, continuer)* he followed up with a right to the jaw

fool around VI (a) *(perdre du temps, traîner)* stop fooling around and get up! (b) *(faire l'imbécile, jouer)* don't fool around with that glue or you'll get it all over you; stop fooling around with that computer! (c) FAM *(avoir une aventure)* she thinks her husband is fooling around behind her back

fork out FAM 1 VT SÉP *(payer, allonger)* I have to fork out the cash for everything just because I have a better-paid job than him
2 VI *(casquer, allonger)* we're all going to have to fork out

freak out VI FAM (a) *(piquer une crise, péter les plombs)* Mum will freak out when she sees that you've dyed your hair blue
(b) *(s'éclater)* look at him freaking out on the dancefloor!

frighten away/off VT SÉP *(effrayer, faire fuir)* we keep a couple of Doberman to frighten off potential burglars; don't look so grim or you'll frighten people away

frown on VT INSÉP *(désapprouver)* they all frowned on my suggestion;

her parents frowned on her marriage to a man so much younger

G

gain on VT INSÉP *(rattraper)* they're gaining on us

gear up 1 VI *(se préparer)* the shops are already gearing up for Christmas
2 VT SÉP (a) *(préparer)* shops are getting geared up for the January sales (b) *(augmenter)* we must gear up production to meet the demand

get about VI (a) *(se déplacer)* he doesn't get about much these days (b) *(se répandre, circuler)* a rumour has got about that you're leaving

get across 1 VI (a) *(traverser)* there are no traffic lights there so I found it difficult to get across (b) *(être compris, passer)* our message is not getting across
2 VT SÉP (a) *(faire traverser ou passer)* the flooding will prevent them from getting much-needed supplies across the river (b) *(faire comprendre)* did you get your point across to her?

get ahead VI *(réussir, arriver)* he got ahead in life; if you want to get ahead, you have to work extremely hard *(c.-à-d. obtenir de l'avancement)*

get along VI (a) *(partir, s'en aller)* I must be getting along (b) *(aller, se passer)* how are you getting along in the new house? (c) *(s'entendre)* I wish I got along better with my neighbours

get around 1 VI (a) *(se déplacer)* elderly people often find it hard to get around; *(avoir une vie sociale importante)* that young man really gets around! (b) *(se répandre)* I wonder how that story got around
2 VT INSÉP *(éviter, contourner)* there's no getting around it, you'll have to tell him what happened; can we get around this difficulty?

get at VT INSÉP (a) *(atteindre)* I can't get at that shelf, it's too high (b) *(découvrir)* he intends to get at the truth (c) *(vouloir dire)* do you mind telling me what you're getting at? (d) FAM *(critiquer, s'en prendre à)* his father is always getting at him (e) FAM *(acheter)* the trial could not continue because a number of witnesses had been got at and refused to testify

get away 1 **VI** **(a)** *(s'en aller, partir)* I usually get away by six; will they manage to get away this year? **(b)** *(s'échapper, s'enfuir)* the terrorists got away in a stolen car
2 **VT SÉP** *(emmener, éloigner)* get that child away from the road!; *(prendre, arracher des mains)* the policeman managed to get the gun away

get away with **VT INSÉP** **(a)** *(s'enfuir avec)* the thieves got away with the old lady's life savings **(b)** *(s'en tirer avec)* he got away with a small fine **(c)** *(locution)* that child gets away with murder! *on laisse tout faire à ce gamin!*

get back 1 **VI** **(a)** *(reculer)* get back from the edge of the cliff!
(b) *(rentrer, revenir)* when did you get back?; I must be getting back soon
2 **VT SÉP** **(a)** *(récupérer)* I'll get it back from him tomorrow
(b) *(rendre)* get the file back to me as soon as you can

get back at **VT INSÉP** *(se venger de)* I'll get back at you for that

get back to **VT INSÉP** **(a)** *(se remettre à, reprendre)* I must get back to work soon **(b)** *(rappeler (au téléphone), reparler à)* can we get back to you on that point later?

get behind 1 **VI** *(prendre du retard)* I've got so behind that I'm working late every night this week
2 **VT INSÉP** *(se cacher derrière)* get behind that tree

get by 1 **VI** **(a)** *(passer)* the car could not get by because of the roadworks **(b)** *(s'en sortir, se débrouiller)* he thinks he'll get by without studying; it must be difficult getting by on so little money; do you think I'll get by in Greece without speaking the language?
2 **VT INSÉP** **(a)** *(passer à côté de)* can I get by you? **(b)** *(échapper à)* his latest book did not get by the censor

get down 1 **VI** **(a)** *(descendre)* get down at once!
(b) *(se coucher, se cacher)* get down or she'll see us
(c) *(sortir de table)* may I get down?
2 **VT SÉP** **(a)** *(descendre)* will you get my case down for me?
(b) *(faire baisser)* the doctors have got his temperature down at last

(c) *(noter)* I didn't manage to get that down, she was speaking too quickly
(d) *(déprimer)* this kind of weather gets everybody down
(e) *(avaler)* her throat is so swollen she can't get anything down; get this soup down and you'll soon feel better

get down to VT INSÉP *(se mettre à)* when are you going to get down to your homework?

get in 1 VT SÉP (a) *(faire venir)* I was so worried about the baby that I got the doctor in
(b) *(rentrer, faire rentrer)* just let me get the washing in before the rain starts; farmers are only now getting their crops in
(c) *(réussir à faire)* she got some last-minute revision in the night before the exam
(d) *(placer, caser)* she was talking so much I couldn't get a word in
(e) *(faire admettre ou entrer)* these excellent exam results will get you in anywhere
(f) *(faire élire, assurer l'élection de)* it was the government's mistakes that got the opposition in
(g) *(planter, semer)* you should get your bulbs in earlier than this
2 VT INSÉP *(entrer dans)* the smoke from the camp fire got in their eyes; *(monter dans)* get in the car!
3 VI (a) *(entrer)* if they didn't have a key, how did they get in?
(b) *(rentrer (à la maison))* we got in about 4 a.m.
(c) *(arriver)* when does the train get in?
(d) *(être admis)* he applied to Oxford but he didn't get in
(e) *(être élu)* she got in with a very small majority

get in on VT INSÉP *(prendre part à)* they'd all like to get in on the deal

get into 1 VT INSÉP (a) *(mettre, enfiler)* she got into her clothes; *(rentrer dans)* she hasn't been able to get into any of her clothes since the baby was born
(b) *(entrer dans)* only a small percentage of candidates get into university; the thieves got into the house through an open window
(c) *(arriver à, prendre à, pour des sautes d'humeur)* I don't know what's got into her these days
(d) *(s'impliquer, se lancer dans)* he wants to get into politics
(e) *(locutions)* there's no need to get into a panic *ce n'est pas la peine de paniquer*; you'll get into trouble *tu vas avoir des*

ennuis; they've got badly into debt *ils se sont sérieusement endettés*
(f) *(se faire à, s'habituer à)* she'll soon get into our ways
(g) *(s'intéresser à)* he got into Eastern religions; *(rentrer dans)* everyone says this is an excellent book, but I just can't get into it
2 VT SÉP (a) *(mettre dans)* did you manage to get everything into the suitcase?; you got me into this mess, now get me out of it
(b) *(faire entrer à ou dans)* he got his friend into the club
(c) *(entraîner dans)* you're the one who got us into this
(d) *(mettre de ou dans)* she knows just what to do to get her father into a good mood; don't get her into one of her rages

get in with VT INSÉP (a) *(se faire bien voir de)* if you want to get in with him, tell him how much you enjoyed his singing
(b) *(fréquenter)* she's worried about her daughter getting in with a bad crowd

get off 1 VI (a) *(descendre, d'un véhicule)* he got off at the traffic lights
(b) *(s'en aller, partir)* I have to be getting off to work
(c) *(sortir du travail, finir)* I'd like to get off early tomorrow
(d) *(s'en tirer)* he shouldn't have got off; you got off lightly! *(c.-à-d. à bon compte)*
(e) *(lâcher)* hey! get off! that's my book!
(f) *(s'endormir)* I couldn't get off at all last night
2 VT SÉP (a) *(envoyer)* it's time to get the children off to bed; I must get this letter off in time to catch the last post
(b) *(enlever de)* get your hands off that child; get those football boots off the chair
(c) *(tirer d'affaire, faire acquitter)* he has a reputation for always getting his clients off
(d) *(prendre, comme congé)* maybe I could get the afternoon off
(e) *(obtenir de, tenir de)* I got it off the woman next door
(f) *(dispenser de)* the burns were not very serious but they got him off work
(g) *(endormir)* it always takes ages to get her off

get off with VT INSÉP BR (a) FAM *(avoir une touche avec, flirter avec)* she used to get off with a different guy every night (b) *(s'en tirer avec)* he got off with just a fine

get on 1 VI (a) *(monter, dans un bus, un train, etc.)* where did you get on?

(b) *(aller, se passer)* how did you get on at the dentist's?; *(se débrouiller)* how is the old man going to get on without his dog?
(c) *(avancer, progresser)* if he wants to get on, the best thing he can do is work hard; time is getting on *(c.-à-d. il se fait tard)*
(d) *(se faire vieux)* my grandmother is getting on
(e) *(s'entendre)* we don't get on
2 **VT SÉP** *(mettre)* I can't get the lid on; get your coat on and we'll be off; *(faire monter dans, mettre dans)* you won't be able to get that on the bus, it's far too big; I got her on (the train) with seconds to spare

get on for **VT INSÉP** *(approcher)* she must be getting on for 90 but she's very active; *(être presque)* it's getting on for four o'clock; there were getting on for 500 guests at the wedding

get onto **VT INSÉP** (a) *(trouver, trouver le nom de)* how did you get onto me? (b) *(prendre contact avec)* I'll get onto the bank about it (c) *(en venir à)* I'd like to get onto the question of expenses

get on with **VT INSÉP** (a) *(continuer, poursuivre)* please get on with what you're supposed to be doing; I would like to get on with my reading; that will do to be going on with *(c.-à-d. ça ira pour le moment)* (b) *(progresser ou avancer avec)* how are you getting on with the painting? (c) *(s'entendre avec)* I don't get on with my parents

get out 1 **VI** (a) *(sortir, partir)* I told her to get out
(b) *(être libéré, sortir)* when does he get out?
(c) *(sortir (de chez soi))* she doesn't get out much; he ought to get out more
(d) *(s'ébruiter)* how did the news get out?
2 **VT SÉP** (a) *(sortir)* I got my purse out to pay the delivery man; get your books out and turn to page 54
(b) *(libérer)* our prime concern must be to get the hostages out
(c) *(dire, sortir)* he couldn't get a word out when they told him his wife had had triplets; *(donner, publier)* we have to get this report out by Monday
(d) *(éliminer, au cricket)* John got their best batsman out for ten

get out of 1 **VT INSÉP** (a) *(partir de, sortir de)* let's get out of here; he got out of the country before the police came looking for him; the children get out of school at about three o'clock
(b) *(échapper à)* he always gets out of the washing up

(c) *(perdre, pour une habitude)* I've got out of the habit of studying
2 **VT SÉP** (a) *(sortir de)* get the big pot out of the cupboard; *(obtenir de)* the detective finally got the truth out of the suspect
(b) *(tirer, pour une satisfaction, etc.)* I don't see what pleasure he gets out of all this studying; *(profiter de)* she really gets the most out of life, doesn't she?

get over 1 **VI** (a) *(traverser)* the Channel Tunnel makes it easier to get over to France (b) *(passer, pour une opinion, etc.)* her ideas don't get over to her audience very well
2 **VT INSÉP** (a) *(se remettre de)* he hasn't got over the shock of his wife's death yet; I'm getting over it gradually (b) *(surmonter, vaincre)* they've managed to get over their marital problems; you must get over these silly fears
3 **VT SÉP** (a) *(faire traverser à)* it's not easy getting fifty children over a busy road (b) *(faire passer, pour une opinion, etc.)* you got your point over very well

get over with **VT SÉP** *(en finir avec)* once I got my appointment with the dentist over with, I thoroughly enjoyed my day off; can we get this over with quickly?

get round 1 **VI** (a) *(arriver chez qn)* he won't get round until later, we may as well have dinner now (b) *(se répandre)* the news is getting round quickly
2 **VT INSÉP** (a) *(échapper à, contourner)* there's no getting round it, you'll have to own up; how did they get round the export regulations? (b) *(persuader)* I can always get round my father
3 **VT SÉP** *(convertir)* you've got me round to your way of thinking

get round to **VT INSÉP** *(réussir à ou trouver le temps de s'occuper de)* I'll get round to it eventually, I promise

get through 1 **VI** (a) *(passer)* the cars could not get through because the pass was blocked with snow; will the message get through?
(b) *(obtenir la communication téléphonique)* the lines must be down, I can't get through
(c) **AM** *(finir)* the evening class does not usually get through until nine o'clock
(d) *(réussir un examen, être reçu)* only three of the class didn't get through

2 **VT INSÉP** (a) *(franchir)* you will not be able to get through the roadblock
(b) *(réussir)* I got through my exams second time around
(c) *(finir, achever)* will you get through your homework in time to come to the match?
(d) *(utiliser)* he gets through a dozen shirts a week
(e) *(faire passer, pour le temps)* since she retired, she's been finding it difficult to get through the days
3 **VT SÉP** (a) *(faire parvenir)* they got the food supplies through just in time
(b) *(faire comprendre)* I finally got it through to him that I wasn't interested
(c) *(faire réussir un examen)* it was your essay that got you through

get to **VT INSÉP** (a) *(se rendre à)* how do we get to their house from here? (b) *(pouvoir, réussir à)* did you actually get to speak to the Prime Minister? (c) *(commencer à)* you know, I've got to wondering if maybe he's right after all (d) **FAM** *(vexer, énerver)* she really got to me with her sarcastic remarks; don't let it get to you! *(c.-à-d. ne t'énerve pas pour ça !)*

get together 1 **VI** *(se réunir)* when can we get together to discuss the project?; *(rencontrer)* he's getting together with the bank manager tomorrow
2 **VT SÉP** *(rassembler, ramasser)* get your things together

get up 1 **VI** (a) *(se lever, de son lit)* it's time to get up (b) *(se lever, se mettre debout)* he got up to address the audience (c) *(se lever, se préparer)* there's a storm getting up
2 **VT SÉP** (a) *(réveiller)* will you get me up early tomorrow?
(b) *(monter)* how are we going to get this up to the top floor?
(c) *(gagner)* we'll get up speed when we reach the motorway
(d) *(organiser)* we've got up a petition to protest about the closure (e) *(habiller)* the children are always nicely got up

get up to **VT INSÉP** (a) *(arriver à, en être à)* I've got up to the fifth chapter (b) *(faire, pour des bêtises)* those children are always getting up to mischief; I don't want you getting up to anything while I'm out

give away **VT SÉP** (a) *(donner)* I gave it away to someone who needed it more (b) *(conduire à l'autel)* her uncle is to give her away
(c) *(trahir, dénoncer)* who gave us away?; *(locution)* to give the game away *vendre la mèche*

give in 1 VT SÉP *(rendre, remettre)* give your homework in; I gave the wallet in to the police
2 VI *(céder)* try not to give in to temptation; *(donner sa langue au chat)* I give in, tell me what the answer is

give off VT SÉP *(produire, dégager)* this fire gives off a lot of heat; something is giving off a bad smell

give onto VT INSÉP *(donner sur)* the windows give onto the main road so it's a noisy flat

give out 1 VT SÉP (a) *(distribuer)* they were giving out leaflets about abortion (b) *(annoncer)* the Chancellor gave out the trade figures today (c) *(produire)* the radiators are not giving out much heat
2 VI (a) *(tomber en panne)* the old car has finally given out
(b) *(s'épuiser, manquer)* supplies have given out; *(être à bout)* my patience is giving out

give over VT SÉP (a) *(confier)* he gave the children over to his mother; *(mettre à la disposition de)* the vicar gave the hall over to the scouts (b) *(consacrer)* they gave the entire evening over to a discussion of the film

give up 1 VT SÉP (a) *(abandonner)* the climbers gave up hope of being found before nightfall; *(laisser tomber)* give it up as a bad job
(b) *(arrêter)* she is giving up chocolate as part of her diet; I've given up trying
(c) *(donner, céder)* I gave up my seat on the bus to a pregnant woman
(d) *(rendre)* the escaped prisoner gave himself up after two days
(e) *(considérer)* to give someone up for dead/lost
(f) *(consacrer)* I gave the entire week up to studying
(g) *(ne plus attendre)* we had almost given you up
2 VI *(se rendre)* don't shoot, we give up; *(donner sa langue au chat)* OK, tell me the answer then, I give up

give up on VT INSÉP *(ne plus attendre, cesser d'attendre)* we gave up on you after waiting for an hour; *(ne plus rien attendre de)* how can a mother give up on her daughter and say she's no good?

gloss over VT SÉP (a) *(passer sur)* she very kindly glossed over my mistakes; I tend to gloss those things over (b) *(ne pas tout dire de, cacher)* he glosses over his past

go about 1 **VI** *(circuler)* there's a story going about that they've separated; there seems to be a virus going about; you can't go about saying things like that *(c.-à-d. il ne faut pas raconter des choses pareilles)*
2 **VT INSÉP** (a) *(s'y prendre)* what's the best way to go about buying a house? (b) *(s'occuper de)* just go about your business as usual

go about with **VT INSÉP** *(fréquenter, sortir avec)* my son has been going about with her for a year now

go after **VT INSÉP** (a) *(suivre, rattraper)* go after them! (b) *(courir après, essayer d'obtenir)* she's going after the world record; she really goes after what she wants

go ahead **VI** (a) *(passer devant)* you go ahead, we'll follow later (b) *(y aller)* if you have something to say to me, just go ahead!; *(mettre en route, poursuivre)* they have decided to go ahead with the wedding; he just went ahead and did it (c) *(avancer, progresser)* the project is going ahead quite satisfactorily

go along **VI** (a) *(marcher le long de)* she met him as she was going along the road (b) *(avancer)* please check your punctuation as you go along

go along with **VT INSÉP** *(accepter)* that's what they decided and I went along with it; *(être d'accord avec)* I cannot go along with you on that; *(se conformer à, respecter)* he went along with his father's wishes

go at **VT INSÉP** *(s'attaquer à ou attaquer, se jeter sur)* he went at the wall with a hammer; the children ignored the sandwiches and went at the cakes instead

go back **VI** (a) *(revenir, retourner)* let's go back some day (b) *(être rendu ou retourné)* when do these library books have to go back?; my new shoes will have to go back - they don't fit properly (c) *(être retardé, pour une montre, etc.)* don't forget that the clocks go back tomorrow (d) *(remonter)* the church has records going back to the 16th century

go back on **VT INSÉP** *(revenir sur)* I cannot go back on my promise to her; he never goes back on his decisions

go by 1 **VI** *(passer)* as the parade was going by...; many years have

gone by since we met; don't let this opportunity go by
2 **VT INSÉP** **(a)** *(juger d'après, se baser sur)* don't go by my opinion – I hate that kind of film; if you go by that clock, you'll miss the train **(b)** *(suivre)* he never goes by the rules; go by your brother's example **(c)** *(être connu sous)* she has been going by her maiden name since the divorce

go down **VI** **(a)** *(se coucher)* the sun is going down
(b) *(couler)* the ship went down with all hands
(c) *(baisser)* house prices may go down; *(descendre)* flood waters are going down
(d) *(déchoir, se dégrader)* my old neighbourhood has really gone down; his family has gone down in the world *(c.-à-d. sa famille a connu des jours meilleurs)*; *(baisser)* she went down in my estimation when I found out what really happened
(e) *(s'incliner, être battu)* Mexico went down to Germany; I won't go down without a fight *(c.-à-d. je me battrai jusqu'au bout)*
(f) *(être reçu)* my suggestion did not go down very well; how did your proposal go down with the director?; British actors often go down well in the States
(g) *(descendre)* some water will help the pill go down; *(se boire)* this wine goes down very nicely, don't you think?
(h) *(rester, laisser sa marque)* she will go down in history as a woman of great courage
(i) *(tomber en panne, planter, pour un ordinateur)* the computer's gone down
(j) *(tomber malade)* he went down with flu on the first day of the holidays, the poor thing

go for **VT INSÉP** **(a)** *(aller chercher)* he went for a doctor
(b) *(attaquer)* what was I supposed to do when she went for me with a knife?; we heard them going for each other in the street
(c) *(viser, essayer de décrocher ou d'obtenir)* with his next jump, he's going for the gold medal; she's going for his job; **FAM** go for it! *(c.-à-d. vas-y, fonce !)*
(d) **FAM** *(aimer)* I don't really go for that idea; he really goes for her in a big way *(c.-à-d. il est vraiment fou d'elle)*; *(préférer)* she's always gone for the tall, dark and handsome type
(e) *(concerner, s'appliquer à)* what I said goes for both of you
(f) *(servir à)* his twenty years of service went for nothing

go in VI (a) *(entrer, rentrer)* it's cold, let's go in (b) *(se cacher, pour le soleil)* the sun's gone in

go in for VT INSÉP (a) *(faire, se lancer dans, s'adonner à)* they have decided to go in for catering (b) FAM *(s'intéresser à, aimer)* he doesn't go in for team sports; my parents don't go in for opera (c) *(participer à, prendre part à)* are you going in for the four hundred metres?

go into VT INSÉP (a) *(entrer dans ou à)* our special training programme is now going into its third year; she has to go into hospital (b) *(faire carrière dans)* she wants her daughter to go into teaching (c) *(commencer à)* the car went into a skid; he nearly went into hysterics *(c.-à-d. il a failli avoir une crise de nerfs)*; *(aborder)* we won't go into that for the moment (d) *(s'embarquer dans)* my grandmother then went into a long and detailed description of her childhood

go off 1 VI (a) *(partir)* she has gone off with the man next door; he's gone off on some business of his own (b) *(s'avarier, pour de la nourriture, tourner, pour du lait, etc.)* the milk has gone off (c) *(s'éteindre)* the lights went off all over the city last night (d) *(sonner)* the alarm went off at the usual time; *(partir)* he said that the gun just went off in his hand (e) *(être reçu, se passer)* how did the play go off?; my presentation went off well/badly

2 VT INSÉP *(ne plus aimer ou s'intéresser à)* I've gone off him since I found out how unpleasant he is; she says she has gone off Spain

go on 1 VI (a) *(continuer)* go on, what did he say then?; just go on with what you were doing; do we have enough coffee to be going on with or should I buy some more?

(b) *(aller, pour un vêtement)* your coat won't go on unless you wear a different sweater; *(aller, se mettre, pour un couvercle, etc.)* the lid goes on this way

(c) *(s'allumer)* the street lights go on when it gets dark

(d) FAM *(ne pas cesser de parler)* once he starts, he goes on and on

(e) *(se passer)* what's going on?

(f) *(passer)* as time went on, I realized that I'd made the right decision

2 VT INSÉP (a) *(commencer, se mettre à)* most people go on a diet at least once

(b) *(être guidé par, se fonder ou s'appuyer sur)* I have nothing concrete to go on, I just don't trust him
(c) *(approcher, aller sur, pour un âge)* she's going on forty-five
(d) FAM *(en pincer pour, aimer)* my sister is really gone on the boy next door; I don't go much on abstract art

go on at VT INSÉP FAM *(s'en prendre à, embêter)* my parents keep going on at me to get a job

go out VI (a) *(sortir)* they were just about to go out; *(sortir de chez soi)* she doesn't go out much these days; we're going out for dinner
(b) *(sortir, fréquenter)* she's been going out with him for years
(c) *(être éliminé)* I bet his team goes out in the first round
(d) *(s'éteindre)* put some wood on the fire before it goes out; the lights went out
(e) *(être envoyé)* has that letter gone out?
(f) *(locution)* I went out like a light *je me suis endormi tout de suite*
(g) *(passer de mode, se démoder)* jeans will never go out
(h) *(descendre, pour la marée)* the tide has gone out

go over 1 VI (a) *(aller, à un endroit précis)* I went over and tapped him on the shoulder (b) *(passer, changer)* they've gone over to the Conservative Party; he's thinking about going over to cigars (c) *(passer, être reçu)* my suggestion didn't go over at all well
2 VT INSÉP (a) *(examiner)* we should go over the accounts
(b) *(revoir, repasser)* let's go over your speech a second time
(c) *(discuter de, parler de)* we must have gone over this point a dozen times already

go round 1 VI (a) *(rendre visite, aller)* you ought to go round and see him; she's gone round to her mother's (b) *(suffire)* there won't be enough to go round *(c.-à-d. il n'y en aura pas assez pour tout le monde)* (c) *(faire un détour)* there was a road accident so we had to go round the long way (d) *(tourner)* everything is going round
2 VT INSÉP (a) *(prendre, pour un chemin)* I went round the long way to be sure of not getting lost (b) *(visiter, faire le tour de)* we must have gone round every museum in town; she went round the neighbourhood looking for her cat (c) *(suffire à)* is the roast big enough to go round everyone?

go through 1 VI *(être accepté ou conclu)* the deal has gone through; *(être prononcé)* when does the divorce go through?

2 **VT INSÉP** (a) *(souffrir)* she has gone through a lot in recent years (b) *(examiner, étudier)* the detective went through the witness's statement very carefully (c) *(fouiller (dans))* I've gone through all the papers and I still can't find it (d) *(répéter, réciter)* how often do you have to go through your lines before you know them by heart? (e) *(user)* children go through a lot of shoes; *(consommer)* we've gone through six pints of milk in two days (f) *(être voté)* the bill went through Parliament last week

go through with **VT INSÉP** *(aller jusqu'au bout de, exécuter)* he decided at the last moment that he couldn't go through with the wedding; management went through with its threat to close the factory

go together **VI** (a) *(aller bien ensemble)* do these colours go together? (b) *(se fréquenter, sortir ensemble)* we've been going together for a long time

go towards **VT INSÉP** *(être consacré à, contribuer à)* the proceeds from the fête are going towards a new village hall

go under 1 **VI** (a) *(couler)* it's too late, he's gone under (b) **FIG** *(couler, être en faillite)* his business is going under and there isn't much he can do about it
2 **VT INSÉP** *(être connu sous)* since the divorce she's been going under her old name of Williams

go up **VI** (a) *(monter)* just go up, he's expecting you (b) *(monter, augmenter)* the patient's temperature had been going up for some time; house prices are going up again (c) *(se lever)* the curtain will go up at eight o'clock (d) *(être détruit)* the building went up in flames; *(locution)* his hopes went up in smoke *ses espoirs sont partis en fumée*

go with **VT INSÉP** (a) *(aller de pair avec)* mathematical skills usually go with an ability to play chess (b) *(aller avec)* change your tie, it doesn't go with that shirt

go without 1 **VI** *(s'en passer)* those are too dear – if you don't like any of the others you'll just have to go without
2 **VT INSÉP** *(se passer de)* I went without breakfast so I wouldn't be late

grow apart **VI** *(s'éloigner, pour des amis, etc.)* they have grown apart over the years

grow in VI *(repousser)* your hair will grow in soon

grow out of VT INSÉP (a) *(devenir trop grand pour, ne plus rentrer dans)* he has grown out of those shoes we bought just a few months ago (b) *(devenir trop mûr pour)* I've grown out of my friends; *(passer l'âge de, perdre l'habitude de)* when are you going to grow out of biting your nails?

grow up VI (a) *(grandir, devenir adulte)* children grow up so fast nowadays (b) *(se comporter comme un adulte)* I wish you would grow up! (c) *(se développer)* a theory has grown up that...

guard against VT INSÉP *(se prémunir contre, se protéger de)* take vitamin C to guard against colds

H

hammer home VT SÉP (a) *(enfoncer, au marteau)* be sure to hammer all the nails home (b) *(insister sur)* we hammered home the importance of wearing seat belts

hammer out VT SÉP (a) *(aplatir au marteau, débosseler)* I'll have to hammer these dents out (b) *(élaborer, mettre au point, avec difficulté)* they have finally managed to hammer out an agreement on the withdrawal of troops

hand back VT SÉP *(rendre, rapporter)* I'll hand it back to you as soon as I've finished

hand down VT SÉP (a) *(passer, d'un endroit plus haut)* hand that plate down to me (b) *(transmettre, donner en héritage)* she handed the necklace down to her granddaughter (c) *(prononcer, pour une sentence)* the sentence will be handed down soon

hand in VT SÉP *(rendre, remettre)* I want you to hand in your essays tomorrow

hand out VT SÉP (a) *(distribuer)* I've offered to hand leaflets out (b) *(donner, distribuer, pour des conseils, etc. non désirés)* you can always rely on him to hand out advice

hand over 1 VT SÉP (a) *(passer, donner)* hand over your wallet (b) *(remettre)* she handed the papers over to the lawyer for

safekeeping (c) *(transmettre, passer)* he will be handing over the reins of power very soon; we now hand you over to our foreign affairs correspondent *(c.-à-d. nous passons maintenant l'antenne à...)*
2 VI *(laisser la place, donner la parole)* I now hand over to the weatherman; *(passer le pouvoir)* when will he be handing over to the new chairman?

hang about/around FAM 1 VI (a) *(poireauter, attendre)* I had to hang about for ages before he finally arrived (b) *(traîner)* don't hang about or we'll never finish
2 VT INSÉP *(fréquenter, traîner dans)* I don't want you hanging about amusement arcades

hang back VI *(rester en arrière)* if you have a contribution to make to the discussion, please don't hang back; *(se retenir)* I hung back from saying anything as it wasn't really my place to do so

hang down VI *(descendre, tomber)* her hair hung down in ringlets

hang in VI FAM *(s'accrocher, tenir le coup)* hang in there, we'll get you out soon; he'll just have to hang in until a better job comes along

hang on 1 VI (a) *(se tenir, s'accrocher)* hang on tight (b) FAM *(attendre)* can you hang on for a couple of minutes?
2 VT INSÉP (a) *(écouter attentivement)* the audience was hanging on the speaker's every word *(c.-à-d. le public buvait les paroles ou était suspendu aux lèvres de l'orateur)* (b) *(dépendre de)* the fate of the project hangs on the availability of supplies

hang on to VT INSÉP (a) *(s'accrocher à, se cramponner à)* he hung on to the cliff face (b) *(conserver, garder)* I'd hang on to those documents if I were you

hang out VI (a) *(sortir, dépasser)* your shirt tails are hanging out (b) FAM *(traîner habituellement)* I'm looking for Bill – any idea where he hangs out? (c) FAM *(tenir bon ou insister pour obtenir)* I'm hanging out for a rise

hang together VI *(être plausible, tenir debout)* the plot of the film doesn't hang together

hang up 1 **vi** *(raccrocher (le téléphone))* don't hang up until you've heard what she has to say; hang up immediately 2 **vt sép** *(accrocher, suspendre)* hang your coat up

happen along **vi Fam** *(arriver par hasard)* then, thank goodness, a policeman happened along

hark back to **vt insép** *(revenir à ou sur, pour un sujet)* he keeps harking back to the war

have around **vt sép** *(avoir sous la main)* it's always a good idea to have some candles around

have back **vt sép** (a) *(récupérer)* can I have it back? (b) *(inviter chez soi en retour)* we're having them back next Saturday

have in **vt sép** (a) *(appeler, faire venir)* we'll have to have the plumber in to fix that leak (b) *(inviter chez soi)* the old ladies across the street like having people in for tea (c) *(locution)* to have it in for someone *avoir une dent contre quelqu'un*

have off **vt sép** (a) *(enlever)* the doctor had the plaster off in no time at all (b) *(se faire enlever)* she's having the plaster off next week (c) **Br Fam** *(s'envoyer en l'air)* he's been having it off with a different woman every weekend for years

have on **vt sép** (a) *(porter, pour des vêtements)* he looks totally different when he doesn't have his business suit on (b) **Br Fam** *(taquiner, faire marcher)* didn't you realize I was having you on? (c) *(avoir... à faire, avoir... de prévu)* she has a lot on this week; I have something else on, I'm afraid (d) *(avoir des preuves contre)* he told the police they had nothing on him – he'd been in hospital at the time (e) *(mettre, installer)* once we have the roof rack on, we'll be ready to go

have out **vt sép** (a) *(se faire enlever)* he's in hospital having his appendix out (b) *(s'expliquer sur)* let's have this out once and for all *(c.-à-d. mettons les choses au point une fois pour toutes)*

have up **vt sép** (a) *(monter, installer)* they worked all night to have the exhibits up in time for the opening (b) *(inviter, pour qn qui habite en bas de chez soi ou dans le sud)* he had them up (to his flat) for tea; we're having them up from London for the weekend

head for **vt insép** (a) *(aller à, se rendre à)* where is he headed for?; let's head for home (b) *(aller droit à)* the country is heading for civil war; she's heading for a disappointment if she thinks he's going to propose

head off VT SÉP (a) *(détourner l'attention de, occuper)* head Mum off for a couple of minutes while I finish wrapping her present
(b) *(prévenir, éviter)* to head off accusations of favouritism...

head up VT SÉP *(présider, être à la tête de)* how many committees does she head up?

hear of VT INSÉP (a) *(connaître)* I've never heard of her; *(entendre parler, être au courant)* the whole town had heard of his success
(b) *habituellement à la forme négative (accepter, laisser)* I won't hear of you going to a hotel when we've got a spare room

hear out VT SÉP *(écouter jusqu'au bout)* please hear me out; the committee heard her out before reaching a decision

heat up 1 VI (a) *(se réchauffer)* the room will soon heat up (b) FIG *(s'animer, se dégrader)* the discussion heated up and turned into an argument
2 VT SÉP *(faire chauffer)* heat up some milk; *(réchauffer)* a bowl of soup will heat you up

hide out VI *(se cacher)* he's hiding out in some hotel to get away from his fans

hit back 1 VI *(riposter)* he hit back with accusations that they were accepting bribes
2 VT SÉP *(renvoyer)* hit the ball back; *(rendre un coup)* he hit her so she hit him back

hit off VT SÉP (a) *(imiter)* he hits the Prime Minister off very well
(b) FAM *(locution)* we hit it off immediately *le courant est tout de suite passé entre nous*

hit on VT INSÉP *(trouver)* I've hit on a possible solution

hit out VI (a) *(lancer des coups)* all of a sudden he started hitting out
(b) *(attaquer, s'en prendre à)* all the speakers at the conference hit out at the proposals

hive off 1 VI *(se diversifier, se lancer)* they're hiving off into the retail side of things
2 VT SÉP *(se séparer de)* my boss is furious that the company wants to hive off the research team

hold against VT SÉP *(reprocher à, en vouloir à)* why do you hold my past against me?; she's very naive but you can't hold that against her

hold back 1 VI *(rester silencieux, se retenir)* I held back while the two of them discussed old times; he held back from making any comment
2 VT SÉP (a) *(retenir, contenir)* security guards held the fans back; he held back his rage (b) *(empêcher de progresser)* your poor performance in maths is holding you back (c) *(ne pas dire, cacher)* she's holding something back, I know she is; don't hold anything back

hold down VT SÉP (a) *(maintenir au sol, maîtriser)* it took two of us to hold him down (b) *(limiter, empêcher de monter)* the government must take action to hold down interest rates (c) *(avoir, occuper, pour un emploi)* she is holding down a fairly high-powered job; *(garder, pour un emploi)* can he hold this job down?

hold forth VI *(disserter, pérorer)* she held forth at great length on the benefits of aromatherapy *(c.-à-d. elle a fait un long discours sur...)*

hold in VT SÉP (a) *(rentrer)* for heaven's sake, hold your stomach in (b) *(retenir, contenir)* she shouldn't hold her emotions in

hold off 1 VI (a) *(ne pas se mettre à tomber, pour la pluie)* the rain seems to be holding off *(c.-à-d. on dirait qu'il ne va pas pleuvoir)* (b) *(s'abstenir)* hold off from smoking for a few weeks
2 VT SÉP *(tenir à distance)* the troops held off the enemy; *(repousser)* the remaining men managed to hold off the attack until reinforcements arrived

hold on VI (a) *(garder)* hold on to this contract for me (b) *(s'accrocher)* hold on tightly!; *(bien tenir)* hold on to your hat! (c) *(tenir le coup)* I can't hold on much longer (d) *(attendre)* hold on, how do I know I can trust you?

hold out 1 VI (a) *(durer)* our supplies will not hold out for long (b) *(tenir le coup)* can you hold out until the doctor gets here?
2 VT SÉP (a) *(tendre)* she held out her hand (b) *(offrir, pour un espoir, une possibilité)* the doctor doesn't hold out much hope for a complete recovery

hold out on VT INSÉP *(ne pas dire à, cacher à)* you've been holding out on me – I didn't know you played the saxophone

hold to 1 **VT INSÉP** *(s'en tenir à, maintenir)* he held to his decision
2 **VT SÉP** *(faire tenir)* we held him to his promise

hold up 1 **VI** (a) *(tenir debout)* the centuries-old house continues to hold up (b) *(tenir le coup, rester calme)* she held up magnificently under the strain
2 **VT SÉP** (a) *(lever)* she held her face up to the sun
(b) *(maintenir, faire tenir)* the tent is held up with just a couple of pegs
(c) *(retarder)* bad weather is holding the project up
(d) *(faire un hold-up dans)* armed men held up another bank yesterday

hold with **VT INSÉP BR** *(approuver)* I don't hold with private education

hole up **VI FAM** *(se terrer, se planquer)* the bank robbers decided to hole up for a while

home in on **VT INSÉP** (a) *(se diriger automatiquement sur ou vers)* the missiles can home in on the heat of aircraft engines (b) *(mettre l'accent sur, faire remarquer)* she homed in on my one mistake

hook up 1 **VI** (a) *(s'agrafer)* the dress hooks up at the back (b) *(faire une émission en duplex)* we will be hooking up with European networks to bring you this very special programme
2 **VT SÉP** *(agrafer, pour des vêtements)* hook me up

hot up **FAM** 1 **VI** *(chauffer, pour des paroles, le ton d'une conversation, etc.)* the argument hotted up when one of them swore at the other; things are hotting up again on the industrial relations front
2 **VT SÉP** *(augmenter, hâter)* they are hotting up the pace

hunt down **VT SÉP** (a) *(rechercher, traquer)* they are being hunted down by state and federal police (b) *(dénicher, débusquer)* he was finally hunted down

hunt out **VT SÉP** *(dénicher, trouver, avec difficulté)* I've hunted out those old family photographs you wanted to see

hurry along 1 **VI** *(se presser, se dépêcher)* you're hurrying along as if we were late; hurry along please, the museum is now closed
2 **VT SÉP** *(activer, accélérer)* I'm trying to hurry the project along but it's not easy; you can't hurry these things along

hurry up 1 VI *(se dépêcher)* do hurry up or we'll be late
2 VT SÉP *(faire aller plus vite, faire accélérer)* I'll go and hurry them up; *(activer, accélérer)* could you hurry things up a bit, please, the deadline is fast approaching

I

ice over VI *(geler)* this river is too fast-flowing to ever ice over

ice up VI *(givrer, geler)* the crash was attributed in part to the plane's wings having iced up; I can't get the key in – the lock must have iced up

improve on VT INSÉP *(améliorer)* we have to improve on last year's performance; she'll have to improve on that score with her next jump

iron out VT SÉP (a) *(enlever au fer)* I'll iron out these creases in your shirt for you (b) FIG *(faire disparaître, aplanir)* have you ironed out your differences?; *(résoudre)* there are one or two little problems that must be ironed out

J

jack in VT SÉP BR FAM (a) *(laisser tomber, plaquer)* I'm going to jack this job in as soon as I can (b) *(la fermer, la boucler)* jack it in!

jack up VT SÉP (a) *(soulever avec un cric)* he had to jack up the car to change the wheel (b) FAM *(augmenter, faire grimper)* they've jacked up the price of petrol again

jam in(to) 1 VT SÉP (a) *(coincer)* the crowd were jamming him in (b) *(entasser, bourrer, mettre)* can you jam anything else in?; he had jammed as many quotations as he could find into the essay
2 VI *(s'entasser)* hundreds of people jammed in to hear her speech

jam on VT SÉP *(appuyer à fond sur, écraser)* I had to jam on my brakes or I would have hit him; *(enfoncer complètement, à fond)* she jammed her hat on and marched out

jam up VT SÉP *(bloquer, encombrer, créer des embouteillages sur)* Sunday motorists in search of a good spot for a picnic have jammed up the roads

jar on VT INSÉP *(irriter, porter sur)* that constant banging is jarring on my nerves

jazz up VT SÉP FAM *(mettre de l'ambiance dans, animer)* it's very dull in here tonight – couldn't we jazz things up a bit?; *(égayer)* jazz up a plain dress with some costume jewellery

jockey for VT SÉP *(essayer d'obtenir, surtout pour des emplois, des fonctions)* everyone is jockeying for the position of chairperson

jog along VI *(avancer, suivre son rythme)* the work is jogging along

join in 1 VI *(participer)* I want everyone to join in
2 VT INSÉP *(prendre part à)* I joined in the fun; they all joined in the chorus *(c.-à-d. ils ont tous repris le refrain en chœur)*

join on 1 VI *(s'attacher, se fixer)* where does this bit join on?
2 VT SÉP *(attacher, accrocher)* they've joined on another carriage

join up 1 VI (a) *(s'engager dans l'armée)* he joined up as soon as war was declared (b) *(se rencontrer, se rejoindre)* the two groups will join up here
2 VT SÉP *(joindre, assembler, raccorder)* join the ends up

jot down VT SÉP *(prendre rapidement, noter rapidement)* he jotted down a few notes for his speech; just jot it down

jump at VT INSÉP *(saisir, sauter sur)* I jumped at the chance of a holiday in Spain; when he offered her the position she jumped at it

jump down 1 VI *(sauter)* there aren't any steps, you'll have to jump down; he jumped down from the window
2 VT INSÉP FAM *(locution)* to jump down someone's throat *rembarrer ou engueuler quelqu'un*

jump on 1 VI *(monter)* there was a bus sitting at the traffic lights so he decided to jump on
2 VT INSÉP FAM (a) *(se jeter sur, agresser)* the hooligans jumped on the old man at the corner of the street (b) *(passer un savon à, engueuler)* he jumps on me for the least little thing

K

keel over VI (a) *(chavirer)* the lifeboat keeled over (b) *(s'évanouir)* he keels over at the sight of blood; *(tomber)* the hat stand just keeled over

keep at 1 VT INSÉP (a) *(continuer à travailler)* if he wants to get into university, he'll have to keep at his maths (b) *(harceler)* she kept at me until I agreed
2 VT SÉP *(faire travailler)* the boss kept us hard at it all morning

keep away 1 VI *(ne pas s'approcher)* keep away from the cooker!; I knew you had visitors so I kept away *(c.-à-d. je savais que tu avais de la visite donc je ne suis pas venu)*; *(ne pas succomber, résister)* she can't keep away from chocolates
2 VT SÉP *(tenir éloigné, empêcher d'approcher)* keep him away from me

keep back 1 VI *(rester en arrière, ne pas s'approcher)* a policeman was telling people to keep back
2 VT SÉP (a) *(tenir éloigné, empêcher d'approcher)* the security guards at the concert had trouble keeping the fans back from the stage (b) *(retenir)* I couldn't keep back my tears; *(ne pas dire, cacher)* she's keeping something back from us (c) *(faire redoubler, pour un élève)* he has been kept back a year
(d) *(retenir, retarder)* am I keeping you back?

keep down 1 VI *(ne pas se lever ou se relever)* keep down or he'll see us
2 VT SÉP (a) *(ne pas lever, baisser)* the policemen surrounding the house were told to keep their heads down; please keep your voice down, some people are trying to concentrate
(b) *(garder, pour la nourriture)* I think it must be a virus, I haven't been able to keep anything down for days
(c) *(limiter, empêcher d'augmenter)* the government is not doing anything to keep inflation down; he's trying to keep his weight down *(c.-à-d. il essaie de garder la ligne)*; *(empêcher de proliférer)* it's a full-time job keeping the weeds down in this garden

keep from 1 VT SÉP (a) *(cacher à)* they kept the news from the old lady for as long as possible; what are you keeping from me?
(b) *(empêcher de)* the climber hung on to his partner's hand to keep him from falling over the edge; I'm trying to keep

you from harm *(c.-à-d. j'essaie de te protéger)* (c) *(distraire de)* I mustn't keep you from your work
2 **VT INSÉP** *(s'empêcher de)* he was such a boring speaker that I couldn't keep from nodding off

keep in with **VT INSÉP** *(rester en bons termes avec)* if you want to keep in with him, just agree with everything he says

keep off 1 **VI** *(ne pas approcher)* that's my property, keep off!
2 **VT INSÉP** (a) *(ne pas s'approcher de, ne pas marcher sur)* keep off the grass (b) *(éviter)* they tactfully kept off the subject of divorce; the doctor has ordered him to keep off alcohol
3 **VT SÉP** (a) *(éloigner, protéger de)* this cream will keep the mosquitoes off; Mum said to keep our hands off the cakes *(c.-à-d. de ne pas toucher)* (b) *(enlever, ne pas porter, pour un vêtement)* don't keep your coat off for long or you'll get cold

keep on 1 **VI** (a) *(continuer)* if they keep on like this much longer, I'm going to call the police (b) **FAM** *(parler sans cesse)* he keeps on about his kids
2 **VT SÉP** (a) *(garder, pour un employé)* we can't afford to keep the cleaning woman on (b) *(garder, pour un vêtement)* make sure the baby keeps her gloves on

keep on at **VT INSÉP** *(faire des remontrances, harceler)* the headmaster keeps on at his pupils about their behaviour

keep out 1 **VI** (a) *(ne pas entrer)* danger – keep out!
(b) *(ne pas s'attirer)* try to keep out of trouble; *(ne pas se mêler à, ne pas intervenir)* I'm keeping out of this argument
2 **VT SÉP** (a) *(empêcher d'entrer)* lock the door to keep people out; *(protéger de, empêcher d'entrer)* these boots are supposed to keep the rain out (b) *(locution)* keep out of the reach of children *ne pas laisser à la portée des enfants* (c) *(ne pas mêler)* I'll do my best to keep you out of this

keep to 1 **VT INSÉP** (a) *(respecter)* we must keep to the agenda and introduce new subjects for discussion; people should keep to their promises (b) *(ne pas s'écarter de, rester à ou sur)* keep to the right
2 **VT SÉP** (a) *(maintenir à)* we are endeavouring to keep delays to a minimum (b) *(locution)* to keep something to oneself *garder quelque chose pour soi*

keep up 1 **VI** (a) *(continuer)* if this snow keeps up much longer the roads will be blocked

(b) *(suivre, pour une vitesse ou un rythme)* she dictated so quickly that her secretary couldn't keep up
(c) *(rester en contact)* have you kept up with them since they moved away?
2 **VT SÉP** (a) *(maintenir, empêcher de tomber)* he needs a belt to keep his trousers up; keep your spirits up! *(c.-à-d. ne te laisse pas abattre !)*
(b) *(maintenir, continuer)* we kept up a fairly regular exchange of letters until quite recently; keep it up, you're doing fine
(c) *(suivre)* it seems impossible for him to keep this pace up
(d) *(entretenir)* the garden hasn't been kept up very well
(e) *(empêcher de dormir, garder éveillé)* our dinner guests kept us up until three o'clock this morning

kick about/around 1 **VI FAM** *(traîner)* don't leave the paper kicking about; find yourself something to do instead of kicking around
2 **VT SÉP** (a) *(donner des coups de pied dans)* they're not doing any harm kicking a ball around *(c.-à-d. jouer au ballon)* (b) **FAM** *(marcher sur les pieds de, maltraiter)* you've kicked me around long enough (c) **FAM** *(débattre)* we kicked the proposal around for a while but finally decided against it

kick in **VT SÉP** *(enfoncer à coups de pied)* we lost our key and had to kick the door in; **FAM** *(locution)* I'll kick his teeth in! *je vais lui casser la figure!*

kick off 1 **VI** (a) *(donner le coup d'envoi)* when do they kick off?
(b) **FAM** *(commencer)* our speaker will now answer questions – who's going to kick off?; let's kick off with a situation report
2 **VT SÉP** (a) *(enlever d'un coup de pied)* it's always such a relief to kick your shoes off (b) **FAM** *(expulser de, virer de)* they're going to kick him off the team for misconduct

kick out 1 **VI** *(ruer)* the mules kicked out whenever anyone approached; *(donner des coups de pied)* she would kick out at anyone who came near
2 **VT SÉP FAM** *(foutre dehors)* his wife has kicked him out and he's got nowhere to go

kick up **VT SÉP FAM** *(faire, créer, pour des ennuis, des problèmes)* he'll kick up an awful fuss when he finds out *(c.-à-d. il en fera toute une histoire quand il le saura)*

knock about/around 1 **VI** = **kick about/around** 1

2 **VT SÉP FAM** (a) *(battre)* he knocks her about regularly (b) *(défoncer, abîmer)* the car was knocked about a good bit but the driver is unharmed (c) *(ballotter)* we were really knocked about in the back of the truck (d) **FAM** *(débattre)* we knocked the idea about for a while

knock back **VT SÉP** (a) **FAM** *(descendre, pour une boisson)* he's knocking the whisky back a bit, isn't he? (b) **FAM** *(coûter)* how much did that knock you back? (c) **BR** *(rejeter)* she knocked him back; *(refuser)* they knocked the invitation back

knock down **VT SÉP** (a) *(démolir)* the council wants to knock those houses down (b) *(renverser)* the car that knocked her down was moving much too fast; *(envoyer au tapis)* the champion knocked his opponent down in the first round (c) *(faire baisser son prix à qn)* we're trying to knock them down to something we can afford; *(baisser le prix de)* she knocked it down a fair bit (d) **BR** *(adjuger)* both paintings were knocked down to dealers

knock off 1 **VI FAM** *(cesser le travail, finir)* I'll try to knock off early
2 **VT SÉP** (a) *(faire tomber, renverser)* there's water everywhere, the cat must have knocked the vase off
(b) *(baisser de, pour un prix)* could you knock a pound or two off?
(c) **FAM** *(faire vite fait, torcher)* she knocks those sketches off by the dozen
(d) **FAM** *(piquer, faucher)* those watches that he's trying to sell have probably been knocked off
(e) **FAM** *(descendre, buter)* she's terrified he'll be knocked off for informing on the gang leader
(f) **FAM** *(locution)* knock it off! *arrête ton char!*

knock out **VT SÉP** (a) *(assommer, mettre K.O.)* the challenger knocked the champion out with a single punch; *(anesthésier, endormir)* will they knock you out or just give you a local anaesthetic?
(b) *(éliminer)* that's her knocked out of Wimbledon already!
(c) **FAM** *(crever, épuiser)* those children have knocked me out
(d) **FAM** *(épater)* his performance absolutely knocked me out
(e) *(détruire)* the government jets knocked out two rebel encampments; the storm has knocked out power supplies to a great many homes
(f) *(débourrer)* knocking his pipe out, he said...

knock over VT SÉP *(faire tomber, renverser)* he knocked several people over as he ran away; a bus knocked her over

knock together 1 VI *(s'entrechoquer)* my knees were knocking together at the thought of the interview
2 VT SÉP FAM *(faire à la hâte, bricoler à la va-vite)* I've promised to knock a tree house together for the kids

knock up 1 VI BR *(faire des balles, s'échauffer)* the players are allowed two minutes to knock up
2 VT SÉP (a) BR *(réveiller, en frappant à la porte)* will you knock me up at six o'clock? (b) FAM *(bricoler, préparer à la hâte)* if you don't mind leftovers, I'll knock a quick meal up for you (c) FAM *(mettre en cloque)* he's knocked her up

know of VT INSÉP (a) *(savoir)* has Bill arrived? – not that I know of (b) *(avoir entendu parler de)* I don't know him personally, but I know of him; *(connaître sur ou de)* nothing is known of her whereabouts

knuckle under VT INSÉP *(céder)* I won't knuckle under to threats

L

lash down 1 VT SÉP *(arrimer, fixer)* the lorry driver lashed the tarpaulin down
2 VI *(pleuvoir à verse)* it's lashing down

lash into VT INSÉP BR (a) *(attaquer)* the two men lashed into each other (b) *(attaquer verbalement, se déchaîner contre)* I lashed into her for making such silly mistakes

lash out 1 VI (a) *(donner des coups de pied ou de poing)* he lashed out at the police officer who was trying to arrest him; FIG *(fustiger)* she lashes out at anyone who opposes her (b) BR FAM *(faire une folie, claquer son fric)* I think I'll lash out and treat myself to a new coat
2 VT SÉP BR FAM *(claquer, pour de l'argent)* they lashed out a couple of thousand pounds on that holiday to the States

last out 1 VI (a) *(tenir)* how long will he last out?; I don't think I can last out at this job (b) *(suffire)* will our water last out?
2 VT SÉP *(passer)* she is not expected to last out the night; we have enough supplies to last out the winter

laugh off VT SÉP *(se moquer de, rire de)* he laughed off everyone's warnings

launch into VT INSÉP *(se lancer dans)* he launched into a glowing description of the car he had just bought

launch out VI *(se diversifier)* the company is going to launch out and add textiles to its product range; *(locution)* to launch out on one's own *se mettre à son compte*

lay about VT INSÉP FAM *(attaquer, taper sur)* the old lady laid about him with her stick

lay down VT SÉP (a) *(poser)* he laid his glass down on the table; *(déposer, pour les armes)* the rebels have announced that they will lay down their arms (b) *(renoncer à, sacrifier)* she laid down her life for her beliefs (c) *(établir, stipuler)* it is laid down in the regulations; *(locution)* to lay down the law *faire la loi*

lay in VT SÉP *(amasser, faire entrer)* we have laid in enough canned goods to feed an army; you had better lay some wood in

lay off 1 VI FAM *(arrêter)* I've had as much criticism as I can take, so lay off
2 VT INSÉP FAM *(laisser tranquille, ficher la paix à)* my sister doesn't want to go out with you so lay off her
3 VT SÉP *(licencier)* the company will be laying 350 employees off within the next few weeks

lay on VT SÉP *(installer, fournir)* water and electricity are both laid on at the cottage; extra buses will be laid on if necessary; *(offrir)* I'll lay on a meal for everyone

lay out VT SÉP (a) *(étendre, étaler)* lay the pattern out on the floor (b) *(préparer)* she always lays her clothes out the night before (c) *(faire la toilette de, pour un défunt)* the old lady was laid out for her relatives to view her (d) *(aménager)* I don't like the way the office has been laid out (e) *(assommer, mettre K.O.)* he laid me out with one blow (f) *(dépenser, pour de l'argent)* your parents have laid out a considerable sum on your education

lay up VT SÉP BR (a) *(clouer au lit)* this flu has laid her up (b) *(désarmer, pour un navire)* the severely damaged vessel will be laid up for repair; *(mettre au garage)* my car is laid up

lead on 1 VI *(aller ou marcher devant)* lead on, you know the way better than I do
2 VT SÉP (a) *(faire marcher)* he led her on with promises of marriage; you led me on to believe that the job was mine (b) *(amener)* this leads me on to my second point; *(inciter)* it was those so-called friends of his that led him on to do it

lead up VI (a) *(mener à, conduire à)* a narrow path led up to the house (b) *(précéder)* in the years leading up to the Declaration of Independence...; *(déclencher)* these events led up to the war (c) *(préparer à, mener à)* her opening remarks were plainly leading up to a full-scale attack on her critics; what are you leading up to? *(c.-à-d. où voulez-vous en venir ?)*

lean on VT INSÉP (a) *(dépendre de, compter sur)* his mother leans on him for advice (b) *(faire pression sur)* the company is leaning on her to take early retirement

leave behind VT SÉP (a) *(ne pas prendre, laisser)* drivers are advised to leave their cars behind and use public transport; I think we should leave the children behind (b) *(oublier, laisser)* I came out in such a rush that I left my keys behind (c) *(distancer, devancer)* when it comes to maths, she leaves most of the others far behind

leave off 1 VT SÉP *(ne pas (re)mettre)* it was such a beautiful day I left my coat off; who keeps leaving the lid off the coffee jar?; she wants to leave most of her relations off the guest list
2 VI *(s'arrêter)* we'll carry on from where we left off; BR FAM *(arrêter)* leave off, will you!

leave out VT SÉP (a) *(oublier, omettre)* you've left out an entire line (b) *(exclure)* I felt completely left out at the party; the old lady decided to leave her son-in-law out of her will (c) *(ne pas mêler, laisser en dehors)* leave me out of this (d) *(laisser sorti)* I'll leave out the instructions for the washing machine; *(laisser dehors)* do you want to leave the car out?

let down VT SÉP (a) *(faire descendre)* they let a rope down to the men stranded on the beach; *(dénouer)* she let her hair down (b) *(décevoir)* you must stop letting people down like this (c) *(rallonger)* she always has to let down the hems of her daughter's clothes (d) *(dégonfler)* the boys let his tyres down as a joke

let in 1 VT SÉP (a) *(laisser entrer)* don't let him in; these shoes are letting water in *(c.-à-d. ces chaussures prennent l'eau)* (b) *(mettre au courant)* they let me in on the secret
2 VI *(prendre l'eau, etc.)* are your boots letting in?

let in for VT SÉP *(causer)* your absence let us all in for a lot of extra work; *(s'engager dans)* he didn't realize what he was letting himself in for

let off VT SÉP (a) *(faire exploser)* animal rights activists have let off a number of bombs (b) *(produire)* the fire was letting off a lot of smoke (c) *(faire grâce à)* he was let off because of lack of evidence; the judge let him off with a fine (d) *(lâcher, libérer)* the teacher lets us off early on Fridays (e) *(déposer, d'un véhicule)* I asked the taxi driver to let me off at the corner

let on VI FAM (a) *(dire, pour un secret)* he never let on that he was married; I'm pregnant but don't you let on
(b) *(prétendre, faire croire)* he likes to let on that he went to university

let out VT SÉP (a) *(laisser sortir, libérer)* they're letting him out on parole soon; *(reconduire)* my secretary will let you out; don't get up, I'll let myself out *(c.-à-d. ne vous levez pas, je connais le chemin)* (b) *(révéler, vendre la mèche)* he let the truth out; who let it out that we had a party? (c) *(laisser échapper, émettre)* she let out a yelp of pain (d) BR *(louer)* they let out rooms to students (e) *(élargir, pour des vêtements)* I'm either going to have to go on a diet or let all my clothes out

let up VI *(cesser, arrêter, pour quelque chose qui a duré longtemps)* I wish this rain would let up; don't you ever let up?

lie back VI (a) *(s'allonger)* you lie back and rest (b) *(ne rien faire)* he just lay back and let the rest of us do the work

lie in VI *(faire la grasse matinée)* most people lie in on Sundays; I wish I could have lain in this morning

lie up VI (a) *(rester au lit)* the doctor says she's to lie up for a couple of days (b) *(se cacher)* the police are convinced that the wanted men are lying up somewhere (c) *(ne pas être utilisé)* that boat has been lying up for years

light up 1 VI (a) *(s'illuminer)* his face suddenly lit up; the room seemed

to light up when she came in (b) *(allumer une cigarette, etc.)* he lit up and sighed with contentment
2 **VT SÉP** (a) *(éclairer, illuminer)* the fireworks lit up the sky (b) *(allumer)* they both lit up their pipes

line up 1 **VI** *(faire la queue)* people are already beginning to line up outside the cinema
2 **VT SÉP** (a) *(faire aligner)* the headmaster lined everybody up in the playground (b) *(arranger, prévoir)* I've lined a date up for you; he's got something else lined up for tomorrow

listen in **VI** *(écouter)* it's fascinating listening in on other people's conversations; do you mind if I listen in?

live down **VT SÉP** *(pardonner à)* they'll never let him live that down; *(faire oublier à)* he won't let her live it down that she made one stupid mistake; you'll never live this down! *(c.-à-d. tu n'as pas fini d'en entendre parler!)*

live in/out **VI** *(habiter/ne pas habiter sur place)* they have at least three maids living in; I would rather live out than stay in a hall of residence

live off **VT INSÉP** (a) *(vivre de)* she lived off what she earned as a cleaner; *(se nourrir de, ne manger que)* that child would live off ice cream if he could (b) *(vivre aux crochets de)* he lives off his parents

live on 1 **VI** *(durer)* the memory of their sacrifice will live on
2 **VT INSÉP** (a) *(vivre de, se nourrir de)* she lives on fruit and vegetables (b) *(vivre de)* this salary is not enough to live on *(c.-à-d. ce salaire n'est pas suffisant pour vivre)*

live up to **VT INSÉP** (a) *(être à la hauteur de)* the holiday didn't live up to our expectations (b) *(se montrer digne de ou à la hauteur de)* there's no point in trying to live up to my sister's reputation

load down **VT SÉP** *(charger, surcharger)* he was loaded down with packages; I'm loaded down with work

load up 1 **VI** *(charger)* there are a number of ships waiting to load up
2 **VT SÉP** *(charger)* we loaded the car up with everything we needed

lock away **VT SÉP** *(mettre sous clé)* lock those papers away for the night; *(mettre sous les verrous, incarcérer)* the police said they could lock him away for ten years

lock in VT SÉP *(emprisonner)* she's locked in a cell with three other women; *(enfermer)* you almost locked me in

lock out VT SÉP (a) *(enfermer dehors)* they've gone to bed and locked me out (b) *(lock-outer)* the company has threatened to lock its employees out unless they return to work immediately

lock up 1 VI *(fermer à clé)* you go to bed, I'll lock up
2 VT SÉP (a) *(fermer à clé)* could you lock the house up?
(b) *(mettre sous clé)* lock up your valuables; *(enfermer)* the dogs are locked up every night; *(incarcérer, mettre sous les verrous)* he was locked up for fraud

long for VT INSÉP *(avoir très envie de, attendre avec impatience)* I'm longing for the holidays

look after VT INSÉP *(s'occuper de)* we've been looking after our grandchildren for the weekend; the car has been well looked after

look at VT INSÉP (a) *(regarder)* look at that gorgeous man! (b) *(examiner, regarder)* I'll need to get someone in to look at that damp patch (c) *(considérer, voir)* he doesn't look at it that way at all; *(prendre en considération)* they won't even look at the idea

look back VI (a) *(regarder derrière soi, se retourner)* he stopped and looked back (b) *(regarder en arrière, dans le temps)* looking back over the last five years, do you have any regrets?

look down on VT INSÉP *(mépriser)* he looks down on anyone who hasn't gone to university

look for VT INSÉP (a) *(chercher)* I'm really looking for something a bit bigger (b) *(attendre)* it's not the result we were looking for

look forward to VT INSÉP *(attendre avec impatience)* you must be looking forward to their visit; I look forward to hearing from you soon *(c.-à-d. dans l'attente de vous lire)*

look in VI *(passer, faire une courte visite)* I'll look in again tomorrow; they looked in for a minute

look into VT INSÉP *(étudier, examiner)* the company has promised that it will look into my complaint

look on 1 VI *(regarder)* a crowd looked on as firemen fought the blaze

2 VT INSÉP *(considérer)* they look on her as a daughter; I used to look on him with envy

look onto VT INSÉP *(donner sur)* our house looks onto open fields

look out 1 VI (a) *(regarder dehors)* she opened the window and looked out (b) *(faire attention)* look out, you're very close to the edge
2 VT SÉP *(chercher, trouver)* look out a scarf for me; she has promised to look those letters out

look out for VT INSÉP (a) *(ouvrir l'œil pour trouver, guetter)* you could always ask the garage to look out for a good second-hand car (b) *(s'occuper de)* he promised his parents he would always look out for his younger brother (c) *(faire attention à)* look out for the bones in this fish

look over VT SÉP (a) *(examiner, étudier)* look over the papers carefully before you sign them; *(observer, jauger)* I'm sure I've been invited for the weekend just so his mother can look me over (b) *(visiter)* we're looking over a flat this evening

look to VT INSÉP *(compter sur)* you must stop looking to other people to solve your problems

look up 1 VI (a) *(lever les yeux)* she looked up when I entered the room; he didn't even look up from his book (b) *(s'améliorer)* his business must be looking up if he's bought a new car
2 VT SÉP (a) *(rendre visite à, passer voir)* you must look us up again (b) *(chercher, dans un livre, etc.)* look it up in the encyclopedia

look up to VT INSÉP (a) *(lever la tête pour regarder)* he's so tall I have to look up to him (b) *(admirer, respecter)* everyone looks up to her for her courage

loosen up 1 VT SÉP (a) *(relaxer, détendre)* a nice massage will loosen you up (b) *(assouplir)* they've promised to loosen up the rules
2 VI (a) *(se détendre)* he began to loosen up once the meal was served (b) *(se montrer moins sévère)* will they loosen up on immigration? (c) *(s'échauffer)* the athletes take a couple of minutes to loosen up

lose out VI *(être perdant)* you're the one who'll lose out; he lost out on a deal

louse up VT SÉP FAM *(gâcher, foutre en l'air)* you're always lousing things up for me; he really loused that race up

M

make for VT INSÉP (a) *(se diriger vers)* he was making for the exit when they stopped him (b) *(mener à, contribuer à)* handling a complaint in that way does not make for good customer relations

make of 1 VT SÉP (a) *(comprendre quelque chose à)* can you make anything of these instructions? (b) *(accorder de l'importance à)* you're making too much of this – I've known him since we were children; strangely, the press isn't making much of this scandal
2 VT INSÉP *(penser de)* well, what do you make of that?

make off VI *(partir, se sauver)* the boys made off at a run when they saw the policeman

make off with VT INSÉP *(partir avec, prendre)* who's made off with the scissors again?; don't leave your bag lying around, someone might make off with it

make out 1 VT SÉP (a) *(remplir, faire)* make the cheque out to me (b) *(distinguer, voir)* can you make out who it is? (c) *(déchiffrer)* he can't make out his own handwriting (d) *(comprendre)* I can't make her out at all (e) *(prétendre)* don't make yourself out to be something you're not; the insurance company is making out that I was negligent
2 VI FAM *(se débrouiller)* how is she making out in her new job?

make over VT SÉP *(céder)* she has made her entire estate over to her granddaughter

make up 1 VT SÉP (a) *(maquiller)* she was heavily made up
(b) *(inventer)* she is making the whole thing up, it's not true
(c) *(préparer, faire)* the chemist made up the prescription; would you make these up into three separate packages?
(d) *(augmenter)* for your birthday, I'll make your savings up to the price of a new bike
(e) *(locution)* to make it up with someone *se réconcilier avec quelqu'un*
2 VT INSÉP (a) *(rattraper, compenser)* overtime will be necessary to make up the time we lost because of the weather

(b) *(former, composer)* the community is made up primarily of old people
(c) *(compléter)* we need two more players to make up the team
3 VI *(se réconcilier)* haven't you two made up yet?

make up for VT INSÉP *(compenser)* the pay doesn't make up for the poor conditions; *(se faire pardonner pour)* how can I make up for forgetting your birthday?; *(rattraper)* he's certainly making up for lost time now

make up to 1 VT SÉP *(locution)* I promise I'll make it up to you someday *tu peux être sûr que je te revaudrai ça (un jour)*
2 VT INSÉP *(flatter, se faire bien voir de)* they got the money by making up to the old man; *(faire des avances à)* don't try making up to me

map out VT SÉP (a) *(tracer)* have you mapped out the route yet?
(b) *(organiser, prévoir)* I've mapped out a programme

mark up VT SÉP (a) *(marquer)* the menu is marked up on the blackboard (b) *(augmenter le prix de, majorer)* most restaurants mark up wine by about three hundred percent

marry off VT SÉP *(marier, par arrangement)* she married off her daughter to an aristocrat

measure up 1 VT SÉP (a) *(mesurer)* after measuring up the timber...
(b) *(prendre la mesure de)* she measured her mother's new boyfriend up with one glance
2 VI *(être à la hauteur)* I don't think you're going to measure up to the job

meet up VI *(se rencontrer, se retrouver)* let's meet up again soon

meet with VT INSÉP (a) *(rencontrer)* the proposal has met with fierce opposition; rescue attempts have so far met with failure; the suggestion met with acclaim (b) *(avoir rendez-vous avec, rencontrer)* the senator is meeting with his advisors next week

melt away VI (a) *(fondre complètement)* the ice has melted away
(b) *(se disperser)* the onlookers melted away after the initial excitement

melt down VT SÉP *(fondre)* the gold jewellery will have been melted down by now and will be impossible to identify

mess about/around FAM 1 VT SÉP (a) *(se moquer de, faire tourner en bourrique)* first we're going, then we're not going – I wish you would stop messing me about! (b) *(changer l'ordre de, de façon gênante)* they've messed the programmes around again 2 VI BR (a) *(faire l'idiot)* stop messing about! (b) *(traîner)* would you stop messing about and get on with your work (c) *(bricoler, s'occuper)* he's been messing about in the garden all day (d) *(tripoter, jouer avec)* don't mess around with something that doesn't belong to you

mess up VT SÉP (a) *(mettre en désordre, salir)* don't mess the kitchen up (b) FAM *(gâcher, ficher en l'air)* you've really messed your marriage up; by changing his mind at the last minute he's messed things up for all of us

miss out 1 VT SÉP *(omettre, oublier)* have I missed anyone out? 2 VI *(rater son coup)* you missed out there; *(être désavantagé)* he missed out because he couldn't afford to go to college

miss out on VT INSÉP *(manquer, rater)* you missed out on a great concert

mix up VT SÉP (a) *(mélanger)* mix up all the ingredients in a large bowl (b) *(embrouiller)* don't talk to me when I'm trying to count or you'll mix me up (c) *(confondre)* he mixes her up with her mother (d) *habituellement au passif (impliquer, mêler)* everyone in that family is mixed up in something dishonest

move along 1 VT SÉP *(faire partir, faire circuler)* the police had to move the crowd along
2 VI (a) *(se pousser)* move along and let the lady sit down (b) *(partir, s'en aller)* I really ought to be moving along (c) *(passer)* moving along to my next question...

move in 1 VT SÉP (a) *(envoyer)* the government has decided to move troops in to quell the riots in the city (b) *(installer)* when are they going to move the bookcase in?
2 VI (a) *(avancer, s'approcher)* troops are now moving in on the beleaguered capital (b) *(emménager)* people are moving in next door

move on 1 VT SÉP *(faire partir, faire circuler)* the police moved us on
2 VI (a) *(poursuivre son chemin, circuler)* a policeman told me to move on (b) *(passer)* can we move on to the next item on the agenda?

move out 1 **VT SÉP** *(sortir)* you'll have to move the car out of the garage; *(faire déménager)* they're being moved out of their homes to make way for a new road; *(retirer)* the new government has promised to move its soldiers out
2 **VI** (a) *(déménager)* the people next door have decided to move out (b) *(se retirer)* troops are already moving out

move up 1 **VT SÉP** (a) *(faire monter, faire passer)* he's been moved up a class (b) *(promouvoir)* they've moved him up to be assistant manager (c) *(faire avancer)* another division has been moved up
2 **VI** (a) *(se pousser)* move up and let me sit down (b) *(avancer)* troops are moving up to the combat zone

muddle along/on **VI** *(se débrouiller)* they were muddling along quite happily before management brought in a team of consultants to look at efficiency

muddle up **VT SÉP** *(mélanger, confondre)* he's managed to muddle the dates up; *(embrouiller)* you're muddling me up

muscle in **VI FAM** *(s'imposer, arriver en force)* a lot of big companies are muscling in; I'm not going to let anyone muscle in *(c.-à-d. je ne vais laisser personne s'immiscer dans mes affaires)*; *(locution)* to muscle in on someone's territory *piétiner ou marcher sur les plates-bandes de quelqu'un*

N

narrow down 1 **VI** *(se réduire, se résumer)* the question narrows down to this...
2 **VT SÉP** *(réduire)* we've narrowed the candidates down to four

nod off **VI FAM** *(s'endormir, s'assoupir)* to my embarrassment, I nodded off in the middle of the board meeting

notch up **VT SÉP FAM** *(marquer, remporter)* she has notched up yet another win

O

open onto **VT INSÉP** *(donner sur)* the back door opens onto a paved courtyard

open out 1 VI (a) *(s'ouvrir, s'épanouir)* the roses are beginning to open out (b) *(s'étendre)* miles of wheatfields opened out before us
2 VT SÉP *(ouvrir, déplier)* it's difficult to open out your newspaper on a crowded train

open up 1 VI (a) *(ouvrir)* police, open up!; the shopkeeper was just opening up when I passed (b) *(s'ouvrir)* another couple of warm days and the roses will have opened up; new markets are opening up all the time; there are some new shops opening up on the high street (c) *(s'ouvrir, pour une personne)* he never opens up to anybody
2 VT SÉP (a) *(ouvrir)* when did you open the shop up this morning? (b) *(ouvrir, pour une affaire)* opening up a restaurant in this part of town is a risky venture (c) *(commencer à exploiter)* the rainforest is being opened up for development

opt out VI *(choisir de ne plus participer, se retirer)* I'm opting out of the committee because I have too many other commitments

own up VI *(avouer)* I know it was you I saw so you might as well own up; he rarely owns up to his mistakes

P

pack away 1 VT SÉP (a) *(ranger)* maybe we packed our winter clothes away a little too soon (b) FAM *(se goinfrer de, bouffer)* I've never seen anyone who can pack it away like you (c) FAM *(expédier, envoyer)* I packed the kids away to bed
2 VI *(se replier, se ranger)* this tent packs away easily

pack in 1 VT SÉP (a) *(entasser, faire rentrer)* you can't possibly pack anything more in (b) BR *(attirer, en grand nombre)* her latest film is packing them in (c) FAM *(arrêter)* go next door and tell them to pack that noise in (d) FAM *(laisser tomber, plaquer)* he's decided to pack his job in; are you going to pack him in or not?
2 VI BR FAM *(tomber en panne)* the lawnmower's packed in again

pack off VT SÉP FAM *(envoyer, expédier)* I'll call you back once I've packed the kids off to school

pack out VT SÉP FAM *(remplir à craquer)* the fans packed the hall out; the pub was packed out so we went somewhere else

pack up VI (a) *(faire ses bagages)* pack up, we're not staying here another night (b) BR *(dételer, arrêter le travail)* are you packing up already? (c) BR FAM *(tomber en panne)* the lawnmower has just packed up so I can't cut the grass

palm off VT SÉP FAM *(fourguer)* be careful he doesn't try to palm any rotten fruit off on you; *(refiler)* they're palming the children off on us for the weekend; *(se débarrasser de)* the last time I complained, the company palmed me off with a standard letter

pass away 1 VT SÉP *(passer)* we read to pass the time away
2 VI *(s'éteindre, mourir)* the old lady passed away in her sleep

pass by 1 VI (a) *(passer)* luckily a taxi was passing by just at that moment (b) *(passer, venir)* she passed by to say hello
(c) *(passer, pour le temps)* time is passing by, are you going to meet the deadline?
2 VT INSÉP *(passer devant)* we pass by that house every morning
3 VT SÉP *(locution)* life is passing me by *je n'ai pas l'impression de vivre*; life has passed her by *elle n'a pas vraiment vécu*

pass off 1 VI *(se dérouler)* the ceremony passed off without a hitch
2 VT SÉP *(faire passer)* he passed her off as a duchess

pass on 1 VI (a) *(s'éteindre, mourir)* when did your father pass on?
(b) *(passer)* why don't we pass on to the next item on the agenda and come back to this later?
2 VT SÉP *(transmettre, dire, pour une information)* don't pass this on, but...; *(passer, donner)* I passed the file on to him yesterday

pass out 1 VI *(s'évanouir)* I always pass out at the sight of blood
2 VT SÉP *(distribuer)* he passed out copies of the memo to the people at the meeting

pass over 1 VT SÉP *(oublier, ignorer)* they've passed me over for promotion again
2 VI *(s'éteindre, mourir)* the clairvoyant began to talk about "our loved ones who have passed over"

pass up VT SÉP (a) *(passer)* pass me up the light bulb (b) *(laisser passer)* imagine passing up a job like that!; she has had to pass up the offer

patch up VT SÉP (a) *(rafistoler, réparer)* I've managed to patch up the car so that it gets us into town at least; *(soigner rapidement)* the army doctor just patched him up and sent him back to the front
(b) *(locution)* to patch things up with someone *se réconcilier, se rabibocher avec quelqu'un*

pay back VT SÉP (a) *(rembourser)* have you paid back that money yet? (b) *(rendre la monnaie de sa pièce à)* I'll pay you back for this! *(c.-à-d. tu me le paieras !)*

pay off VT SÉP (a) *(licencier)* the company is going to pay half its labour force off at the end of the month (b) *(rembourser)* in ten years' time, we'll have paid the mortgage off (c) FAM *(acheter, corrompre)* the policeman admitted to having been paid off

pay out VT SÉP (a) *(dépenser)* he's had to pay out a lot on car repairs lately (b) *(payer)* the wages were paid out this morning (c) *(laisser filer, pour une corde)* pay out some more rope

pay up 1 VT SÉP (a) *(payer, pour une dette)* has she paid up what she owes you? (b) *(payer complètement)* my subscription is paid up
2 VI *(payer)* I've asked him twice to pay up but I'm still waiting

pick off VT SÉP (a) *(gratter)* I spilled some paint on the carpet and had to pick it off when it dried in; *(ramasser)* pick those papers off the floor (b) *(abattre)* the sniper picked them off one by one

pick on VT INSÉP (a) *(choisir)* why pick on me to answer? (b) FAM *(harceler, s'en prendre à)* stop picking on him, he's doing his best

pick out VT SÉP (a) *(choisir)* I've picked out one or two patterns you might like; he picked out the best peaches (b) *(identifier)* she picked the man out from the identity parade; *(repérer)* I picked you out immediately – you were the only one wearing a red coat (c) *(rehausser, mettre en valeur)* the panels on the door are picked out in a deeper shade of the colour used on the walls (d) *(retrouver, pour un air)* he can pick out a few tunes on the piano but that's all

pick up 1 VT SÉP (a) *(ramasser, prendre)* he picked up a book and started to read

(b) *(passer prendre, aller chercher)* will you pick up my prescription at the chemist's?; when did he say he would be picking us up?; *(faire monter)* the bus stopped to pick up passengers
(c) *(dénicher)* they picked up that wonderful old table at an auction; I picked it up cheap *(c.-à-d. je l'ai acheté bon marché)*
(d) FAM *(draguer)* he picks up a different woman every night
(e) *(attraper, pour une maladie)* she's constantly picking up colds
(f) *(prendre, pour des habitudes, un accent, etc.)* that child has picked up some very bad habits; *(apprendre)* he managed to pick up the rules of bridge quite quickly
(g) *(pincer, arrêter par la police)* he's been picked up for shoplifting
(h) *(revenir sur, reprendre)* to pick up my story,...
(i) *(relever, découvrir)* the police have picked up a trail that might lead them to the suspect
(j) *(capter)* you can pick up a lot of foreign stations with a short-wave radio
(k) *(reprendre, corriger)* please pick me up if I make any mistakes
(l) FAM *(remonter, requinquer)* a weekend away will pick her up; what would really pick me up would be a holiday in the sun
2 **VI** (a) *(s'améliorer)* the weather is picking up; *(se rétablir, aller mieux)* he's been quite ill but he's picked up in the last day or two
(b) *(continuer, reprendre)* let's pick up where we left off

pile up 1 **VI** *(s'accumuler)* the work tends to pile up at this time of year
2 **VT SÉP** *(faire un tas de, entasser)* pile the leaves up there; *(accumuler)* they're piling up the evidence against him

pin down **VT SÉP** (a) *(coincer, immobiliser)* they were pinned down by wreckage; he has his opponent pinned down on the canvas
(b) *(forcer à se décider)* I've tried to pin her down to a time
(c) *(définir)* it's just one of those feelings that are very difficult to pin down; *(identifier)* I was sure I had seen him before but I couldn't pin him down

pipe down **VI** FAM (a) *(faire moins de bruit, la mettre en sourdine)* I wish you two would pipe down while I'm trying to watch television

(b) *(se la boucler)* just pipe down about it, OK?; *(rabattre son caquet)* he finally piped down when he realized she knew more about it than he did

play about/around VI *(s'amuser, jouer)* it's about time he stopped playing around and settled down; you shouldn't play around with people's feelings

play along 1 VI *(coopérer)* if that's what you've decided then I'm quite happy to play along
2 VT SÉP *(faire marcher, manipuler)* he's just playing her along until he gets what he wants

play back VT SÉP *(repasser, pour un enregistrement)* play that last bit back

play down VT SÉP *(minimiser)* she played down the extent of her injuries; the government is trying to play down its involvement

play off VI *(jouer un match de barrage)* the two teams will play off next week

play off against VT SÉP *(monter... contre)* she's playing David off against James; you take pleasure in playing people off against each other, don't you?

play on 1 VI *(continuer à jouer)* the orchestra played on despite the bomb scare
2 VT INSÉP *(jouer sur)* the government is playing on people's fears

play out VT SÉP (a) *(jouer)* that was quite a scene they played out for our benefit (b) *habituellement au passif (être épuisé, être dépassé)* he's played out as a world-class boxer
(c) *(accompagner en musique la sortie de)* the organist played the congregation out

play up BR FAM 1 VI (a) *(faire des siennes, causer des problèmes)* the car is playing up again (b) *(faire de la lèche)* he plays up to anyone who can further his career
2 VT SÉP *(embêter, causer des problèmes à)* the baby has been playing me up all day

plough back (AM = **plow back**) VT SÉP *(réinvestir)* all the profits are ploughed back into the company

plug in VT SÉP *(brancher)* plug the iron in

plug up VT SÉP *(colmater, boucher)* that gap will have to be plugged up

plump for VT INSÉP FAM *(arrêter son choix sur, opter pour)* I see you plumped for a car instead of a holiday

point out VT SÉP (a) *(montrer)* can you point him out? (b) *(signaler, faire remarquer)* he pointed out that two people were missing

point up VT SÉP *(souligner, faire resssortir)* why point up the difficulties?; the accident points up the need for proper health and safety measures

poke about/around 1 VI (a) *(fouiller, fureter)* poke about and see what you can find; the dog was poking about in the bushes (b) *(fourrer son nez partout)* that social worker is always poking about
2 VT INSÉP *(fouiller ou fouiner dans)* I love poking about antique shops

poke out 1 VI *(dépasser)* the label on your coat is poking out
2 VT SÉP (a) *(sortir)* she opened the window and poked her head out (b) *(déloger)* careful or you'll poke my eye out! *(c.-à-d. fais attention, ou tu vas me crever un œil !)*

polish off VT SÉP FAM (a) *(finir, avaler)* the two of them polished that whole bowl of pasta off between them! (b) *(écraser)* he polished his opponent off in three straight sets

polish up VT SÉP (a) *(polir, astiquer)* the silver needs to be polished up (b) *(améliorer)* I'm going to evening classes to polish up my Spanish

pop off VI FAM (a) *(partir)* they're popping off home to pick up their kids (b) *(clamser, claquer)* more people pop off in the winter than at any other time of year

pop in VI FAM *(passer, faire une petite visite)* he popped in to say hello

pop out VI FAM *(sortir un instant)* I only popped out for five minutes; *(faire un saut)* I'll pop out to the tobacconist's

pop up VI FAM *(surgir)* a head popped up through the trap door; this question has popped up again *(c.-à-d. est revenue sur le tapis)*

pore over VT INSÉP *(être plongé dans)* he spends all his time poring over old manuscripts

pour out 1 VI *(sortir en masse)* smoke was pouring out of the windows; *(sortir à flots, jaillir)* once she had composed herself, the words just poured out
2 VT SÉP (a) *(servir)* will I pour out the tea?; *(verser)* pour some sugar out into a bowl (b) *(raconter, déballer)* I hope you didn't mind me pouring out my troubles like that

print out VT SÉP *(imprimer)* the text is edited on screen and then printed out to be sent back to the author

prop up VT SÉP *(consolider)* they've had to prop the castle walls up; *(soutenir)* the regime is being propped up by the military; *(appuyer)* he propped himself up against the gate; FAM he's always propping up the bar *(c.-à-d. c'est un vrai pilier de bar)*

pull away 1 VT SÉP *(retirer)* she pulled her hand away; *(arracher)* she pulled the book away from him; *(éloigner)* he pulled me away from the window
2 VI (a) *(démarrer, s'ébranler)* the train slowly pulled away (b) *(s'écarter)* the dog pulled away when I tried to pat it (c) *(se détacher, prendre de l'avance, dans une course)* she's beginning to pull away

pull down VT SÉP (a) *(baisser)* pull the blind down (b) *(démolir, abattre)* how many more buildings are they going to pull down? (c) AM FAM *(se faire, gagner, pour de l'argent)* considering his qualifications, he doesn't pull down much of a salary

pull in 1 VT SÉP (a) *(attirer)* the play is really pulling people in (b) *(arrêter, embarquer)* the police pulled him in for questioning
2 VI (a) *(se garer, s'arrêter)* pull in here; we'll pull in to the next garage we see (b) *(arriver, pour un train ou un bus)* the coach pulled in two hours late

pull off VT SÉP (a) *(enlever, retirer)* help me pull the dirty sheets off the bed; he pulled off his clothes (b) *(réussir)* I never thought we would pull it off; he has pulled off a remarkable achievement

pull out 1 VT SÉP (a) *(sortir, en tirant)* my car's stuck in the mud, you'll have to pull me out; *(arracher)* he's having a tooth pulled out tomorrow (b) *(retirer)* the president has promised that all troops will be pulled out by the end of the year
2 VI (a) *(déboîter)* look in your mirror before you pull out (b) *(se retirer)* troops have begun to pull out

pull over 1 **VT SÉP** (a) *(tirer, amener)* he pulled the chair over to the window (b) *(faire tomber)* be careful or you'll pull the filing cabinet over on top of you
2 **VI** *(se mettre sur le côté, s'arrêter)* the policeman asked us to pull over; *(se rabattre)* she's pulling over to let the other cars past

pull through 1 **VT SÉP** *(faire tenir, permettre de tenir le coup)* he says it was his faith that pulled him through
2 **VI** *(guérir)* I think we can confidently say that she will pull through

pull together 1 **VT SÉP** (a) *(préparer)* I've pulled together a few suggestions (b) *(locution)* pull yourself together! *ressaisis-toi !*
2 **VI** *(concentrer ses efforts, coopérer)* we must pull together on this

pull up 1 **VT SÉP** (a) *(approcher, prendre)* he pulled up a chair and joined us; *(remonter, lever)* pull the blind up (b) *(arrêter, en voiture)* he was pulled up by the police (c) *(réprimander)* she pulled him up about his bad language
2 **VI** (a) *(s'arrêter)* why are you pulling up?; the horse pulled up lame (b) *(remonter, revenir, dans une course)* he is beginning to pull up, but I think he's left it too late

push about **VT SÉP** *(malmener)* he didn't hit her but he was pushing her about

push ahead **VI** (a) *(avancer, progresser)* research on this is pushing ahead in various countries (b) *(persévérer, continuer, malgré les difficultés)* I think we should push ahead nonetheless

push along 1 **VT SÉP** *(pousser)* I saw her pushing a pram along
2 **VI FAM** *(filer, se sauver)* I suppose I should be pushing along soon

push around **VT SÉP FAM** *(marcher sur les pieds de)* I'm not going to let him push us around like this

push for **VT INSÉP** *(demander, faire pression pour obtenir)* the company is pushing for more government funding

push off 1 **VT SÉP** (a) *(faire tomber)* they pushed me off the ladder (b) *(pousser, soulever)* push the lid off
2 **VI FAM** (a) *(filer, mettre les bouts)* everyone's pushing off at five o'clock; *(dégager)* I wish you would push off and let me

finish what I'm doing **(b)** *(pousser au large, déborder)* we pushed off in the early hours of the morning

push on 1 **VI** *(continuer)* we decided to push on
2 **VT SÉP** **(a)** *(forcer, pour mettre)* you need to push it on quite firmly **(b)** *(encourager)* both runners are being pushed on by the crowd

push through 1 **VT INSÉP** *(se frayer un chemin à travers)* we'll have to push through the crowd
2 **VT SÉP** *(imposer, réussir à faire voter ou passer)* the government is pushing this bill through

push up **VT SÉP** **(a)** *(remonter, relever)* you have to push up the handle **(b)** *(faire monter)* excessive wage increases are pushing up inflation

put about **VT SÉP** *(faire circuler, faire courir)* who put that rumour about?; it's being put about that she's pregnant *(c.-à-d. le bruit court que...)*

put across **VT SÉP** *(faire passer, pour des idées)* he didn't put that across very well; a politician who certainly knows how to put herself across *(c.-à-d. s'imposer)*

put away **VT SÉP** **(a)** *(ranger, remettre à sa place)* put your wallet away, I'm paying for this; *(garer)* could someone put the car away for the night? **(b)** *(économiser, mettre de côté)* she puts something away every month for her holidays **(c)** **FAM** *(bouffer, pour de la nourriture, descendre, pour de l'alcool)* you should see how much junk food he can put away!; *(picoler)* he's down at the pub every night putting it away **(d)** **FAM** *(enfermer, dans une prison, etc.)* that maniac should be put away somewhere

put back **VT SÉP** **(a)** *(remettre)* put that back where you found it **(b)** *(repousser, remettre, à une autre date, etc.)* the meeting's been put back till next month **(c)** *(retarder, pour une montre, une horloge, etc.)* isn't this the week we put the clocks back?

put down **VT SÉP** **(a)** *(poser)* put that down before you drop it
(b) *(déposer, laisser)* if you put me down at the next corner, I can walk the rest of the way
(c) *(réprimer)* the revolt was put down by armed police
(d) *(dire du mal de, rabaisser)* he's always putting her down; why do you keep putting yourself down?

(e) *(faire piquer, pour un animal)* the cat's in a great deal of pain, I think we should have her put down
(f) *(verser)* how much do you have to put down as a deposit?
(g) *(écrire)* have you put all the details down?
(h) *(faire atterrir, poser)* the pilot had to put the plane down in a field

put down to VT SÉP *(mettre sur le compte de)* she puts it down to laziness

put forward VT SÉP (a) *(avancer, proposer)* somebody put forward the idea that...; they've put him forward for a knighthood
(b) *(avancer, à une autre date, etc.)* the meeting has been put forward to noon today (c) *(avancer, pour une montre, une horloge, etc.)* did you put your watch forward?

put in 1 VT SÉP (a) *(mettre, dans une valise, armoire, etc.)* have you put everything in? (b) *(installer)* we're having cable TV put in
(c) *(travailler, faire)* I put in a lot of overtime last month; don't you think you should put in a bit of piano practice? (d) *(présenter, inscrire)* we're putting him in for the 500 and 1000 metres
2 VI *(poser sa candidature)* has he put in for that job we saw advertised?

put off VT SÉP (a) *(déposer, laisser)* could you put me off at the corner?; *(faire descendre)* the bus conductor put the boys off because of their behaviour
(b) *(repousser, remettre)* let's put lunch off to another time
(c) *(décommander, annuler un rendez-vous avec)* you can't keep putting him off like this – just tell him you don't want to go out with him
(d) *(éteindre)* put the TV off
(e) *(dégoûter)* their stories have put me off foreign travel; that programme on slaughterhouses put him off eating meat for a while
(f) *(déranger, gêner)* you would think that all those people standing round watching would put her off

put on VT SÉP (a) *(mettre, pour un vêtement, etc.)* put your coat on; she put on her glasses
(b) *(prendre, affecter)* she puts on a posh accent sometimes; the boss can put on a show of being fierce *(c.-à-d. faire semblant de)*; FAM don't worry, he's just putting it on *(c.-à-d. ne t'inquiète pas, c'est du cinéma)*

(c) *(jouer, monter)* they're not putting Hamlet on again, are they?; *(passer)* why can't they put on something decent on TV for a change?
(d) *(prendre, pour du poids, etc.)* he's put on a few inches round the waist
(e) *(ajouter)* the tax increase will put another 10p on a gallon of petrol
(f) *(allumer)* put the radio on

put onto VT SÉP *(indiquer à)* I can put you onto a good lawyer; *(mettre sur la piste de, amener à soupçonner)* what put the police onto him as the culprit?

put out VT SÉP (a) *(mettre dehors, sortir)* have you put the dustbin out?
(b) *(préparer, sortir)* remember to put the side plates out as well
(c) *(tendre)* she put her hand out
(d) *(sortir, publier)* we'll be putting out a new edition very soon
(e) *(éteindre)* put the light out
(f) *(endormir, pour un malade)* the drug will put you out very quickly
(g) *(énerver)* everyone was put out by the two-hour delay
(h) *(déranger)* would one more guest put you out?; I don't want to put anyone out
(i) *(se démettre)* don't lift that table or you'll put your back out again

put through VT SÉP (a) *(faire accepter, faire passer)* a bill has been put through Parliament (b) *(passer à, pour une communication téléphonique)* will you put me through to the book department, please? (c) *(causer à)* you've put your mother through a great deal of worry with your behaviour

put up VT SÉP (a) *(lever)* put up your hand if you know the answer
(b) *(construire, ériger)* a new block of flats is being put up just behind their house
(c) *(accrocher au mur)* I want to put up a few more pictures in this room
(d) *(augmenter)* car manufacturers are putting their prices up again
(e) *(héberger)* could you put us up while we're in town?
(f) *(mettre)* a lot of people have put their houses up for sale
(g) *(présenter)* we are not putting up any candidates
(h) *(opposer)* they put up a lot of resistance; she put up a

good fight but had to concede defeat in the end *(c.-à-d. elle s'est bien défendue mais...)*

put up with VT INSÉP *(tolérer, supporter)* why do you put up with that kind of behaviour?; it's a lot to have to put up with

Q

quieten down 1 VI (a) *(se calmer)* if you lot don't quieten down I'm going to get very cross; business always quietens down after Christmas (b) *(s'assagir)* he's quietened down a lot since he got married
2 VT SÉP *(calmer, faire taire)* it took me ages to quieten the class down; the nurse tried to quieten the child down but he kept crying for his mother

R

rain off (AM = rain out) VT SÉP *toujours au passif (annuler à cause de la pluie)* the match was rained off

rattle through VT INSÉP (a) *(rouler en faisant un bruit de ferraille)* the two old cars rattled through the streets (b) *(expédier)* she tends to rattle through her work; the speaker rattled through his talk

read out VT SÉP *(lire à haute voix)* he read out the names of the injured

read up on VT INSÉP *(étudier)* the play might have meant more to you if you'd read up a bit on the events it depicted

rein in 1 VT SÉP (a) *(ramener au pas)* the girl reined her pony in and turned back towards the stables (b) *(maîtriser, réfréner)* he tried very hard to rein in his anger; *(restreindre, diminuer)* the council wants to rein in its spending on sports facilities
2 VI *(ralentir, l'allure d'un cheval)* they reined in so they could talk

rest up VI *(se reposer)* the doctor has told him to rest up

ring back BR 1 VT SÉP *(rappeler, au téléphone)* he's not in but I'll ask him to ring you back

2 **VI** *(rappeler, au téléphone)* could you ring back in half an hour?

ring in **VI** **BR** *(téléphoner)* you ought to have rung in to say you were ill and couldn't come to work

ring off **VI** **BR** *(raccrocher)* I must ring off now, there's someone at the door

ring out **VI** *(résonner, retentir)* her voice rang out; *(sonner)* the church bells were ringing out

ring up **BR** 1 **VT SÉP** *(téléphoner à)* why not ring her up and ask?
2 **VI** *(téléphoner)* I'll ring up and find out

rip off **VT SÉP** (a) *(arracher)* as soon as they got their hands on the presents, the children ripped the paper off (b) **FAM** *(arnaquer)* let's choose another restaurant – I was ripped off the last time I was at this one (c) **FAM** *(braquer)* they ripped off a bank; *(piquer)* he ripped off our idea

rip up **VT SÉP** *(déchirer en petits morceaux)* just rip his letter up and forget the whole business

root for **VT INSÉP** *(soutenir, encourager)* which side are you rooting for?; the candidate I root for invariably loses

rough out **VT SÉP BR** *(ébaucher)* could you rough out a publicity campaign?

rough up **VT SÉP** (a) *(ébouriffer)* don't rough up my hair (b) **FAM** *(tabasser)* he was roughed up by some thugs; *(malmener)* they roughed her up a bit but she's all right

round down **VT SÉP** *(arrondir, au chiffre inférieur)* the price will be rounded down

round off **VT SÉP** (a) *(arrondir)* round off the edges (b) *(clore, terminer)* we rounded the meal off with coffee and liqueurs; she rounded off her presentation with a joke

round on **VT INSÉP** *(s'en prendre à, attaquer)* he rounded on his tormentors

round up **VT SÉP** (a) *(rassembler)* about this time of year the cattle are rounded up; round everyone up for the meeting, will you?
(b) *(arrondir, au chiffre supérieur)* just round the bill up to £50

rub down VT SÉP *(bouchonner)* the groom will rub your horse down; *(sécher)* he rubbed himself down with the towel

rub in VT SÉP (a) *(faire pénétrer, en frottant ou en massant)* rub the cream in well (b) FAM *(insister sur, rappeler)* I know I was wrong, don't keep rubbing it in!

rub off 1 VT SÉP *(enlever, en frottant)* rub those dirty marks off the wall; *(effacer)* the teacher rubbed the equations off the blackboard
2 VI (a) *(s'en aller, partir, en frottant)* the stain won't rub off
(b) FIG *(déteindre)* I hope his bad behaviour doesn't rub off on you

rub out VT SÉP (a) *(enlever, en frottant)* try rubbing the stain out with a damp cloth (b) *(effacer, gommer)* don't rub out your calculations (c) AM FAM *(liquider, descendre)* one of the key witnesses to the shooting was rubbed out by a gang member

run about/around 1 VT INSÉP *(courir)* I spent all day running about the shops looking for a birthday present
2 VI *(courir partout)* the children were running about on the beach; I've been running about all day looking for you! *(c.-à-d. j'ai passé ma journée à te chercher partout!)*

run across VT INSÉP *(rencontrer par hasard, tomber sur)* if you should run across John give him my regards; I've run across a word I don't know

run away with VT INSÉP (a) *(partir avec, s'enfuir avec)* his daughter has run away with a married man; *(se sauver avec)* one of his employees has run away with the week's takings
(b) *(submerger, envahir pour un sentiment, l'imagination, etc.)* she tends to let her imagination run away with her *(c.-à-d. elle a tendance à se laisser emporter par son imagination)*
(c) *(locution)* don't go running away with the idea that it will be easy *n'allez pas croire que ce sera facile*
(d) *(remporter)* they ran away with nearly all the medals

run back 1 VI (a) *(revenir en courant)* I ran back to the car (b) *(revenir, vers son/sa conjoint(e))* he'll come running back once he realizes what he's missing
2 VT SÉP *(raccompagner, ramener en voiture)* don't worry about the last bus, I'll run you back

run down 1 VI (a) *(descendre, en courant)* run down and see who's at the door

(b) *(s'essouffler)* the government is accused of letting the industry run down; *(s'arrêter, pour une horloge, etc.)* don't wind up the clock until it has completely run down; *(se décharger)* you've let the battery run down

2 **VT SÉP** **(a)** *(renverser, par un véhicule)* she was run down by a bus

(b) *(dire du mal de, rabaisser)* you shouldn't run everyone down like that

(c) *(décharger)* remember to switch off the lights or they'll run the battery down; *(baisser la production de)* the factory is being deliberately run down

(d) *(retrouver après de longues recherches, dénicher)* the police finally ran him down in Brighton

run in 1 **VI** *(entrer en courant)* she came running in to tell us

2 **VT SÉP** **(a)** **BR** *(roder)* it will be another couple of weeks before we've run the new machine in **(b)** **FAM** *(arrêter, pincer)* the police ran him in for drunk driving

run into **VT INSÉP** **(a)** *(rentrer dans)* he ran into an old lady as he raced for his train **(b)** *(tomber sur, rencontrer par hasard)* guess who I ran into last week! **(c)** *(s'élever à)* the cost will run into millions

run off 1 **VI** *(partir en courant)* he ran off when he saw me coming; *(partir, s'enfuir)* he's run off with the woman next door

2 **VT SÉP** **(a)** *(tirer, photocopier)* will you run off six copies of this? **(b)** *(écrire rapidement, pondre)* she runs these magazine articles off in her spare time **(c)** *(perdre en courant)* he's a bit overweight and wants to run off a few pounds

run out 1 **VI** **(a)** *(s'épuiser, venir à manquer)* money is running out; your time is running out *(c.-à-d. vous n'avez plus beaucoup de temps)* **(b)** *(expirer, venir à expiration)* my passport is going to run out soon

2 **VT SÉP** *(éliminer, au cricket)* he was run out for ten

run out of **VT INSÉP** *(être à bout de)* I have run out of patience with you; *(manquer de, être à court de)* we're running out of butter; they ran out of petrol *(c.-à-d. ils sont tombés en panne d'essence)*

run over 1 **VI** **(a)** *(faire un saut)* I won't be a minute, I'm just running over to the shops **(b)** *(dépasser le temps imparti ou le temps d'antenne)* the live broadcast of the football match ran over into the next programme **(c)** *(déborder)* the sink is running over

2 **VT INSÉP** *(examiner rapidement)* the doctor will want to run over your case history; *(récapituler)* let's run over the arrangements one last time
3 **VT SÉP** (a) *(amener en voiture)* I'm running Mum over to her sister's, do you want to come? (b) *(renverser en voiture)* he ran an old lady over

run through 1 **VT INSÉP** (a) *(consommer)* we ran through several cases of wine over the Christmas holidays (b) *(revoir, répéter)* would you like me to run through your speech with you?
2 **VT SÉP** *(transpercer d'un coup d'épée)* the coachman ran the highwayman through

run up 1 **VI** (a) *(monter, en courant)* run up and fetch my purse for me (b) *(accourir)* people ran up to see if they could help
2 **VT SÉP** (a) *(coudre rapidement ou à la hâte)* the dressmaker said she could run the suit up for me in a couple of days (b) *(laisser s'accumuler)* you've run up a lot of bills this month (c) *(hisser, pour un drapeau)* they run the flag up on special occasions

rush at **VI** *(se jeter sur)* he rushed at the burglar

rush through **VT SÉP** (a) *(envoyer d'urgence)* the necessary equipment has been rushed through to the rescue workers (b) *(exécuter d'urgence)* could you rush my order through? (c) *(faire passer à toute allure)* they rushed us through Customs; *(faire dépêcher pour finir)* you rushed me through lunch and now you're rushing me through dinner – what's the hurry?

rustle up **VT SÉP FAM** *(préparer ou faire en vitesse, pour un plat ou une boisson)* could you rustle up a meal for me?

S

save up 1 **VI** *(faire des économies)* if you want a new motorbike you'll have to start saving up, won't you?
2 **VT SÉP** (a) *(économiser)* you should save up part of your pocket money for Christmas presents (b) *(garder, mettre de côté)* I always save up the money-off coupons in all the magazines

score off 1 **VT SÉP** *(rayer, barrer)* score his name off the guest list

2 **VT INSÉP** *(prendre l'avantage sur, marquer un point sur, dans un débat)* the speaker scored off the government when he reminded them of their campaign promises

score out **VT SÉP** **BR** *(rayer, barrer)* score any mistakes out neatly

scrape along **VI** *(se débrouiller, financièrement)* she's scraping along until her next pay cheque

scrape by **VI** *(se débrouiller, financièrement)* he's just been scraping by since he lost his job *(c.-à-d. il arrive tout juste à joindre les deux bouts...)*

scrape through 1 **VT INSÉP** *(passer de justesse, remporter de justesse)* the government will probably just scrape through the next election
2 **VI** *(passer de justesse, réussir de justesse)* I don't mind scraping by, as long as I pass the exam

scrape together/up **VT SÉP** *(réunir ou trouver, avec beaucoup de difficulté)* I'll scrape the money together somehow

scream out 1 **VI** *(pousser un grand cri)* the pain made him scream out
2 **VT SÉP** *(crier)* the sergeant major screamed out his orders

screw up **VT SÉP** **(a)** *(visser)* screw it up tightly **(b)** *(froisser, chiffonner)* she screwed the letter up and threw it in the bin **(c)** **BR** *(plisser)* she screwed up her eyes **(d)** **FAM** *(bousiller, faire foirer)* this rush job has screwed up my plans for the weekend; you screwed the whole thing up – next time let me do the talking **(e)** **FAM** *(rendre dingue, mettre dans tous ses états)* he claims it was his parents that screwed him up; she's all screwed up over that affair with the married man

see about **VT INSÉP** **(a)** *(s'occuper de)* you'll have to see about those cracks in the ceiling **(b)** *(considérer, voir)* I'll see about it; **FAM** so they're going to win, are they? well, we'll see about that

see across **VT SÉP** *(faire traverser)* she saw me across the road

see in 1 **VI** *(voir à l'intérieur)* they always keep the curtains drawn so people can't see in
2 **VT SÉP** *(faire entrer)* see the guests in, could you, please?

see off **VT SÉP** *(dire au revoir à, à la gare, à l'aéroport)* who's coming to see you off?

see out 1 **VI** *(voir dehors)* another passenger changed seats with the little boy so he could see out
2 **VT SÉP** (a) *(raccompagner à la porte)* my husband will see you out, doctor (b) *(tenir jusqu'à la fin de, passer)* we've got enough food to see the week out

see over/round **VT INSÉP** *(visiter)* would you like to see round our new house?

see through 1 **VT INSÉP** *(ne pas se laisser duper ou tromper par)* why do you persist with these stories when everyone can see through them?
2 **VT SÉP** *(aider à traverser, pour une période difficile)* friends and neighbours are seeing them through this bad time; *(suffire à... pour)* a couple of hundred gallons of oil should see us through the winter

see to **VT INSÉP** *(s'occuper de)* let your husband see to the baby – you relax for a bit; *(réparer)* you should get the brakes seen to

see up **VT SÉP** *(accompagner, à un étage supérieur)* do you know where his room is or do you want me to see you up?

seize up **VI** (a) *(se gripper, se bloquer)* if you don't put some oil in soon the engine will seize up (b) *(s'ankyloser)* my knee always seizes up in the cold weather

seize (up)on **VT INSÉP** *(sauter sur, saisir, pour une occasion, une idée, etc.)* it seemed like an excellent idea and we seized on it immediately *(c.-à-d. nous l'avons tout de suite adoptée)*

sell off **VT SÉP** *(solder, liquider)* the shoe shop is closing down soon and has started to sell off its stock

sell out 1 **VT SÉP** (a) *habituellement au passif (ne plus avoir en stock)* how can a supermarket be sold out of butter?; the tickets are sold out *(c.-à-d. tous les billets ont été vendus)* (b) *(trahir)* the rebel leaders were accused of selling out their supporters
2 **VI** (a) *(liquider son stock)* all of the shops I tried had sold out (b) *(vendre son affaire)* they are selling out since they want to retire (c) *(renier ses principes)* we will negotiate but we will never sell out

sell up 1 **VT SÉP** *habituellement au passif (forcer à vendre)* something has to be done to prevent farmers being sold up and losing their livelihood

2 **VI** *(vendre son affaire)* since she can no longer run the business on her own, she has decided to sell up

send away **VT SÉP** *(envoyer, faire partir)* he's too young to be sent away to school *(c.-à-d. il est trop jeune pour être envoyé en internat)*

send away for **VT INSÉP** *(se faire envoyer, demander par correspondance)* send away for your free gift now; you should send away for an application form

send down **VT SÉP** (a) *(faire descendre)* the tenants upstairs sent their daughter down with the rent money (b) *(faire baisser)* the rumours have sent share prices down (c) **BR FAM** *(envoyer en prison)* the judge sent her down for two years (d) **BR** *(expulser de l'université)* all of the students involved in the incident were sent down for a term

send for **VT INSÉP** *(appeler, faire venir)* I think we should send for the doctor

send in **VT SÉP** (a) *(faire entrer)* send Mr Martin in as soon as he arrives, please (b) *(envoyer)* a lot of viewers have sent in comments on the programme we aired last week

send off **VT SÉP** (a) *(envoyer, poster)* have you sent that letter off yet? (b) *(expulser, pour un joueur)* he was sent off for spitting at the referee

send on **VT SÉP** (a) *(faire suivre)* would you send on any letters that come for me?; *(expédier, par avance)* we've decided to send our luggage on so we don't have as much to carry (b) *(faire entrer sur le terrain)* the coach decided to send him on

send out **VT SÉP** (a) *(envoyer, poster)* those invitations should have been sent out a week ago (b) *(faire sortir, renvoyer)* the teacher sent him out of the classroom for talking; *(envoyer dehors)* send the children out to play (c) *(émettre)* the satellite has stopped sending out signals

send out for 1 **VT INSÉP** *(envoyer quelqu'un chercher, se faire apporter)* do you want to send out for a sandwich?
2 **VT SÉP** *(envoyer chercher)* send him out for coffee for everyone

send up **VT SÉP** (a) *(lancer, dans le ciel)* the crew sent up a distress rocket (b) *(faire monter)* news of the takeover bid sent the company's share prices up (c) **BR** *(parodier)* politicians are very easy to send up; *(se moquer de)* don't you know when you're being sent up? (d) AM FAM *(envoyer en taule, coffrer)* he was sent up for armed robbery

serve out VT SÉP (a) *(distribuer, servir)* you can start serving out the soup while I finish preparing the main course (b) *(finir)* my father had only just served out his apprenticeship when the war started; *(purger)* he served out a prison sentence

set about VT INSÉP (a) *(se mettre à, pour une corvée)* she set about the washing up (b) *(commencer à)* be sure to take expert advice before you set about rewiring the house (c) *(s'en prendre à, physiquement ou verbalement)* the old lady set about the boys with her stick; Mum set about me for leaving my room in such a mess

set against VT SÉP (a) *(monter contre)* something must have set him against the idea; it was her friends who set her against me (b) *(déduire)* some expenses can be set against taxes (c) *(étudier à la lumière de)* we must set the government's promises against its performance in the past

set apart VT SÉP *(distinguer)* what sets her apart from all the other children in my class is her confidence

set aside VT SÉP (a) *(laisser, mettre de côté)* could you set aside what you're working on and do this instead?; let's set that particular aspect of the issue aside for a moment; I've decided to set aside some money every week (b) *(annuler)* the Supreme Court has set aside the decision

set back VT SÉP (a) *(mettre en retrait)* the cottage is set back quite a bit from the road (b) *(retarder)* the strike has set the company back at least a month in its deliveries (c) FAM *(coûter)* that new car must have set him back a bit; will it set me back more than a thousand?

set down VT SÉP (a) *(poser)* you can set those cases down in the hall (b) BR *(laisser descendre, déposer)* the bus stopped to set down one or two passengers (c) *(fixer, pour des lois)* permissible levels of pollution are set down in the regulations (d) *(noter)* the policeman set down the details in his notebook

set forth VT SÉP *(présenter, exposer)* would you like to set forth your suggestions to the committee?; this document sets forth a detailed description of the service provided

set in VI *(se déclarer)* the doctors are worried that gangrene might set in; *(arriver)* winter seems to be setting in early this year

set off 1 VT SÉP (a) *(faire exploser)* terrorists have set off yet another bomb in a crowded street (b) *(déclencher, provoquer)* what set the argument off? (c) *(faire rire, pleurer, etc.)* that last joke of his set us all off; if you say any more you'll only set her off again; he is so allergic to pollen that even a vase of flowers sets him off (d) *(mettre en valeur, réhausser)* those velvet curtains really set the room off (e) *(déduire)* can I set these expenses off against my tax liability?
2 VI *(partir, se mettre en route)* we'll have to set off at dawn

set on 1 VT SÉP *(lâcher sur, pour une attaque)* if you don't get off my land immediately, I'll set the dogs on you; *(mettre aux trousses de)* they set the police on his trail
2 VT INSÉP *(attaquer)* travellers were often set on by highwaymen

set out 1 VT SÉP (a) *(étaler, présenter)* a mouthwatering display of desserts was set out on a side table (b) *(indiquer, présenter)* this document sets out the steps that must be taken
2 VI (a) *(partir, se mettre en route)* they set out late last night (b) *(commencer)* I didn't realize when I set out just how long the job was going to take me (c) *(locution)* to set out to do something *vouloir faire quelque chose*

set to 1 VI *(commencer à travailler, s'y mettre)* isn't it about time that we set to and cleaned out the garage?
2 VT INSÉP *(commencer)* when are the builders going to set to work?

set up 1 VI *(s'établir, s'installer)* they've decided to set up in business for themselves; she's setting up as a hairdresser
2 VT SÉP (a) *(installer, monter)* marquees will be set up on the front lawn (b) *(organiser, prendre, pour un rendez-vous, etc.)* I'd like to set up an appointment with a careers adviser; *(constituer)* a task force will be set up to investigate the matter (c) *(installer)* he's set her up in a flat of her own (d) FAM *(monter un coup contre)* there's no point in claiming you were set up – no one will believe you

settle down 1 VI (a) *(s'installer)* I had just settled down with a book when the phone rang (b) *(se calmer)* settle down, please, children (c) *(se concentrer sur, se mettre à)* he must settle

down to his homework **(d)** *(se ranger)* when are you going to settle down and get married?
2 **VT SÉP** **(a)** *(installer)* just let me settle the baby down for the night **(b)** *(calmer)* I couldn't settle my class down at all today

settle for **VT INSÉP** *(se contenter de, accepter)* we haven't got any drink at all, I'm afraid – will you settle for a cup of coffee?; is that a fixed price for the house or would the seller settle for less?

settle in 1 **VI** *(s'installer)* once we're settled in, we'll invite you round; *(s'habituer, s'adapter)* he'll soon settle in at the job
2 **VT SÉP** *(aider qn à trouver ses marques)* I'm just going to settle the new secretary in and then I'm having a holiday

settle on **VT INSÉP** *(décider de, après réflexion)* have you settled on a date for the wedding yet?

settle up **VI** **(a)** *(régler la note)* can I leave you to settle up? **(b)** *(régler ses comptes)* he said he would settle up with us later

shake off **VT SÉP** **(a)** *(enlever en secouant, secouer)* shake the snow off your coat before you come in **(b)** *(se débarrasser de, pour une maladie, une habitude, etc.)* I can't seem to shake this cold off; *(échapper à)* she shook the detective off by going into the ladies and leaving by a back door

shake up **VT SÉP** **(a)** *(agiter)* shake it up a bit, all the solids are at the bottom; don't shake the champagne bottle up **(b)** *(secouer, pour un coussin, etc.)* let me shake your pillows up for you **(c)** *(secouer, bouleverser)* the news of the accident shook her up; I was badly shaken up by my narrow escape **(d)** **FAM** *(remanier)* this committee needs shaking up a bit; *(secouer les puces à, secouer)* he needs shaking up

shell out **VT SÉP FAM** *(payer, casquer)* I'm not going to shell out any more on that motorbike of his; how much do we each have to shell out for petrol?

shoot down **VT SÉP** **(a)** *(abattre, pour une personne, un avion, etc.)* he was shot down over France; the guerrillas claim to have shot down three planes in the last week **(b)** **FAM** *(démolir, pour un argument, etc.)* she shot his argument down; if he doesn't like your proposal he'll shoot it down

shoot out 1 **VI** *(jaillir)* the water shot out of the hose

2 **VT SÉP** *(lancer, tendre d'un geste vif)* she shot out her hand and grabbed him before he could fall

shoot up 1 **VI** (a) *(monter en flèche)* house prices have shot up in the last year; *(se lever)* hands were shooting up all over the room to ask questions (b) *(se shooter, se piquer)* a government poster showing kids shooting up
2 **VT SÉP** *(détruire par les bombardements)* the runways are so badly shot up that they are unusable

shop around **VI** *(comparer les prix des produits)* it pays to shop around

shout down **VT SÉP** *(rejeter avec violence)* union members shouted down management's proposal; *(empêcher de parler en criant)* don't shout her down – listen to what she has to say

show off 1 **VI** *(crâner, frimer)* he was flexing his muscles and generally showing off
2 **VT SÉP** (a) *(faire admirer)* I think I'll go for a drive round town and show off the new car (b) *(mettre en valeur)* wearing white always shows off a tan

show up 1 **VI** (a) *(ressortir, se voir)* the dirt really shows up on a pale carpet (b) **FAM** *(se pointer)* he showed up wearing a new suit; she's always showing up late
2 **VT SÉP** (a) *(rendre manifeste, faire apparaître)* the loss of export markets shows up the company's failure to modernize
(b) *(faire honte à)* I don't want you showing me up in front of people, so don't tell any of your crude jokes
(c) *(accompagner, en haut)* the porter will show you up to your room

shrug off **VT SÉP** *(ignorer, ne pas tenir compte de)* he shrugs off all criticism

shut away **VT SÉP** *(enfermer, mettre à l'écart)* he's been shut away in prison for the last year; ever since her husband's death, she has shut herself away

shut down **VT SÉP & VI** = **close down**

shut in **VT SÉP** *(enfermer)* shut the dog in

shut off 1 **VT SÉP** (a) *(éteindre, couper)* the electricity had to be shut off (b) *(isoler)* don't they feel shut off living in the depths of the countryside?

2 **VI** *(s'arrêter)* the kettle shuts off automatically when the water is boiling

shut out **VT SÉP** (a) *(enfermer dehors)* the door's locked, they've shut us out; I've forgotten my key and now I'm shut out
(b) *(empêcher d'entrer)* he drew the curtains to shut out the light; *(cacher)* we're going to plant some trees to shut out the view of the railway line (c) **FIG** *(exclure)* people want to help – why do you insist on shutting them out?

shut up 1 **VT SÉP** (a) *(enfermer)* the cat got accidentally shut up in the airing cupboard (b) *(fermer)* they're away shutting up their cottage for the winter (c) **FAM** *(faire taire)* shut those kids up, I'm trying to concentrate
2 **VI FAM** *(la boucler, la fermer)* don't tell me to shut up!; please can you shut up for five minutes?

shy away **VI** *(se reculer nerveusement)* she shied away when he tried to put his arm around her

shy away from **VT INSÉP** *(éviter (de), par peur)* he has shied away from driving ever since the accident

sift out **VT SÉP** (a) *(enlever, en passant au tamis)* sift out any impurities (b) *(éliminer)* we have sifted out the most obviously unsuitable candidates

sign away **VT SÉP** *(signer l'abandon de)* read the small print to be sure you're not signing away any of your rights

sign for **VT INSÉP** *(signer, pour un reçu)* there's a registered letter for you – will you sign for it, please?

sign in 1 **VI** *(signer en arrivant, signer le registre d'entrée)* it's a rule of the club that all visitors must sign in
2 **VT SÉP** *(faire entrer, en signant pour)* I'm a member, so I can sign you in

sign off **VI** (a) *(terminer l'émission)* they usually sign off for the day at midnight; he always signs off with that catchphrase (b) *(phrase utilisée en fin de lettre : je vous quitte)* I think I'll sign off now and go to bed

sign on **VI BR** *(s'inscrire au chômage, pointer au chômage)* how long do you have to be out of work before you can sign on?; I have to sign on every second Monday

sign up 1 VT SÉP *(embaucher, engager)* the committee wants to sign up more volunteers to help with the fundraising campaign 2 VI (a) *(se faire embaucher)* he signed up as a crew member (b) *(s'engager dans l'armée)* my uncle tried to sign up when he was only 15 (c) *(s'inscrire, pour un cours)* she has signed up for a class in car maintenance

simmer down VI *(se calmer)* I'll tell you what he said once I've simmered down

single out VT SÉP *(sélectionner, distinguer)* why single her out for praise? after all, we all contributed to the success of the project *(c.-à.d. pourquoi est-ce elle qu'on a félicitée ?...)*

sink in VI (a) *(pénétrer, pour un liquide, etc.)* pour the syrup over the cake and allow it to sink in (b) *(faire son effet, être compris)* his remark didn't sink in until she was halfway down the stairs

sit about/around VI *(rester à ne rien faire, attendre sans rien faire)* we had to sit about in the airport lounge for two hours

sit back VI (a) *(s'installer confortablement dans un fauteuil, etc.)* I just want to sit back, put my feet up and watch some TV (b) *(rester sans rien faire)* we can't just sit back and do nothing if we think something's wrong

sit down 1 VI *(s'asseoir)* you'd better sit down, I've got some bad news 2 VT SÉP *(faire asseoir)* the doctor sat her down and explained the operation

sit in VI (a) *(assister, sans participer)* do you mind if I sit in on the class? (b) *(faire un sit-in)* students used to sit in regularly in the sixties

sit in for VT INSÉP *(remplacer)* the chairwoman is ill and has asked me to sit in for her at the meeting

sit on VT INSÉP (a) *(être membre de)* how many people sit on the committee? (b) *(garder le silence sur)* reporters were asked to sit on the news until the hostages were safely out of the country (c) *(garder sous le coude)* the company decided to sit on the consultant's recommendations (d) FAM *(fermer le bec à, faire taire)* I'm sorry I had to sit on you like that but you were about to be indiscreet

sit out VT SÉP (a) *(ne pas danser)* I'd rather sit this one out (b) *(supporter jusqu'à la fin)* we sat the concert out to the bitter end but it didn't get any better

sit up 1 VI (a) *(se tenir assis)* she was sitting up in bed when I arrived; sit up straight! *(c.-à-d. tiens-toi droit ou redresse-toi !)* (b) *(s'asseoir)* sit up, I've brought you breakfast in bed (c) *(rester éveillé, rester debout)* we sat up until midnight waiting for them to arrive
2 VT SÉP *(asseoir, redresser)* the nurse sat the old man up

size up VT SÉP *(jauger, observer)* she looked round the room, sizing everyone up

skim off VT SÉP *(enlever avec une écumoire)* let the soup cool and then skim off any fat on the surface; FIG *(récupérer)* he always skims off the best applicants for his department

skim over/through VT INSÉP *(parcourir)* the lawyer skimmed over his client's statement

slap on VT SÉP FAM (a) *(appliquer n'importe comment ou à la va-vite)* just slap some paint on and that will hide the marks (b) *(ajouter)* the government has slapped ten pence on the cost of a gallon of petrol

sleep around VI FAM *(coucher à droite et à gauche)* before she met her husband she had quite a reputation for sleeping around

sleep in VI (a) *(se lever en retard, ne pas se réveiller à l'heure)* this is the third morning this week I've slept in and been late for work (b) *(être logé sur place)* she has two maids sleeping in

sleep off VT SÉP *(dormir pour faire passer ou se remettre de quelque chose)* he's upstairs sleeping off his hangover

sleep on 1 VI *(continuer à dormir)* let her sleep on for as long as she likes
2 VT INSÉP *(remettre au lendemain, pour une décision)* you don't have to make your mind up now – sleep on it and then call me; I'll sleep on it *(c.-à-d. la nuit porte conseil)*

sleep together VI *(coucher ensemble)* when did you start to sleep together?

sleep with VT INSÉP *(coucher avec)* she's been sleeping with him for a year

slip away VI *(s'éclipser, partir discrètement)* she slipped away from the party; *(passer vite)* the time just slips away when I'm with him *(c.-à-d. je ne vois pas le temps passer quand je suis avec lui)*

slip by 1 VI *(passer vite)* the time has slipped by
2 VT INSÉP *(échapper à l'attention de)* how did that mistake manage to slip by you?

slip in 1 VI *(entrer discrètement ou sans se faire remarquer)* I just slipped in for five minutes
2 VT SÉP *(placer, glisser)* she slipped in a remark about his affair

slip off 1 VI *(s'éclipser)* we didn't see you go – when did you slip off?
2 VT SÉP *(enlever, ôter)* she slipped off her coat

slip on VT SÉP *(enfiler, pour un vêtement)* she slipped a dressing gown on and ran to answer the door

slip out VI (a) *(sortir discrètement, s'esquiver)* we slipped out halfway through the concert (b) *(échapper, pour des remarques)* I didn't mean to give the secret away, it just slipped out

slip up VI FAM *(faire une gaffe)* slip up one more time and you're fired

slow down/up 1 VI *(ralentir)* slow down, there's a speed limit here; slow down, I can't understand what you're saying
2 VT SÉP *(ralentir, retarder)* can't you walk any faster? you're slowing everyone down

smooth down VT SÉP (a) *(lisser)* smooth down your hair – it's sticking up all over the place (b) *(calmer, apaiser)* he's really very upset – give me a few minutes to smooth him down

smooth out VT SÉP (a) *(faire disparaître (en lissant), pour des plis, etc.)* she smoothed out the creases from the tablecloth (b) *(résoudre, pour des difficultés)* we have a little problem we hope you can help us smooth out

smooth over VT SÉP *(apaiser)* the chairman smoothed over the dispute with a light remark; *(arranger)* I smoothed things over

snap out VT SÉP *(lancer, dire d'un ton sec)* the sergeant snapped out an order

snap out of VT INSÉP *(se sortir de, pour une humeur)* you must snap out of this depression

snap up VT SÉP FAM *(sauter sur, s'arracher, pour une marchandise intéressante)* the towels are so cheap people are snapping them up

snarl up VT SÉP BR *(bloquer)* because of the accident, traffic is all snarled up on the motorway

snow under VT SÉP FAM *habituellement au passif (submerger)* we have been snowed under with orders

soldier on VI *(persévérer)* I know you're all very tired but if you could soldier on till the project is finished, I'd be very grateful

sort out VT SÉP (a) *(ranger)* I've sorted out all those tools that you had just thrown in the drawer (b) *(trier)* I've sorted out some books for you to take away with you (c) *(régler, résoudre)* maybe he needs some counselling to sort out his problems (d) *(arranger, fixer)* we need to sort out a date for the next meeting (e) FAM *(régler son compte à, verbalement ou physiquement)* it's about time someone sorted him out

sound off VI *(râler)* she is always sounding off about rude shop assistants

sound out VT SÉP *(demander l'opinion de)* I want to recommend you for the job but I thought I should sound you out first and see if you'd be interested

spell out VT SÉP (a) *(épeler)* it's rather an unusual name so I'll spell it out for you (b) *(expliquer bien clairement)* the chairman spelled out what a strike would mean for the company's future; do I have to spell it out for you?

spin out VT SÉP *(faire durer, économiser)* I have to spin my spending money out until the end of the holiday

splash down VI *(amerrir, pour un engin spatial)* the capsule splashed down at 13.00 hours just off Haiti

splash out 1 VI FAM *(faire des folies)* let's splash out for once and stay in the best hotels

2 VT INSÉP *(claquer)* she splashed out a lot of money on a camera

split up 1 VT SÉP (a) *(fendre)* he split the wood up into small pieces (b) *(partager, répartir)* we're going to split the money up among our children (c) *(séparer)* the teacher split the boys up

2 VI *(se séparer, pour un couple)* I hear they're splitting up

spring up VI **(a)** *(se lever brusquement)* several hands sprang up **(b)** *(grandir, pousser)* hasn't Lisa sprung up this year! **(c)** *(surgir, apparaître brusquement)* weeds are springing up all over the garden after the rain; the company sprang up almost overnight

square up VI **(a)** *(faire les comptes, régler ses comptes)* can we square up later?; I'll square up with you when I get paid if that's all right **(b)** *(se préparer à se battre, se mettre en garde)* the two men were so angry with each other that they began to square up **(c)** *(faire face)* it was wonderful the way you squared up to that bully

stamp out VT SÉP *(enrayer, réprimer)* the military government has vowed to stamp out unrest

stand by 1 VI **(a)** *(rester là sans rien faire ou sans intervenir)* people just stood by and watched the policeman being beaten up
(b) *(attendre)* viewers were told to stand by for further developments; *(se tenir prêt)* the police were standing by to disperse the crowd
2 VT INSÉP *(honorer, tenir)* the government has promised to stand by its election promises

stand down VI *(démissionner, se retirer)* he will stand down as chairman of the football club at the end of the year

stand for VT INSÉP **(a)** *(se présenter à, pour une élection)* I have decided to stand for the chairmanship of the committee; she is standing for election **(b)** *(représenter, vouloir dire)* what does the F stand for in JFK? **(c)** *(tolérer)* I won't stand for that kind of behaviour

stand in VI *(assurer le remplacement)* Mr Wilson has very kindly agreed to stand in at short notice for our scheduled speaker

stand out VI **(a)** *(se distinguer)* he is so tall that he stands out in a crowd; what makes her stand out is her platinum blonde hair **(b)** *(tenir bon, résister)* we are standing out against management's attempts to break our strike

stand up 1 VI **(a)** *(se lever)* everyone stood up when the president entered the room **(b)** *(être valable, pour un argument)* the prosecution hasn't got enough evidence for the charge to stand up

2 VT SÉP FAM *(poser un lapin à, faire faux bond à)* that's the second time this month I've been stood up!

stand up for VT INSÉP *(défendre, se battre pour)* my parents stood up for me when I was in trouble; stand up for what you believe in

stand up to VT INSÉP *(affronter, faire face à)* I admired the way she stood up to that aggressive drunk

start off 1 VI (a) *(partir)* the runners will be starting off in the coolness of the early morning (b) *(commencer)* to put your audience at ease, start off with a joke or two; *(débuter)* he started off as a cashier
2 VT SÉP (a) *(commencer)* start your presentation off with a brief history of the problem (b) *(déclencher)* what started the alarm off?; *(faire rire, pleurer, etc.)* there's the baby crying again – what started her off this time?

start up 1 VI (a) *(démarrer)* she heard a car starting up next door (b) *(s'installer, ouvrir, pour une affaire, un commerce)* there's a new dry cleaner's starting up on the corner
2 VT SÉP (a) *(faire démarrer, mettre en marche)* start the engines up (b) *(ouvrir, pour une affaire, un commerce)* they're starting up another restaurant

stay off 1 VI (a) *(rester chez soi, ne pas aller au travail, à l'école)* he's decided to stay off and see if he can cure this cold (b) *(ne pas se mettre à tomber, pour la pluie)* do you think the rain will stay off until the washing's dry?
2 VT INSÉP *(ne pas aller à)* can I stay off school today? *(c.-à-d. est-ce que je peux rester à la maison aujourd'hui ?)*

stay out VI (a) *(ne pas rentrer chez soi)* I can't stay out late like I used to, not when I have work the next day (b) *(poursuivre la grève)* the women have decided to stay out until their demands are met

step in VI *(intervenir)* the government should step in and order the strikers back to work

step up VT SÉP *(accélérer, augmenter)* research into this disease must be stepped up; the company is stepping up production of the vaccine

stick around VI FAM *(rester dans les parages)* stick around, we may need you

stick out 1 **VI** (a) *(dépasser, sortir)* the label on your dress is sticking out; his ears stick out *(c.-à-d. il a les oreilles décollées)* (b) *(se faire remarquer)* she sticks out because of the way she dresses
2 **VT SÉP** *(sortir ou passer... par)* stick your head out the window and see if they're coming

stick to **VT INSÉP** (a) *(coller à)* the cloth is sticking to the table (b) *(s'en tenir à, suivre, pour une décision, des plans, etc.)* she's sticking to her plans despite her parents' opposition; it's a very tough exercise regime – do you think you'll stick to it?; *(se contenter de)* if red wine gives you a headache, stick to white

stop by 1 **VT INSÉP** *(passer à)* stop by the post office on your way home
2 **VI** *(passer)* we'll stop by and see you next week

stop off **VI** *(faire une halte, faire étape)* they're stopping off at Bali for a couple of days on their way back

stop over **VI** *(faire escale)* we stopped over at Singapore on the flight to Sydney

straighten out 1 **VT SÉP** (a) *(ajuster, tirer, pour des tissus)* she straightened out the crumpled bedclothes (b) *(résoudre, mettre au clair)* we need to straighten a few things out in this relationship
2 **VI** *(devenir droit, pour une route, etc.)* after twisting and turning for a couple of hundred yards, the path finally straightened out

straighten up 1 **VT SÉP** (a) *(mettre d'aplomb, mettre droit)* can you straighten up that picture for me? (b) *(mettre de l'ordre dans, ranger)* straighten your room up a bit, it's very untidy
2 **VI** *(se dresser)* she straightened up and rubbed her back

strike back **VI** (a) *(répondre)* the government struck back at its critics with a strong defence of its actions (b) *(marquer à son tour)* two minutes later, the home team struck back

strike off **VT SÉP** *(rayer, barrer)* your name has been struck off (the list)

strike out 1 **VT SÉP** *(éliminer, rayer)* strike out whichever answer does not apply
2 **VI** (a) *(donner des coups, frapper)* he struck out at his opponent (b) *(aller, dans une direction précise)* we're all tired, let's strike out for home (c) *(locution)* I'm striking out on my own *je m'installe à mon compte*

strike up 1 **VT SÉP** **(a)** *(commencer à jouer)* the orchestra struck up a waltz **(b)** *(commencer, engager)* he immediately struck up a conversation with me; they struck up a friendship at school *(c.-à-d. ils se sont liés d'amitié à l'école)*
2 **VI** *(commencer à jouer, pour un orchestre, etc.)* the band struck up

string along **VT SÉP FAM** *(faire marcher)* that garage is just stringing you along – the car can't possibly be repaired; he just strung her along till he'd taken all her money and then he vanished

string up **VT SÉP FAM** *(pendre)* they should string child abusers up from the nearest lamp post

strip down **VT SÉP** *(démonter complètement)* the garage can't find the fault without stripping down the engine completely

strip off 1 **VT SÉP** *(faire tomber)* the wind stripped all the leaves off the trees; *(enlever)* he stripped off all his clothes and jumped into the water; we'll have to strip off about six layers of paint from this door
2 **VI** *(se déshabiller)* strip off and let the doctor examine you

sum up 1 **VT SÉP** **(a)** *(résumer)* the chairman summed up the committee's discussions **(b)** *(jauger, apprécier d'un coup d'œil)* he summed us up immediately; he began his address by summing up the situation
2 **VI** *(récapituler, résumer)* when summing up, the judge warned the jury against jumping to conclusions

summon up **VT SÉP** *(rassembler, pour le courage, les forces)* I summoned up all my courage and asked to speak to the manager

swallow up **VT SÉP** *(engloutir)* the sea swallowed them up; they were soon swallowed up by the mist *(c.-à-d. ils furent bientôt noyés dans la brume)*

swear in **VT SÉP** *(faire prêter serment à, assermenter)* as soon as the witness had been sworn in, the lawyer began questioning her; the new president was sworn in today

sweat out **VT SÉP** **(a)** *(se débarrasser de... en transpirant)* have a sauna and sweat your cold out **(b)** *(locution)* oh, just leave him to sweat it out, he'll find out soon enough *oh, laisse-le donc se débrouiller tout seul...)*

switch back VI *(revenir à, retourner à)* we tried electricity but we've decided to switch back to gas

switch off/on BR 1 VT SÉP *(allumer/éteindre un appareil électrique, un interrupteur, etc.)* switch the radio off/on
2 VI *(s'allumer, s'éteindre, pour une source électrique)* where does the power switch off/on?

switch over VI *(changer de chaîne, de station, pour la télévision ou la radio)* shall I switch over? the news is on the other side

switch round VT SÉP *(changer de place, échanger)* someone switched the drinks round and the Duchess got the poison by mistake

T

tail away/off VI *(diminuer, s'affaiblir)* the noise of the lorry tailed away in the distance; *(baisser peu à peu)* her voice tailed off as she realized that no one was listening

tail back VI BR *(former un bouchon, être arrêté)* the traffic tailed back all the way to the intersection

take aback VT SÉP *(étonner, déconcerter)* his ignorance really took me aback; *(prendre par surprise)* the enemy was completely taken aback by the speed of our attack

take after VT INSÉP *(ressembler à, tenir de, pour des enfants et leurs parents)* don't blame me, it's her father she takes after

take apart VT SÉP (a) *(démonter)* the radio hasn't worked since he took it apart (b) FAM *(critiquer)* the critics have really taken her new film apart

take around VT SÉP *(faire visiter)* would you like someone to take you around?

take away 1 VI *(enlever)* the fact that he lost in the first round doesn't take away from his overall skill *(c.-à-d. ...n'enlève rien à son talent)*
2 VT SÉP (a) *(soustraire, retrancher)* what do you get if you take 28 away from 70? (b) *(emmener)* they took her father away in an ambulance last night (c) *(emporter, pour des plats tout faits)* how about some curry to take away?

take back VT SÉP (a) *(rapporter)* take these library books back, will you? (b) *(reprendre, chercher)* when is Tony coming to take back those records you borrowed? (c) *(retirer, pour des commentaires)* now that I know her better, I take back all that I said about her (d) *(accepter le retour de, reprendre)* will the shop take it back if it doesn't fit?; she's a fool to take him back (e) *(rappeler à, pour un souvenir, etc.)* these old songs take me back to when I was a teenager

take down VT SÉP (a) *(descendre, décrocher)* it's time we took the curtains down for a wash; take all your posters down (b) *(démonter, enlever)* when are the workmen going to take down the scaffolding?; the shops still haven't taken down their Christmas decorations (c) *(prendre en note, noter)* the reporter took down very little of what was said at the meeting

take in VT SÉP (a) *(amener quelque part)* take your coat in to the cleaner's tomorrow
(b) *(recueillir)* they take in all the stray cats in the neighbourhood; *(héberger, prendre)* she has to take in lodgers to make ends meet
(c) *(reprendre, pour un vêtement)* could you take this skirt in?
(d) *(comprendre, absorber)* he reeled off so many facts and figures that I couldn't take them all in
(e) *(inclure, comprendre)* the Prime Minister's tour will take in a number of urban renewal projects
(f) *(aller voir)* do you want to take in a movie?; let's take in a few of the sights first
(g) *(rouler, tromper)* he took the old lady in by telling her he had known her son; don't be taken in by appearances *(c.-à-d. ne vous laissez pas tromper par les apparences)*

take off 1 VI (a) *(décoller, pour un avion)* we took off an hour late
(b) FAM *(décoller, prendre son essor)* the company's sales really took off last month
(c) FAM *(partir)* they're taking off for France next week; *(quitter le travail)* he's taking off early tonight
2 VT SÉP (a) *(enlever, ôter)* take your hat off; *(retirer)* the policeman was taken off the murder enquiry because he knew the people involved
(b) *(amputer)* they had to take her leg off below the knee
(c) *(réduire)* he needs to take a few pounds off *(c.-à-d. il doit*

perdre du poids); the saleswoman took a couple of pounds off because of this stain *(c.-à-d. elle a baissé le prix de deux livres...)*
(d) *(prendre, comme congé)* why don't you take the rest of the day off?
(e) *(imiter)* he takes off the president extremely well

take on VT SÉP **(a)** *(avoir la charge, la responsabilité de)* when I married you I didn't realize I'd be taking on your whole family too; she's exhausted with all the extra work she's been taking on recently
(b) *(recruter, embaucher)* that new electronics firm took on 200 people this week
(c) *(se battre contre)* why did you agree to take him on? – he's twice your size; *(jouer contre)* it was a mistake to take on the best snooker player in the club
(d) *(prendre, pour un air, un sens)* his face took on a cunning look; life has taken on a whole new meaning since I met you
(e) *(prendre à bord)* the train made an unscheduled stop to take on passengers

take out VT SÉP **(a)** *(sortir)* if you want to work in the garage, you'll have to take the car out; *(faire partir)* washing won't take that stain out, the dress will have to be dry cleaned
(b) *(enlever, arracher)* I'm having two teeth taken out tomorrow
(c) *(retirer, pour de l'argent)* how much do you think we need to take out of our account?
(d) *(emmener, inviter)* he took her out to dinner at a lovely restaurant
(e) *(souscrire à)* have you taken out insurance on the new car?; *(prendre)* how about taking out a subscription to this computer magazine?
(f) *(passer, pour la colère, etc.)* why should he take his anger out on us?
(g) FAM *(locution) (fatiguer)* kids take a lot out of you; that really took it out of me
(h) FAM *(détruire)* our men took out three enemy encampments

take over 1 VI *(prendre le pouvoir, la direction, etc.)* the new chairman will take over next week; *(envahir)* we ought to do something about the garden – the weeds are taking over
2 VT SÉP **(a)** *(prendre la direction, le pouvoir de)* she will be taking over the running of the hotel **(b)** *(racheter, absorber)* they were taken over by a Japanese firm

take round VT SÉP (a) *(amener, apporter)* take this cake round to your grandmother's for me (b) *(faire visiter)* the supervisor was asked to take the trade delegates round the factory

take to VT INSÉP (a) *(se prendre d'amitié pour)* I've never really taken to the people next door (b) *(prendre l'habitude de, se mettre à)* he has taken to treating me like an enemy (c) *(s'enfuir dans)* the outlaws took to the hills

take up 1 VI *(continuer, reprendre)* anyway, to take up where I left off, she's been fired

2 VT SÉP (a) *(soulever)* during their search, the policemen even took up the floorboards

(b) *(monter, à l'étage)* take this tray up to your mother

(c) *(raccourcir)* these curtains need to be taken up a couple of inches

(d) *(prendre, occuper)* I've taken up too much of your time; the bed is so large it just about takes up the entire room

(e) *(discuter de, parler de)* I think you should take up the question of training with the personnel manager

(f) *(se mettre à, pour un passe-temps)* he must be mad taking up jogging at his age!; *(prendre, pour un emploi)* when she first took up the appointment she had very little marketing experience

(g) *(accepter)* I'm going to take up that offer of a weekend in the country

(h) *(continuer, reprendre)* her sister took up the thread of the conversation

take up on VT SÉP (a) *(reprendre sur, dans un débat)* the Leader of the Opposition took the Prime Minister up on that last point

(b) *(accepter, pour une offre, etc.)* if they don't take me up on this offer it's their loss not mine; *(faire tenir à, pour une promesse)* have you taken him up on his promise of a lift to work every morning?; I'll take you up on that sometime *(c.-à-d. ça sera pour une prochaine fois)*

take upon VT SÉP *(se charger de, prendre la responsabilité de)* you took that task upon yourself; why did she take it upon herself to call the police?

take up with VT INSÉP *(se lier d'amitié avec, fréquenter)* he's taken up with a bad crowd recently

talk away 1 **VI** *(parler sans arrêt)* the old lady was talking away about her youth
2 **VT SÉP** *(passer... à discuter)* we talked half the night away

talk back **VI** *(répondre avec insolence, surtout pour des enfants)* don't talk back to your father

talk down **VT SÉP** (a) *(convaincre de redescendre, pour quelqu'un qui veut se suicider en sautant)* the police officers managed to talk her down (b) *(faire atterrir par radio-contrôle)* the fog was so thick at the airport that several planes had to be talked down

talk down to **VT INSÉP** *(parler avec condescendance ou comme à un enfant à)* I wish she wouldn't talk down to me – I'm not stupid

talk over **VT SÉP** *(discuter de)* they've decided to talk things over and see if they can reach some kind of agreement

talk round 1 **VT SÉP** *(faire changer d'avis)* Dad won't let me go to the concert – could you try talking him round?
2 **VT INSÉP** *(tourner autour de)* they seemed nervous about tackling the problem directly and just talked round it

tamper with **VT INSÉP** *(trafiquer, falsifier, saboter dans un but criminel)* after the car accident, he claimed that the brakes had been tampered with

tangle up **VT SÉP** (a) *(emmêler)* the kitten tangled all the wool up (b) *habituellement au passif (accrocher)* he got tangled up in the barbed wire when he tried to climb the fence (c) *(mêler)* I'm sure she's tangled up in something dishonest

tangle with **VT INSÉP FAM** *(se disputer avec, se battre avec)* he tangled with a drunk about some stupid football game

tear apart **VT SÉP** (a) *(détruire, déchirer)* the country is being torn apart by civil war (b) *(fouiller, mettre sens dessus dessous)* the police tore the place apart looking for drugs

tear away **VT SÉP** (a) *(déchirer, arracher)* I tore away the wrapping paper (b) *(éloigner, arracher)* if you can tear yourself away from that television for a minute, we could actually have a conversation

tear into **VT INSÉP** (a) *(attaquer, se jeter sur)* the lion tore into the flesh of the deer it had killed (b) **FAM** *(enguirlander, passer un savon à)* the boss tore into me for being late for the meeting

tear off VT SÉP *(détacher, arracher)* she tore the label off the suitcase

tear up VT SÉP (a) *(déchirer en petits morceaux)* his letter made her so angry she tore it up and threw it in the bin (b) FIG *(annuler, déchirer)* the football player threatened to tear up his contract if the club didn't pay him more

tell off VT SÉP *(gronder, réprimander)* I told him off for his cheek

tell on VT INSÉP (a) *(dénoncer)* Mum knows about the practical joke we were planning – someone must have told on us (b) *(se faire sentir sur, avoir un effet négatif sur)* the strain of waiting for news is telling on her

thaw out VI (a) *(se décongeler)* leave the meat to thaw out (b) FIG *(se réchauffer)* have a cup ot tea and thaw out; *(se dégeler, se mettre à l'aise)* he's pretty unsociable but he does thaw out sometimes

thin out 1 VI *(perdre ses cheveux)* he's thinning out on top; *(devenir épars)* audiences are thinning out; his hair is thinning out
2 VT SÉP *(éclaircir)* thin the plants out in autumn

think about VT INSÉP (a) *(penser à)* it's strange that you should have phoned just when I was thinking about you (b) *(penser, envisager de)* I'm thinking about going to the cinema tonight – do you want to come?

think back VI *(essayer de se souvenir, faire un effort de mémoire)* think back and try to remember what had happened; thinking back, I don't believe we did send them a Christmas card *(c.-à-d. en y repensant,...)*

think of VT INSÉP (a) *(penser à, avoir des égards pour)* it's about time she started thinking of herself instead of other people all the time
(b) *(se souvenir de, se rappeler)* I can't think of his telephone number at the moment
(c) *(imaginer)* just think of it, a holiday in the Caribbean!
(d) *(penser de, avoir une opinion sur)* what do you think of the latest fashions?; she thinks very highly of him *(c.-à-d. elle a une très haute opinion de lui)*
(e) *(considérer, envisager)* we wouldn't think of letting our daughter go to Thailand on her own
(f) *(avoir l'idée de, trouver)* who thought of coming to this restaurant?; I've thought of a solution to the problem

think out/through VT SÉP *(élaborer, considérer scrupuleusement)* I don't think you've thought out your plan very thoroughly; let's think things through before we make any firm decision

think over VT SÉP *(bien réfléchir à)* I told him I would think his offer over

think up VT SÉP *(trouver, pour une idée, etc.)* they've thought up a brilliant idea

throw away VT SÉP (a) *(jeter)* throw those old papers away (b) *(gâcher, gaspiller)* she threw away her chance of a place at university; you're just throwing your money away buying all those computer games and DVDs

throw back VT SÉP (a) *(rejeter)* the fish was so small that the angler threw it back (b) *(rejeter en arrière)* she threw her head back

throw in VT SÉP *(donner en prime à ce qui a été acheté)* we took the bed and they threw in the mattress for nothing

throw off VT SÉP (a) *(enlever ou ôter à la hâte)* he threw off his clothes and jumped into the river (b) *(se débarrasser de, pour une maladie, etc.)* I can't seem to throw off this virus

throw out VT SÉP (a) *(jeter)* don't throw those photographs out (b) *(rejeter, pour une proposition)* after discussion, the committee threw the proposal out (c) *(faire sortir, jeter dehors, pour une personne qui se conduit mal)* the boys got thrown out of the cinema for misbehaving

throw together VT SÉP (a) FAM *(bricoler, faire à la hâte, à la va-vite)* it's not very well made, it looks a bit thrown together (b) *(jeter, mettre, rassembler)* he threw some clothes together in a suitcase and raced to the airport (c) *(réunir, rassembler, pour des personnes)* fate threw the two of them together; on such a small cruise ship, everyone is thrown together, like it or not

throw up 1 VI FAM *(vomir)* no wonder you threw up, mixing your drinks like that
2 VT SÉP *(laisser passer, pour une chance, une occasion)* imagine throwing up a chance to go to the United States

tick off VT SÉP (a) *(cocher)* will you tick people's names off as they come in to vote? (b) BR FAM *(réprimander, passer un savon à)* the teacher ticked him off for being late

tick over VI *(marcher, fonctionner, pour une machine ou un commerce, etc.)* the restaurant is ticking over quite well

tide over VT SÉP *(dépanner, avec de l'argent, etc.)* could you lend me twenty pounds to tide me over until the end of the week?

tie down VT SÉP *(accaparer, contraindre)* children tie you down; I don't want to be tied down to any specific date

tie in VI *(correspondre, concorder)* how does the suspect's story tie in with his wife's?

tie up 1 VI *(être lié, se tenir, pour des faits, etc.)* his debts, the robbery, and now a new car – it all ties up
2 VT SÉP *habituellement au passif* (a) *(immobiliser, pour de l'argent)* my capital is tied up in stocks and shares; his money is tied up until he's 25 (b) *(être occupé, par le travail, etc.)* she'll be tied up all afternoon

tighten up VT SÉP (a) *(serrer)* he bent to tighten up his shoelaces (b) *(rendre plus strict, renforcer)* they're tightening up the rules on tax shelters; the company has decided that security must be tightened up

tip off VT SÉP FAM *(avertir, donner un tuyau à)* someone must have tipped him off that the police were on their way; the reporter was tipped off about an interesting story

tone down VT SÉP (a) *(adoucir)* we toned our original colour scheme down (b) FIG *(modérer, édulcorer)* the reporter was told to tone his article down or the paper would be sued

top up VT SÉP BR *(remplir, pour un verre, un réservoir, etc.)* he kept topping my glass up; *(resservir, pour une boisson)* can I top you up?

touch down VI *(atterrir, pour un avion, un engin spatial)* Concorde touched down exactly on schedule

touch up VT SÉP (a) *(retoucher)* this bit of the window frame needs to be touched up; she's just gone to touch up her make-up *(c.-à-d. se remaquiller)* (b) BR FAM *(peloter)* if you don't stop touching me up I'll slap your face

touch (up)on VT INSÉP *(aborder, effleurer)* his speech didn't even touch on the pollution problem

toughen up **VT SÉP** *(endurcir)* he's one of those parents who send their sons to boarding school to toughen them up

trail away/off **VI** *(s'estomper, s'affaiblir, pour une voix ou un bruit)* his voice trailed away with embarrassment

trot out **VT SÉP FAM** *(réciter, sortir, pour des arguments, etc. que l'on a déjà entendus)* don't trot out the same old excuses; he's not going to trot that speech out again, is he?

try for **VT INSÉP** *(essayer d'obtenir)* she is trying for a place at music school; he's trying for the record *(c.-à-d. il essaie de battre le record)*

try on **VT SÉP** *(essayer, pour des vêtements, des chaussures, etc.)* I've been trying dresses on all morning

try out **VT SÉP** *(mettre à l'essai)* the football club is trying him out in goal; *(essayer)* you can have the car for a day to try it out

turn against 1 **VT INSÉP** *(se retourner contre, s'en prendre à)* why have you turned against me?
2 **VT SÉP** *(monter contre)* she claims that her ex-husband is turning their children against her

turn back 1 **VI** *(rebrousser chemin, faire demi-tour)* we turned back because the path had become too faint to follow
2 **VT SÉP** **(a)** *(refuser l'entrée de, refouler)* the refugees were turned back at the border **(b)** *(rabattre)* she reluctantly turned back the bedclothes and got up **(c)** *(retarder, pour une montre, une horloge)* we turned our watches back an hour

turn down **VT SÉP** **(a)** *(rabattre)* since the rain had stopped, he turned his coat collar down **(b)** *(baisser, pour le chauffage, le son, etc.)* turn the heating down a bit; can you turn your music down a bit? **(c)** *(refuser)* I've been turned down for that job I applied for; *(rejeter)* she turned down his offer of a weekend in Paris

turn in 1 **VI FAM** *(aller se coucher)* it's late, why don't we turn in?
2 **VT SÉP** **(a)** *(dénoncer à la police)* his former wife turned him in **(b)** *(rendre)* hundreds of weapons were turned in during the amnesty

turn off 1 **VI** *(tourner, pour un véhicule)* you turn off at the second street on the left

2 VT SÉP (a) *(éteindre, pour la radio, un moteur, etc.)* be sure to turn the stove off; *(fermer)* who didn't turn the tap off? (b) FAM *(dégoûter, souvent d'un point de vue sexuel)* smelly feet really turn me off

turn on 1 VT SÉP (a) *(allumer, pour un appareil, la télévision, etc.)* turn the gas on for me (b) FAM *(plaire énormément, souvent d'un point de vue sexuel)* rock music turns her on; he is turned on by her
2 VT INSÉP (a) *(s'en prendre à, attaquer physiquement ou verbalement)* one of her dogs turned on her; he turned on me when I suggested that he retire (b) *(dépendre de, reposer sur)* the company's success turns on the skills of its employees

turn out 1 VI (a) *(venir, être présent)* not many people turned out for his funeral
(b) *(se révéler, s'avérer)* it's one of those silly stories where the heroine turns out to be a lost heiress
(c) *(donner, à la fin)* how did the cake turn out?; *(se finir)* everything will turn out fine *(c.-à-d. tout va s'arranger, tout ira bien)*
2 VT SÉP (a) *(éteindre)* it's time you turned the light out and went to sleep
(b) *(vider)* I turned out my handbag to look for my keys
(c) *(produire)* we're now turning out 100 computers a day
(d) *(mettre à la porte, expulser)* the old man was turned out of his cottage

turn over 1 VI *(se retourner)* he turned over in bed; *(chavirer)* the lifeboat turned over and sank in seconds
2 VT SÉP (a) *(remettre, livrer)* the suspect was turned over to the police; *(transmettre, donner)* they have turned the running of the restaurant over to their son-in-law (b) *habituellement non séparé (faire un chiffre d'affaires de, gagner autour de)* he must be turning over a good ten thousand a week

turn round 1 VI (a) *(se retourner)* he turned round and looked at her
(b) *(faire volte-face, faire demi-tour)* he just turned round and punched the other guy
2 VT INSÉP *(tourner à, prendre)* turn round the next corner
3 VT SÉP (a) *(renverser la situation, sauver de la faillite)* the company was headed for bankruptcy but the new management team turned it round (b) *(exécuter, traiter)* how

quickly can you turn this order round? (c) *(tourner)* she turned the chair round and sat down

turn up 1 **VI** (a) *(arriver, venir)* he always turns up late; she turned up at the party with her new boyfriend (b) *(être trouvé ou retrouvé)* if you're sure that you lost it in the house, then it's bound to turn up one day (c) *(arriver, se produire)* things always have a habit of turning up when you least expect them to

2 **VT SÉP** (a) *(remonter, relever)* he turned his collar up in the wind (b) *(mettre plus fort, monter)* turn the television up, will you, I can hardly hear; turn the heat up a bit

U

urge on **VT SÉP** *(talonner, pousser)* the marathon runner said he managed to finish the race only because the crowd urged him on; *(inciter)* her family is urging her on to go to university

use up **VT SÉP** *(finir)* use up the last of the milk before it turns sour; *(épuiser)* the children used up all their energy playing

V

verge on **VT INSÉP** *(être au bord de)* I was verging on tears; they are verging on bankruptcy; *(frôler, friser)* his feeling was one of panic verging on hysteria; she's verging on forty

vote down **VT SÉP** *(rejeter, par le vote)* the amendment to the law was voted down

vote in **VT SÉP** *(élire)* the other members of the committee voted her in as chairperson

vote on **VT INSÉP** *(mettre au vote, voter)* union members will be asked to vote on management's latest offer; it was voted on last night

W

wade in VI BR FAM *(se mêler à)* when the fight started, everybody waded in; our discussion wasn't really anything to do with her, but she waded in anyway

wade into VT INSÉP BR FAM *(attaquer, se mettre à)* he got up early and waded into the job of cleaning the windows; *(s'attaquer à, s'en prendre à)* I'm sorry, I shouldn't have waded into you for something so minor

wait behind VI *(rester, en arrière)* she volunteered to wait behind until the doctor came

wait in VI *(rester chez soi, au bureau, etc.)* I was late because I had to wait in for the telephone engineer

wait on 1 VI *(continuer à attendre)* he waited on in the hope that she would eventually arrive
2 VT INSÉP *(servir)* the waitress who was waiting on them seemed to have vanished

wait up VI *(ne pas se coucher, veiller)* don't wait up, I'll be very late

wake up 1 VI (a) *(se réveiller)* she woke up when the church bells started ringing (b) FIG *(ouvrir les yeux)* his mother never did wake up to the fact that he was a thief
2 VT SÉP (a) *(réveiller)* don't wake me up too early tomorrow (b) FIG *(secouer, réveiller)* this country needs waking up

walk into VT INSÉP (a) *(entrer dans)* she walked into the room; *(tomber dans)* the suspect walked right into the trap the police had set for him (b) *(rentrer dans, se cogner à)* I almost walked into a lamp post

walk off 1 VI *(partir)* he walked off and left us standing there
2 VT SÉP *(se promener pour digérer ou faire passer)* let's go out and walk off our Christmas dinner

walk off with VT INSÉP (a) *(remporter haut la main)* she walked off with the first prize in the short-story competition (b) *(voler)* the bank manager has walked off with a million pounds
(c) *(prendre, pour quelque chose qui ne nous appartient pas)* who keeps walking off with the scissors?

walk out VI (a) *(sortir, partir)* she walked out of the room (b) *(se mettre en grève)* hundreds of workers walked out yesterday

walk out on VT INSÉP *(quitter, pour sa famille, son conjoint, etc.)* you can't just walk out on your wife and children!

walk over 1 VT INSÉP *(faire tomber, vaincre, dans un combat)* the champion walked all over another opponent today
2 VI *(aller, faire un saut)* I'll walk over to her place tomorrow

walk through VT INSÉP *(réussir facilement)* you'll walk through the job interview

walk up VI (a) *(monter à pied)* the lift was out of order so we had to walk all the way up (b) *(s'approcher)* a complete stranger walked up and started talking to me

warm up 1 VI (a) *(se réchauffer)* I hope it starts warming up now that spring is here (b) *(s'échauffer, pour des sportifs)* tennis players get a couple of minutes to warm up before the match
2 VT SÉP (a) *(faire chauffer)* warm up some soup for yourself (b) *(mettre de l'ambiance dans)* can't we do anything to warm this dinner party up?; *(chauffer, pour le public, etc.)* the star of the show doesn't appear until the other acts have warmed the audience up

warn off VT SÉP (a) *(déconseiller à)* I was going to buy it but someone warned me off (b) *(demander instamment à... de quitter ou partir de)* he warned them off his land

wash down VT SÉP *(faire passer ou descendre, pour un repas, un médicament, etc. à l'aide d'un verre d'eau ou d'une boisson)* have a glass of water to wash your medicine down

wash off 1 VI *(s'en aller ou partir au lavage)* do you think these stains will wash off?
2 VT SÉP *(enlever en lavant)* just let me wash the oil off my hands

wash out VT SÉP (a) *(rincer)* wash your mouth out, please
(b) *habituellement au passif (être annulé à cause de la pluie)* the women's tennis final has been washed out

wash over VT INSÉP *(ne faire aucun effet à, passer au-dessus de, pour des remarques, etc.)* anything I say just washes over her; his mother's death seems to have washed over him

wash up 1 VI (a) BR *(faire la vaisselle)* whose turn is it to wash up? (b) AM *(se laver)* don't serve supper until I've washed up
2 VT SÉP (a) BR *(laver, pour la vaisselle, etc.)* why I am always left with the greasy pots to wash up? (b) FAM *habituellement au passif (être fichu, pour une carrière, une occasion, etc.)* he's washed up as a boxer (c) *(rejeter, ramener sur le rivage, pour la mer)* a body was found washed up on the beach *(c.-à-d.... échoué sur la plage)*

watch out VI *(faire attention)* watch out for bones when you're eating the fish; watch out, you nearly broke the window

water down VT SÉP (a) *(couper, pour une boisson alcoolisée)* water this down with a drop of soda, will you? (b) FIG *(édulcorer)* the theatre critic accused the editor of watering his review down

wave down VT SÉP *(faire signe à... de s'arrêter)* he didn't see the policeman waving him down

wave on VT SÉP *(faire signe à... de poursuivre sa course)* the border guard waved them on without looking at their passports

wear away VT SÉP *(éroder, ronger)* the sea is wearing the coastline away

wear down VT SÉP (a) *(user)* I've worn the heels of my shoes down (b) *(épuiser, exténuer)* her busy schedule finally wore her down

wear off VI *(disparaître, se dissiper)* the effect of the anaesthetic is wearing off

wear out 1 VT SÉP (a) *(user)* that's the second pair of shoes he's worn out in six months (b) *(épuiser, exténuer)* she's wearing herself out with the preparations for her daughter's wedding
2 VI *(s'user)* the carpet is wearing out

weed out VT SÉP FIG *(éliminer, par sélection)* we have weeded out the least promising candidates

weigh down VT SÉP (a) *(faire plier, courber)* the branches were weighed down with snow; *(surcharger)* don't weigh me down with anything more to carry (b) FIG *(ronger, accabler)* they are both weighed down with grief

weigh in VI (a) *(se faire peser, pour un boxer, un jockey, des bagages)* the champion weighed in at just under the limit; have you weighed in yet? (b) *(intervenir dans une discussion)* I wish she wouldn't keep weighing in with comments that are totally irrelevant

weigh up VT SÉP (a) *(examiner, peser)* weighing up the situation, she decided it was time to leave (b) *(jauger, estimer la valeur de)* he's very good at weighing people up quickly

while away VT SÉP *(passer ou faire passer, en attendant qn ou qch)* how did you while away all those hours you had to spend in the airport lounge?

whip away VT SÉP (a) *(emporter brusquement, par le vent)* a sudden gust whipped my hat away (b) FAM *(enlever brusquement, arracher)* the waiter whipped our plates away before we'd finished eating

whip out 1 VT SÉP *(sortir brusquement d'un sac, d'une poche, etc.)* he whipped out his wallet
2 VI FAM *(courir, filer)* I'm just whipping out to the car for my briefcase

whip round VI (a) *(se retourner brusquement, faire volte-face)* he whipped round and stared at me (b) FAM *(faire un saut)* whip round to the chemist's for me

whip up VT SÉP (a) *(faire vibrer, galvaniser, exalter)* such speeches are intended to whip an audience up (b) *(obtenir)* what can we do to whip up support for the campaign? (c) *(battre au fouet, fouetter)* whip up some cream for me, could you? (d) FAM *(faire à la va-vite, préparer en vitesse, pour un repas)* I whipped up a meal for them

whisk away VT SÉP (a) *(chasser, de la main)* whisk the wasps away from the jam (b) FAM *(emmener à toute vitesse)* the president was whisked away by helicopter

whittle away VT SÉP *(battre en brèche, réduire progressivement)* she is whittling away her opponent's lead; support for the government is being whittled away by its evident failure to control inflation

whittle down VT SÉP *(réduire, avec l'idée d'effort)* we've whittled the number of candidates down

win back VT SÉP *(reprendre, regagner)* he won back all the money he had lost the previous week

win out/through VI *(triompher, l'emporter)* he finally won out over his parents' objections; the strikers won through in the end *(c.-à-d. les grévistes ont fini par obtenir gain de cause)*

win over/round VT SÉP *(rallier, convaincre)* they are trying to win me over to the idea of a camping holiday; *(séduire)* she is charming and has quite won us over

wind down 1 VT SÉP *(réduire progressivement)* the company has decided to wind down its operations in that part of the world
2 VI *(tirer à sa fin)* we went home since the party was winding down

wind up 1 VT SÉP (a) *(remonter, pour un réveil, une horloge)* the clock needs to be wound up (b) *(finir)* we wound up our holiday with a weekend in Paris (c) BR FAM *(asticoter, faire marcher)* he really wound her up with those remarks about her dress; don't you know when you're being wound up?
2 VI = **end up**

winkle out VT SÉP FAM *(arracher, extirper)* I finally winkled the information out of him; it's no good trying to winkle any money out of me

wipe off VT SÉP *(effacer)* the teacher wiped the equation off the board; *(enlever)* wipe that grin off your face!

wipe out VT SÉP (a) *(effacer)* she has completely wiped out the memory of the crash; *(anéantir)* the power failure wiped out three weeks' work (b) *(dilapider, liquider, pour de l'argent)* his gambling debts wiped out his entire fortune (c) *(détruire, exterminer)* enemy fire wiped out the village; whole families have been wiped out by the disease (d) FAM *(épuiser, crever)* I feel wiped out

work in VT SÉP *(mentionner, dans un discours, etc.)* I think we should work something in about the help we received from other people; *(incorporer)* work the other ingredients in gradually

work off VT SÉP *(passer, pour la colère, etc.)* she worked her anger off on the squash court; *(dépenser, pour l'énergie)* I worked off my excess energy chopping wood

work on VT INSÉP (a) *(chercher)* have you got any ideas? – I'm working on it; the police are working on who stole the jewels; *(essayer de résoudre)* he's been working on his emotional problems **(b)** *(utiliser comme base)* we'll have to work on what we have **(c)** *(persuader)* I've tried working on him but without much success

work out 1 **vi** **(a)** *(se passer)* it depends on how things work out **(b)** *(marcher, réussir)* that relationship will never work out **(c)** *(se monter à, s'élever à)* how much do you make that work out at? **(d)** *(faire de l'exercice, s'entraîner)* she's been working out all morning
2 **vt sép** **(a)** *(résoudre)* once you've worked out the exact problem, we can start to think about possible solutions; *(arranger)* they'll have to work things out between themselves, I'm not getting involved **(b)** *(élaborer)* he's worked out a plan

work up **vt sép** **(a)** *(développer, avoir, pour des sentiments, etc.)* I can't work up any enthusiasm for this project **(b)** *(exciter)* she was getting all worked up at the prospect of a holiday

work up to **vt insép** *(se préparer à)* he's working up to proposing to her; *(en venir à)* it was easy to see what she was working up to

wriggle out of **vt insép** *(éviter de, se dérober à, pour une tâche, une obligation, etc.)* why did you let them wriggle out of doing their homework?; you can't wriggle out of this one

write away for **vt insép** *(écrire pour commander, commander par courrier)* if you want to know more, write away for our free brochure

write in **vi** *(envoyer des lettres, écrire)* a great many viewers have written in with their comments about last week's programme

write off 1 **vt sép** **(a)** *(annuler)* his debts have been written off **(b)** *(considérer comme sans valeur, faire une critique très sévère de)* the critics wrote the play off **(c)** **Br** *(démolir, pour les voitures, etc.)* she wrote her father's car off
2 **vi** *(commander par courrier)* I've written off for tickets

write out **vt sép** **(a)** *(rédiger, mettre au propre)* have you written out your essay? **(b)** *(faire, pour un chèque, un reçu)* just write me out a cheque; the shop assistant wrote out the receipt **(c)** *(retirer, pour un rôle dans une série télévisée, etc.)* her part has been written out

write up **vt sép** *(préparer, rédiger)* he's writing up a report on his business trip

Z

zap up VT SÉP FAM *(rendre plus vivant ou plus coloré)* the prose style could do with a bit of zapping up; *(rehausser)* they've certainly zapped up the colour scheme

zero in on VT INSÉP (a) *(se diriger droit sur)* the missile zeroes in on its target from a range of several kilometres (b) *(mettre le doigt sur)* they immediately zeroed in on the one weak point in the argument

zip up 1 VT SÉP *(fermer ou remonter la fermeture Éclair® de)* she zipped her skirt up; zip me up, will you?
2 VI *(se fermer avec une fermeture Éclair®)* the dress zips up at the back

INDEX

Les codes de cet index de verbes renvoient aux modèles de verbes expliqués pages 16 à 18. Le code M9 indique que le verbe est irrégulier (voir pages 22 à 29).

Les verbes en **-ate** et en **-ize** ne figurent pas dans l'index : ils se conjuguent toujours selon le modèle M4.

Pour les verbes commençant par les préfixes **de-**, **dis-**, **mis-**, **out-**, **over-**, **re-** et **un-**, se reporter au second élément.

(Am) indique que l'orthographe américaine est expliquée au modèle M5 page 17.

A

abase M4
abet M5
abhor M5
abide M4 ou M4M9
abide by M4
abjure M4
abolish M2
abridge M4
absolve M4
abuse M4
abut M5
accede M4
access M2
accompany M6
accomplish M2
accrue M4
accuse M4
ache M4
achieve M4
acknowledge M4
acquiesce M4
acquire M4
acquit M5
ad-lib M5
address M2
adhere M4
adjudge M4
adjure M4
admire M4
admit M5
adore M4
advance M4
adventure M4
advertise M4
advise M4
age M4
agree M3
allege M4
allot M5
allude to M4
allure M4
ally M6
amass M2
amaze M4
amble M4
ambush M2
amplify M6
amuse M4
analyse M4
angle M4
announce M4
annul M5
appal M5
appease M4
apply M6
appraise M4
apprentice M4
apprise M4
approach M2
approve M4
arch M2
argue M4
arise M4M9
arouse M4
arrange M4
arrive M4
ascribe M4
assess M2
assuage M4
assume M4
assure M4
astonish M2
atone M4
attach M2
attribute M4
attune M4
avenge M4
aver M5
average M4
awake M4 ou M4M9
axe M4

B

babble M4
baby M6
baby-sit M5M9
baffle M4
bag M5
bake M4
balance M4
bale out M4
ban M5
bandage M4
bandy M6
banish M2
bar M5
barbecue M4
bare M4
barge M4
barrel M5 *(Am)*
barricade in M4
base M4
bash M2
baste M4
bat M5
bathe M4
battle M4
beach M2
bear M1M9
beat M1M9
beatify M6
beautify M6
become M4M9
bed M5
bedazzle M4
bedevil M5 *(Am)*
beetle along M4
befall M1M9
befit M5
befog M5
befuddle M4
beg M5
beget M5M9
begin M5M9
begrudge M4

beguile M4
behave M4
behold M1M9
behove M4
belch M2
belie M7
believe M4
belittle M4
belly out M6
bend M1M9
benefit M1 ou M5
bereave M4 ou M4M9
beseech M2 ou M2M9
beset M5M9
besiege M4
besmirch M2
bespeak M1M9
bestir M5
bestride M4M9
bet M2M9
betake M4M9
betide M4
bevel M5 *(Am)*
bewitch M2
bias M2 ou M5 *(Am)*
bid M5M9
bide M4
bind M1M9
birch M2
bite M4M9
bivouac M8
blab M5
blackleg M5
blame M4
blanch M2
blare M4
blaspheme M4
blaze M4
bleach M2
bleed M1M9
bless M2
blot M5
blotch M2
blow M1M9
blue M4
blur M5
blush M2
bob M5
bode M4
bog down M5
boggle M4
bone M4
bootleg M5
booze M4
bop M5
bore M4
boss about M2
botch M2
bottle M4
bounce M4
box M2
brace M4
brag M5
brake M4
brave M4
breach M2
break M1M9
breathalyse M4
breathe M4
breed M1M9
bribe M4
bridge M4
brim M5
bring M1M9
bristle M4
broach M2
broadcast M1M9
bronze M4
browse M4
bruise M4
brush M2
bubble M4
buckle M4
bud M5
budge M4
bug M5
build M1M9
bulge M4
bulldoze M4
bully M6
bum M5
bundle M4
bungle M4
burgle M4
burn M1 ou M1M9
burnish M2
burst M1M9
bury M6
bus M2 ou M5 *(Am)*
bust M1M9
bustle M4
busy M6
buy M1M9
buzz M2

C

cable M4
caddie M7
caddy M6
cadge M4
cage M4
cajole M4
cake M4
calcify M6
calve M4
camouflage M4
can (tin) M5
cancel M5 *(Am)*
candy M6
cane M4
canoe M4
canvass M2
cap M5
capture M4
care M4
caress M2
caricature M4
carry M6

cascade M4
cash M2
catalogue M4
catch M2M9
cause M4
cave M4
cavil M5 *(Am)*
cease M4
cede M4
censure M4
centre M4
certify M6
chafe M4
challenge M4
chance M4
change M4
channel M5 *(Am)*
chap M5
chaperone M4
char M5
charge M4
chase M4
chat M5
cherish M2
chide M4M9
chime M4
chip M5
chisel M5 *(Am)*
chivvy M6
choke M4
choose M4M9
chop M5
chortle M4
chuckle M4
chug M5
chum up M5
cinch M2
circle M4
circumscribe M4
cite M4
clam up M5
clap M5
clarify M6
clash M2
class M2
classify M6
cleanse M4
cleave M4 ou M4M9
clench M2
climax M2
clinch M2
cling M1M9
clip M5
clog M5
clone M4
close M4
clot M5
clothe M4 ou M4M9
club M5
clue up M4
clutch M2
coach M2
coalesce M4
coax M2
cobble M4
code M4
coerce M4
cohere M4
coincide M4
collapse M4
collide M4
combine M4
come M4M9
commence M4
commit M5
commute M4
compare M4
compel M5
compere M4
compete M4
compile M4
complete M4
comply M6
compose M4
compress M2
comprise M4
compromise M4
con M5
concede M4
conceive M4
conclude M4
concur M5
concuss M2
condense M4
condole M4
condone M4
confer M5
confess M2
confide M4
confine M4
confuse M4
conjecture M4
conjure away M4
connive M4
conserve M4
console M4
conspire M4
constitute M4
consume M4
continue M4
contravene M4
contribute M4
contrive M4
control M5
convalesce M4
convene M4
converge M4
converse M4
convince M4
convulse M4
cop M5
cope M4
copy M6
core M4
corpse M4
corral M5
corrode M4
cosh M2
cost M1M9
counsel M5 *(Am)*
couple M4
course M4

cox M2
crackle M4
cradle M4
cram M5
crane M4
crap M5
crash M2
crate M4
crave M4
crease M4
create M4
creep M1M9
cringe M4
crinkle M4
cripple M4
crop M5
cross M2
crouch M2
crow M1M9
crucify M6
cruise M4
crumble M4
crumple M4
crunch M2
crush M2
cry M6
cube M4
cuddle M4
cudgel M5 *(Am)*
cue M3
cup M5
curdle M4
cure M4
curry M6
curse M4
curtsy M6
curve M4
cut M5M9
cycle M4

D

dab M5
dabble M4
dally M6
dam M5
damage M4
dance M4
dangle M4
dare M4 ou M4M9
dash M2
date M4
dawdle M4
daze M4
dazzle M4
deal M1M9
debauch M2
debug M5
deceive M4
decide M4
declare M4
decline M4
decrease M4
decree M3
decry M6
deduce M4
defer M5
define M4
defy M6
deify M6
delete M4
delude M4
delve M4
demolish M2
demote M4
demur M5
denounce M4
deny M6
deplete M4
deplore M4
depose M4
depress M2
deprive M4
deride M4
derive M4
describe M4
deserve M4
desire M4
despatch M2
despise M4
destine M4
detach M2
deter M5
determine M4
devalue M4
devise M4
devolve M4
devote M4
diagnose M4
dial M5 *(Am)*
dice M4
die M7
dig M5M9
dignify M6
digress M2
dilute M4
dim M5
diminish M2
dimple M4
dine M4
dip M5
dirty M6
disable M4
disadvantage M4
disagree M3
discipline M4
discourage M4
discourse M4
discuss M2
disentangle M4
disgruntle M4
disguise M4
dish M2
disinter M5
dismantle M4
dismiss M2
disparage M4
dispatch M2

dispel M5
dispense M4
disperse M4
dispose M4
dissolve M4
dissuade M4
distance M4
distil M5
distinguish M2
distress M2
distribute M4
ditch M2
dive M4 ou M4M9
diverge M4
diversify M6
divide M4
divorce M4
divulge M4
do M2M9
dodge M4
dog M5
dole out M4
don M5
doodle M4
dope M4
dose M4
doss M2
dot M5
dote on M4
double M4
doze M4
drag M5
drape M4
draw M1M9
dream M1 ou M1M9
dredge M4
drench M2
dress M2
dribble M4
drink M1M9
drip M5
drive M4M9
drivel M5 *(Am)*
drizzle M4
drone M4
drop M5
drowse M4
drug M5
drum M5
dry M6
duel M5 *(Am)*
dupe M4
dwell M1M9
dwindle M4
dye M4
dynamite M4

E

ease M4
eat M1M9
echo M2
eddy M6
edge M4
edit M1
efface M4
effervesce M4
eke out M4
elapse M4
electrify M6
electrocute M4
elope M4
elude M4
embarrass M2
embed M5
embellish M2
embezzle M4
embody M6
emboss M2
embrace M4
emerge M4
emit M5
empty M6
emulate M4
emulsify M6
enable M4
enamel M5 *(Am)*
encircle M4
enclose M4
encompass M2
encourage M4
encroach M2
endorse M4
endure M4
enforce M4
engage M4
engrave M4
engross M2
enhance M4
enlarge M4
enquire M4
enrage M4
enrapture M4
enrich M2
enrol M5
enshrine M4
ensue M4
ensure M4
enthral M5
enthuse M4
entice M4
entitle M4
entrench M2
envisage M4
envy M6
equal M5 *(Am)*
equip M5
erase M4
erode M4
escape M4
establish M2
etch M2
evade M4
evoke M4
evolve M4
examine M4
excel M5
excite M4
exclude M4
excuse M4
execute M4

exemplify M6
exercise M4
exhale M4
exile M4
expedite M4
expel M5
experience M4
expire M4
explode M4
explore M4
expose M4
express M2
extinguish M2
extol M5
extradite M4
exude M4
eye M4

F

face M4
facet M1 ou M5
fade M4
fake M4
fall M1M9
falsify M6
famish M2
fan M5
fancy M6
fare M4
fatigue M4
fax M2
faze M4
feature M4
feed M1M9
feel M1M9
fence M4
ferry M6
fetch M2
fete M4
fib M5
fiddle M4
fight M1M9
figure M4
filch M2
file M4
filigree M3
finance M4
find M1M9
fine M4
finish M2
fire M4
fish M2
fit M5 ou M5M9
fix M2
fizz M2
fizzle M4
flag M5
flake M4
flame M4
flannel M5 *(Am)*
flap M5
flare M4
flash M2
flee M3M9
fleece M4
flesh out M2
flex M2
flinch M2
fling M1M9
flip M5
flit M5
flog M5
flop M5
flounce M4
flourish M2
flush M2
fly M6M9
fob M5
focus M2
fog M5
fondle M4
forage M4
forbid M5M9
force M4
forecast M1M9
forego M2M9
foresee M3M9
foretell M1M9
forge M4
forget M5M9
forgive M4M9
forgo M2M9
format M5
forsake M4M9
forswear M1M9
fortify M6
fox M2
fracture M4
franchise M4
free M3
freeze M4M9
fret M5
fricassee M3
fringe M4
frolic M8
fry M6
fudge M4
fuel M5 *(Am)*
fulfil M5
fumble M4
fume M4
funnel M5 *(Am)*
fur up M5
furnish M2
fuse M4
fuss M2

G

gab M5
gabble M4
gad about M5
gag M5
gainsay M1M9
gamble M4
gambol M5 *(Am)*
game M4
gape M4
garage M4

garble M4
gargle M4
garnish M2
garrotte M4
gas M5
gash M2
gauge M4
gaze M4
gel M5
gen up M5
gesture M4
get M5M9
gibe M4
giggle M4
gild M1 ou M1M9
gird M1 ou M1M9
girdle M4
give M4M9
glance M4
glare M4
glass M2
glaze M4
glide M4
glimpse M4
glorify M6
glory M6
gloss over M2
glue M4
glut with M5
gnash M2
go M2M9
gobble M4
goggle M4
gore M4
gorge M4
gouge M4
grab M5
grace M4
grade M4
grapple M4
grass M2
grate M4
gratify M6
gravel M5 *(Am)*
graze M4
grease M4
grieve M4
grin M5
grind M1M9
grip M5
gripe M4
grit M5
grope M4
gross M2
grouch M2
grovel M5 *(Am)*
grow M1M9
grub M5
grudge M4
grumble M4
guarantee M3
guess M2
guide M4
gum M5
gun M5
gurgle M4
gush M2
gut M5
guzzle M4

H

haemorrhage M4
haggle M4
halve M4
ham M5
handicap M5
handle M4
hang M1 ou M1M9
harangue M4
harass M2
hare M4
harness M2
harry M6
hash M2
hassle M4
hatch M2
hate M4
have M4M9
hear M1M9
heave M4 ou M4M9
heckle M4
hedge M4
hem M5
hew down M1 ou M1M9
hiccup M1 ou M5
hide M4M9
hike M4
hinge M4
hire M4
hiss M2
hit M5M9
hitch M2
hive M4
hoax M2
hobble M4
hobnob M5
hoe M3
hog M5
hold M1M9
hole M4
home M4
hop M5
hope M4
hose M4
hot up M5
house M4
huddle M4
hug M5
hum M5
humble M4
humidify M6
hunch M2
hurry M6
hurt M1M9
hurtle M4
hush M2
hustle M4

I

ice M4
identify M6
idle M4
ignite M4
ignore M4
imagine M4
imbibe M4
imbue M4
immerse M4
impale M4
impeach M2
impede M4
impel M5
impinge M4
implore M4
imply M6
impose M4
impoverish M2
impress M2
improve M4
improvise M4
incense M4
inch M2
incite M4
incline M4
include M4
inconvenience M4
increase M4
incur M5
indemnify M6
index M2
induce M4
indulge M4
infer M5
inflame M4
inflate M4
influence M4
infringe M4
infuse M4
inhale M4
inhere M4
initial M5 *(Am)*
injure M4
inlay M1M9
inscribe M4
inset M5M9
inspire M4
instil M5
institute M4
insure M4
intensify M6
intercede M4
interfere M4
interleave M4
interpose M4
intersperse M4
intervene M4
intone M4
intrigue M4
introduce M4
intrude M4
inure M4
invade M4
inveigle M4
invite M4
invoice M4
invoke M4
involve M4
issue M4
itch M2

J

jab M5
jam M5
jangle M4
jar M5
jazz M2
jet M5
jib M5
jibe M4
jig M5
jiggle M4
jingle M4
jive M4
job M5
jog M5
joggle M4
joke M4
jostle M4
jot down M5
judge M4
jug M5
juggle M4
jumble M4
justify M6
jut M5
juxtapose M4

K

keep M1M9
kid M5
kidnap M5 *(Am)*
kindle M4
kip M5
kiss M2
kit out ou up M5
knee M3
kneel M1 ou M1M9
knife M4
knit M5 ou M5M9
knot M5
know M1M9
knuckle down M4
KO M3 (KO's, etc.)

L

label M5 *(Am)*
lace M4
ladle M4
lag M5
lam M5
lame M4
languish M2
lap M5

lapse M4
lash M2
lasso M3 ou M2
latch on M2
launch M2
lavish M2
lay M1M9
laze M4
lead M1M9
lean M1 ou M1M9
leap M1 ou M1M9
leapfrog M5
learn M1 ou M1M9
lease M4
leave M4M9
lecture M4
lend M1M9
let M5M9
level M5 *(Am)*
levy M6
liaise M4
libel M5 *(Am)*
license M4
lie M7M9
light M1 ou M1M9
like M4
line M4
liquefy M6
live M4
loathe M4
lob M5
lobby M6
lodge M4
log M5
loose M4
lop M5
lope M4
lose M4M9
lounge M4
louse M4
love M4
lug M5
lunch M2
lunge M4
lurch M2
lure M4
lynch M2

M

machine M4
magnify M6
make M4M9
man M5
manage M4
mangle M4
manicure M4
manoeuvre M4
manufacture M4
map M5
mar M5
march M2
marry M6
marshal M5 *(Am)*
marvel M5 *(Am)*
mash M2
masquerade M4
mass M2
massacre M4
massage M4
mat M5
match M2
mate M4
mature M4
mean M1M9
measure M4
meddle M4
meet M1M9
melt M1 ou M1M9
menace M4
merge M4
mesh M2
mess M2
mime M4
mimic M8
mince M4
mine M4
mingle M4
mislay M1M9
mislead M1M9
misread M1M9
miss M2
mistake M4M9
mix M2
mob M5
model M5 *(Am)*
modify M6
mop M5
mope about ou around M4
mortgage M4
mortify M6
motivate M4
move M4
mow down M1 ou M1M9
muddle M4
muddy M6
muffle M4
mug M5
multiply M6
mumble M4
munch M2
muscle in M4
muse M4
muss M2
mute M4
mutiny M6
muzzle M4
mystify M6

N

nab M5
nag M5
name M4
nap M5
needle M4
nerve M4
nestle M4

net M5
nibble M4
nip M5
nobble M4
nod M5
nose M4
nosh M2
notch M2
note M4
notice M4
notify M6
nourish M2
nudge M4
nullify M6
nurse M4
nurture M4
nuzzle M4

O

oblige M4
obscure M4
observe M4
obsess M2
occupy M6
occur M5
offset M5M9
ogle M4
omit M5
ooze M4
oppose M4
oppress M2
ossify M6
outwit M5
overawe M4
overlay M6
owe M4

P

pace M4
pacify M6
package M4
pad M5
paddle M4
page M4
pal up M5
pan M5
panel M5 *(Am)*
panic M8
parachute M4
parade M4
paralyze M4
paraphrase M4
parcel out M5 *(Am)*
parch M2
pare M4
parody M6
parole M4
pass M2
paste M4
pat M5
patch M2
patrol M5
pause M4
pave M4
pay M1M9
pedal M5 *(Am)*
peddle M4
pee M3
peeve M4
peg M5
pen M5
pencil M5 *(Am)*
pep up M5
perceive M4
perch M2
perfume M4
perish M2
perjure M4
permit M5
perplex M2
persecute M4
persevere M4
personify M6
perspire M4
persuade M4
peruse M4
pervade M4
pet M5
petrify M6
phase M4
phone M4
photocopy M6
phrase M4
pickle M4
picnic M8
picture M4
piddle M4
piece together M4
pierce M4
pig M5
pile M4
pillory M6
pin M5
pinch M2
pine M4
pip M5
pipe M4
pique M4
pirouette M4
piss M2
pit M5
pitch M2
pity M6
place M4
plague M4
plan M5
plane M4
plate M4
plead M1 ou M1M9
please M4
pledge M4
plod M5
plop M5
plot M5
plug M5
plunge M4
ply M6
poach M2

poke M4
police M4
polish M2
pollute M4
pop M5
pore over M4
pose M4
possess M2
postpone M4
pot M5
pounce M4
practise M4
praise M4
prance M4
preach M2
precede M4
preclude M4
predispose M4
prefer M5
prefix M2
prejudice M4
prepare M4
presage M4
prescribe M4
preserve M4
preset M5M9
preside M4
press M2
pressure M4
presume M4
prettify M6
price M4
prickle M4
pride M4
prime M4
prise M4
privilege M4
prize M4
probe M4
process M2
procure M4
prod M5
produce M4
profane M4
profess M2
profile M4
program M5
programme M4
progress M2
promenade M4
promise M4
promote M4
pronounce M4
prop M5
propel M5
prophesy M6
propose M4
proscribe M4
prosecute M4
prostitute M4
protrude M4
prove M4
provide M4
provoke M4
prune M4
pry M6
psychoanalyse M4
publish M2
puke M4
pulse M4
pummel M5 *(Am)*
pun M5
punch M2
puncture M4
punish M2
purchase M4
purée M3
purge M4
purify M6
purse M4
pursue M4
push M2
put M5M9
putrefy M6
puzzle M4

Q

quadruple M4
quake M4
qualify M6
quantify M6
quarantine M4
quarrel M5 *(Am)*
quarry M6
quash M2
quench M2
query M6
queue M4
quibble M4
quit M5M9
quiz M5
quote M4

R

race M4
rag M5
rage M4
raise M4
rake M4
rally M6
ram M5
ramble M4
ramify M6
rampage M4
ranch M2
range M4
rankle M4
rap M5
rape M4
rat M5
rate M4
ratify M6
rattle M4
ravage M4
rave M4
ravish M2
raze M4

razz M2
reach M2
read M1M9
reappraise M4
rebel M5
rebuke M4
rebut M5
recap M5
recede M4
receive M4
recess M2
recite M4
recline M4
recompense M4
reconcile M4
reconnoitre M4
rectify M6
recur M5
recycle M4
redo M2M9
redress M2
reduce M4
refer M5
referee M3
refine M4
refit M5 ou M5M9
refresh M2
refurbish M2
refuse M4
refute M4
regale M4
regress M2
regret M5
rehash M2
rehearse M4
reimburse M4
reinforce M4
rejoice M4
relapse M4
relate M4
relax M2
re-lay (carpet) M1M9
relay (information) M1
release M4
relieve M4
relinquish M2
relish M2
relive M4
rely M6
remedy M6
reminisce M4
remit M5
remove M4
rend M1M9
renege M4
renounce M4
repel M5
reply M6
repose M4
repress M2
reprieve M4
reproach M2
reprove M4
repulse M4
repute M4
require M4
requite M4
rescue M4
research M2
resemble M4
reserve M4
reside M4
resolve M4
respire M4
restore M4
resume M4
retch M2
retire M4
retread (tyre) M1
retrench M2
retrieve M4
retrogress M2
rev M5
revel M5 *(Am)*
revenge M4
revere M4
reverse M4
revile M4
revise M4
revive M4
revivify M6
revoke M4
revolve M4
rhyme M4
rib M5
ricochet M1 ou M5
rid M5M9
riddle M4
ride M4M9
ridge M4
ridicule M4
rifle M4
rig M5
rile M4
ring M1M9
rinse M4
rip M5
ripple M4
rise M4M9
rival M5 *(Am)*
rivet M5
rob M5
robe M4
romance M4
rope M4
rot M5
route M4
rove M4
rub M5
rue M4
ruffle M4
rule M4
rumble M4
rummage M4
rumple M4
run M5M9
rupture M4
rush M2
rustle M4
rut M5

S

sabotage M4
sacrifice M4
saddle M4
sag M5
sally M6
salute M4
salvage M4
salve M4
sample M4
sanctify M6
sandwich M2
sap M5
satisfy M6
savage M4
save M4
saw M1M9
say M1M9
scab M5
scale M4
scan M5
scar M5
scare M4
scavenge M4
schedule M4
scheme M4
scorch M2
score M4
scrabble M4
scrag M5
scram M5
scramble M4
scrap M5
scrape M4
scratch M2
screech M2
scribble M4
scrounge M4
scrub M5
scrunch M2
scruple M4
scud M5
scuffle M4
sculpture M4
scurry M6
scuttle M4
scythe M4
search M2
secede M4
seclude M4
secrete M4
secure M4
seduce M4
see M1M9
seek M1M9
seethe M4
seize M4
sell M1M9
send M1M9
sense M4
sentence M4
serenade M4
serve M4
service M4
set M5M9
settle M4
sew M1M9
sex M2
shackle M4
shade M4
shag M5
shake M4M9
sham M5
shamble M4
shame M4
shape M4
share M4
shave M4
shear M1M9
sheathe M4
shed M5M9
shellac M8
shelve M4
shin M5
shine M4M9
shingle M4
ship M5
shit M5 ou M5M9
shoe M4M9
shoot M1M9
shop M5
shore M4
shove M4
shovel M5 *(Am)*
show M1 ou M1M9
shred M5
shrink M1M9
shrivel M5 *(Am)*
shrug M5
shuffle M4
shun M5
shush M2
shut M5M9
shuttle M4
shy M6
side M4
sidle M4
signal M5 *(Am)*
signify M6
silence M4
silhouette M4
simplify M6
sin M5
sing M1M9
singe M4
single out M4
sink M1M9
sip M5
sire M4
sit M5M9
site M4
size up M4
sizzle M4
skate M4
skedaddle M4
sketch M2
skid M5
skim M5
skin M5
skip M5
skive M4

slake M4
slam M5
slap M5
slash M2
slate M4
slave M4
sleep M1M9
slice M4
slide M4M9
slim M5
sling M1M9
slink M1M9
slip M5
slit M5M9
slog M5
slop M5
slope M4
slosh M2
slot M5
slouch M2
slug M5
sluice M4
slum M5
slur M5
smash M2
smell M1 ou M1M9
smile M4
smite M4M9
smoke M4
smooch M2
smudge M4
smuggle M4
snaffle M4
snafu M2
snag M5
snake M4
snap M5
snare M4
snatch M2
sneak M1 ou M1M9
sneeze M4
sniffle M4
snip M5
snipe M4
snitch M2
snivel M5 *(Am)*
snog M5
snooze M4
snore M4
snub M5
snuffle M4
snuggle M4
sob M5
solace M4
sole M4
solidify M6
solve M4
soothe M4
sow M1M9
space M4
span M5
spangle M4
spar M5
spare M4
sparkle M4
speak M1M9
specify M6
speckle M4
speechify M6
speed M1M9 ou M1
spell M1M9 ou M1
spend M1M9
spice M4
spike M4
spill M1M9 ou M1
spin M5M9
spiral M5 *(Am)*
spit M5M9
spite M4
splash M2
splice M4
split M5M9
splurge M4
spoil M1 ou M1M9
sponge M4
spot M5
spread M1M9
spread-eagle M4
spring M1M9
sprinkle M4
spruce up M4
spur M5
spy M6
squabble M4
square M4
squash M2
squat M5
squeeze M4
squelch M2
squiggle M4
squire M4
stab M5
stable M4
stage M4
stake M4
stalemate M4
stampede M4
stand M1M9
staple M4
star M5
starch M2
stare M4
startle M4
starve M4
stash M2
state M4
staunch M2
steady M6
steal M1M9
stem M5
stencil M5 *(Am)*
step M5
stereotype M4
stet M5
stick M1M9
stifle M4
sting M1M9
stink M1M9
stir M5
stitch M2
stoke M4
stone M4

stop M5
store M4
straddle M4
strafe M4
straggle M4
strangle M4
strap M5
streamline M4
stress M2
stretch M2
strew M1 ou M1M9
stride M4
strike M4
string along M1M9
strip M5
stroke M4
strop M5
structure M4
struggle M4
strum M5
strut M5
stub M5
stucco M1 ou M2
stud M5
study M6
stultify M6
stumble M4
stun M5
stupefy M6
style M4
subdue M4
sublease M4
submerge M4
submit M5
subscribe M4
subside M4
substitute M4
subsume M4
subtitle M4
suckle M4
sue M4
suffice M4
suffuse M4
sully M6
sum up M5
sun M5
sunbathe M4
sup M5
supersede M4
supervise M4
supply M6
suppose M4
suppress M2
surface M4
surge M4
surmise M4
surpass M2
surprise M4
survive M4
suss M2
swab M5
swaddle M4
swan around M5
swap M5
swash M2
swat M5
swathe M4
swear M1M9
sweat M1 ou M1M9
sweep M1M9
swell M1 ou M1M9
swerve M4
swig M5
swim M5M9
swindle M4
swing M1M9
swipe M4
swish M2
switch M2
swivel M5 *(Am)*
swoosh M2
swot M5
syringe M4

T

table M4
tackle M4
tag M5
take M4M9
talc M8 ou M1
tally M6
tame M4
tan M5
tangle M4
tap M5
tape M4
tar M5
tarnish M2
tarry M6
taste M4
tat M5
tattle M4
tax M2
taxi M2
teach M2M9
tear M1M9
tease M4
tee M3
teethe M4
telecast M1M9
telephone M4
telescope M4
televise M4
telex M2
tell M1M9
tense M4
terrace M4
terrify M6
testify M6
thatch M2
thieve M4
thin M5
think M1M9
thrash M2
thresh M2
thrive M4 ou M4M9
throb M5

throttle M4
throw M1M9
thrum M5
thrust M1M9
thud M5
tickle M4
tide over M4
tidy M6
tie M7
tile M4
time M4
tin M5
tinge M4
tingle M4
tinkle M4
tip M5
tipple M4
tire M4
toady M6
toddle M4
toe M3
tog up M5
tone M4
tongue M4
top M5
topple M4
torture M4
toss M2
tot up M5
total M5 *(Am)*
tote M4
touch M2
tousle M4
towel M5 *(Am)*
trace M4
trade M4
traduce M4
traffic M8
traipse M4
trample M4
transcribe M4
transfer M5
transfigure M4
transfix M2
transfuse M4
transgress M2
transmit M5
transmogrify M6
transpire M4
transpose M4
trap M5
travel M5 *(Am)*
traverse M4
tread M1M9
treadle M4
treasure M4
treble M4
tree M3
trek M5
trellis M2
tremble M4
trench M2
trespass M2
trickle M4
trifle M4
trim M5
trip M5
triple M4
trot M5
trouble M4
trounce M4
trudge M4
true up M4
trundle M4
truss M2
try M6
tug M5
tumble M4
tune M4
tunnel M5 *(Am)*
tussle M4
tut M5
twiddle M4
twig M5
twin M5
twine M4
twinkle M4
twit M5
twitch M2
type M4
typify M6

U

umpire M4
understand M1M9
undertake M4M9
unify M6
unite M4
unravel M5 *(Am)*
up M5
urge M4
use M4

V

vanish M2
vanquish M2
varnish M2
vary M6
venture M4
verge on M4
verify M6
vet M5
vex M2
videotape M4
vie M7
vilify M6
vitrify M6
voice M4
vote M4
vouch M2
vouchsafe M4
voyage M4

W

wad M5
waddle M4
wade M4
waffle M4
wag M5
wage M4
waggle M4
waive M4
wake M4 ou M4M9
wangle M4
war M5
warble M4
wash M2
waste M4
watch M2
wave M4
wax M2
wear M1M9
weave M4M9
wed M5
wedge M4
weep M1M9
welcome M4
welsh M2
wench M2
wet M5 ou M5M9
wham M5
wheedle M4
wheeze M4
while away M4
whine M4
whip M5
whistle M4
whittle M4
whizz M2
wholesale M4
whoosh M2
whop M5
whore M4
wiggle M4
win M5M9
wince M4
winch M2
wind M1M9
wine M4
winkle M4
wipe M4
wire M4
wise up M4
wish M2
witness M2
wobble M4
worry M6
wrangle M4
wrap M5
wreathe M4
wrench M2
wrestle M4
wriggle M4
wring M1M9
wrinkle M4
write M4M9
writhe M4

Y

yap M5
yodel M5 *(Am)*
yoke M4

Z

zap M5
zero in M2
zigzag M5
zip M5